W9-AUA-020

Barrier-Free Travel

A Nuts and Bolts Guide
for Wheelers
and Slow-Walkers

Candy Harrington

Photographs by Charles Pannell

Demos

Demos Medical Publishing
386 Park Avenue South
New York, NY 10016, USA

© 2005 by Demos Medical Publishing, LLC. All rights reserved. This book is
protected by copyright. No part of it may be reproduced, stored in a retrieval
system, or transmitted in any form or by any means, electronic, mechanical,
photocopying, recording, or otherwise without the prior written permission of
the publisher.

Designed and produced by Reyman Studio

Visit our website at www.demosmedpub.com
http://www.demosmedpub.com

Library of Congress Cataloging-in-Publication Data

Harrington, Candy.
Barrier-free travel : a nuts and bolts guide for wheelers and slow-walkers
/ Candy Harrington ; photographs by Charles Pannell.
p. cm.
Includes index.
ISBN 1-932603-09-3 (pbk. : alk. paper)
1. People with disabilities—Travel. 2. Barrier-free design. I. Title.
HV3022.H37 2005
910'.87—dc22

                          2005000758

Reprinted December 2006

Dedication

To Charles

Contents

Acknowledgments

A PROJECT LIKE this doesn't happen in a vacuum, so indeed there are many people to thank. However, in keeping with my own personal tradition, I'll keep it short and sweet and offer a special word of thanks to the following folks:

To Diana Schneider for making things happen.

To Connie George (recently promoted to PB) for keeping me on my toes and offering valuable input. I couldn't have completed the cruise or travel agent chapters without you.

To Bonnie Lewkowicz for generously sharing her resources and contacts. You set a great professional example.

To Scott Rains for making me think outside the box and for introducing me to Beans Around The World. You added insight and levity to my life.

To the hundreds of *Emerging Horizons* readers who shared their experiences, hints, and resources with me over the years. I've tried to incorporate them all in this book so that they'll be useful to others.

And most importantly, to Charles Pannell for his support, input, and wonderful photos. This book truly is a collaborative effort between us, as Charles is my best critic and greatest inspiration. Not only did he give me many ideas, but he also helped me gently realize when some of my own were fatally flawed. I know it's not easy to shoot access photos, but Charles did a great job, in spite of my constant "input."

Preface
It's *Still* a Jungle Out There!

FOUR YEARS AGO, when I penned the first edition of this book, I began with the proclamation, "It's a jungle out there." Obviously, I was talking about barrier-free travel and my point was that, because of the chaos and uncertainty involved in travel, people who need access accommodations really need reliable information. In fact that was the whole purpose of my book—to give readers tools and resources to prepare for their journey.

Looking back on things, the book did that job quite nicely. In fact, one reviewer even referred to it as "the Bible for barrier-free travel." So, why the need for a second edition if the first one was so darn great? Good question.

Times changes and so do attitudes, resources, and rules. It's still a jungle out there, but it's a more accessible jungle today. In part, this improvement is due to the increased availability of access information and resources, many of which I have included in this second edition. Some access-related rules and regulations have also changed in the past four years. Those updates are included as well.

Airport security procedures have also drastically changed in the past four years. In fact you could say that September 11 forever changed the way we travel. With that in mind, this second edition includes information about security procedures and how they apply to wheelchair-users and slow walkers.

Due to popular demand, this edition also includes an expanded cruise chapter.

And let's not forget the kids. Last year I was asked to pen the accessible travel chapter for *Kids on Wheels*, a book about disability issues as they pertain to children. In the course of my research for that book, I interviewed a lot of parents who travel with their wheeler kids, so I decided to make that research work for my own title as well. Hence the birth of *Taking the Kids*, my chapter devoted to kid travel issues.

Some things remain the same in this second edition. For example, I still relied heavily on reader input for this edition. As the editor of *Emerging Horizons*, I get a lot of feedback from travelers — both good and bad — and I incorporated many of those tips and resources in this edition.

And I still focused on useful information for travelers with a mobility disability in this edition. As with the first edition, I did not include the trite advice found in so many other publications such as "wear comfortable shoes" or (my personal favorite) "ramps are the ideal alternative to stairs and represent the best choice for passengers who use wheelchairs." This book contains useful resources, tips, and tools to help you plan your holiday.

It should be noted that although I've done my best to ensure the accuracy of the information presented in this book, regulations and laws do change. They are also subject to different interpretations. This book should be used only as a general guide, and it should not be considered legal advice. If you want legal advice specific to your situation, consult a lawyer.

Yes, it's still a jungle out there, but it doesn't have to be a bad jungle. In fact, with the right survival skills it's a very pleasant (and even accessible) place. As with the first edition, this book gives you travel survival skills — just more of them. So read on and get ready to explore — there's a whole world waiting for you, and it's getting more and more accessible every day.

Candy Harrington
horizons@EmergingHorizons.com

The contents of this publication are believed to be correct at the time of printing. Nevertheless, the author cannot be held responsible for any errors, omissions, or changes in the information given in this guide, or for the consequences of any reliance on the information provided by the same.

Up, Up, and Away
Air Travel

1

EVERYBODY IS FLYING these days. Indeed, air travel is one of the most popular forms of travel. Unfortunately, for people with disabilities, air travel can also be one of the most problematic areas of travel. Perhaps it's because there are just so many things that can go wrong on any given flight. And then again, perhaps it's due to the mountain of misinformation circulating about accessible travel.

I believe it's a combination of both factors; however, I tend to favor the misinformation theory, mostly because of my own experience with this growing phenomenon. So, what's wrong with a little misinformation? Well, if you rely on it and accept it as the truth, you may be in for a rude awakening when you take off on your holiday and find out that it's incorrect.

Admittedly, it can be difficult to ferret out the wheat from the chaff, as far as misinformation is concerned. This situation is further complicated by the fact that you can't always determine a person's credibility based on his or her position in the community. Just because somebody is a well respected professional does not mean that they're also an expert on accessible travel. The story of Lenny the Lawyer comes to mind here.

I had the great misfortune of meeting Lenny, a well respected corporate lawyer, at a national disability conference a few years ago. I gave a presentation about accessible travel and Lenny was in charge of introducing me. He seemed harmless enough, until he opened his mouth. Lenny knew very little about accessible travel, but he obviously felt the need to include something of substance in his introduction. So he proceeded to tell the audience that Title

II of the Americans with Disabilities Act (ADA) entitles all wheel-chair-users to guaranteed bulkhead seating. Of course, nothing could be further from the truth.

He then informed the audience that he always manages to get bulkhead seats. He elaborated that he merely threatens to file a Title II lawsuit, and *voila*, the seats are his. Now I'm not arguing that Lenny could definitely be a major pain in the backside; in fact, if I were a reservation agent I would most likely give him the darned seats just to get him off the phone. But that's not the way things usually work in real life.

And more important, Lenny the Lawyer did my audience a real disservice by spreading this misinformation. Fortunately, Lenny was not at all interested in hearing my presentation. He left immediately after the introduction, at which point I told the audience the truth.

Although the Lenny incident is quite memorable, it's far from an isolated case. I've seen many other people spread misinformation: travel agents, rehabilitation professionals, and yes, even writers. Misinformation is rampant. So what's a traveler to do? Ask for documentation. If somebody can't back up their claims with hard facts, then there's a good chance that they too are spreading misinformation. It's hard to argue with cold hard facts. With that in mind, let's talk about the facts of air travel.

Air Carrier Access Act

CONTRARY TO THE gospel according to Lenny, the Air Carrier Access Act (ACAA), covers air travel on all U.S.-based airlines. The ACAA outlines procedures that U.S. airlines must follow regarding passengers with disabilities. Among other things, the ACAA mandates that people with a disability cannot be denied boarding solely because of their disability. It also forbids airlines from assessing surcharges for the services mandated by the ACAA. Although many people take these rights for granted, consider the alternative. Here are a few examples.

- KLM, a Dutch based airline, refuses to board nonambulatory passengers who are not accompanied by an able-bodied escort. The official KLM policy on nonambulatory passengers is as follows. "The passenger must be accompanied by an escort. They must fly on a wide body aircraft, on a flight with a duration of over 3 hours; and medical approval must be given (in advance) by KLM's Medical Department in Amsterdam." Even wheelchair athletes and other nonambulatory passengers who live independently have been denied boarding by KLM.
- Wheelchair-users don't fare any better on Norwegian Air Shuttle (NAS), which operates domestic flights throughout Norway. According to the Federation of Organizations of Disabled People, NAS refuses to transport passengers in power wheelchairs because they can't store those wheelchairs in their luggage compartments.

Other non-U.S. airlines have similar policies, as a former Thai Airways passenger recounts. "I was seated on a Thai Airways flight from Bangkok to Sydney, when I was approached by several airline employees and asked to disembark because I was a paraplegic," he said. "I refused, and the next 15 minutes were about as publicly humiliating as it gets. They wanted to know how I could use the toilet if I could not walk. They said I would have to deplane, because I was a safety risk, and I was unable to go to the toilet. I explained to them that I had traveled extensively throughout Southeast Asia on my own. I then showed them my return airline ticket, which proved I had already traveled from New Zealand to Thailand unaccompanied. I guess they decided that I wasn't much of a safety risk after all, as a few minutes later the plane started to taxi down the runway (with me on board)."

One wheelchair-user didn't fare as well with Britannia Airways. "Two weeks prior to our scheduled departure I called to reconfirm our reservations and to make sure our request for boarding assistance was noted," she said. "The customer service agent asked me if we could get to the airplane toilet by ourselves (we can if we have to) and if we use catheters (we don't). I pointed out that even though my husband and I both use a wheelchair, we made this same journey the previous year without incident. This made absolutely no difference to Britannia Airways. They refused to fly us and canceled our reservations."

Some airlines, like Air New Zealand, refuse to assist passengers with transfers. In fact, Air New Zealand's official policy states, "If you are unable to self-lift to transfer between the wheelchair or aisle chair and the aircraft seat, a support person will be required." More specifically, that means you have to provide your own support person if you cannot transfer by yourself.

And finally, Ryanair, the Ireland-based self-touted "low fare airline" actually charges extra to carry some disabled passengers. These charges are not reflected in Ryanair's published fares, because passengers are required to pay them directly to third-party contractors who provide wheelchair assistance at some U.K. airports. Contractors at these airports charge a lift-on and lift-off fee of £12.50 per occurrence. A direct round trip involves two lift-ons and two lift-offs, resulting in extra charges of £50.

According to Ryanair CEO Michael O'Leary, Ryanair only requires people traveling without their own wheelchair to pay these fees directly to the contractors. Interestingly enough, British Midland and Aer Lingus use the same airport facilities and contractors as Ryanair does; however, these airlines don't require their passengers to pay extra for wheelchair assistance. Apparently, British Midland and Aer Lingus absorb the charges into their general operating costs and distribute them equally to all passengers.

Disability rights activists have tried to fight Ryanair on this issue, but to no avail. The fight continues and hopefully, one day Ryanair's discriminatory practices will be a thing of the past. For now, it's best to avoid Ryanair at all costs. Choose an airline that doesn't charge extra for accessible services.

Unfortunately Ryanair is not alone. Nationwide, a domestic

South African airline, also charges passengers for wheelchair assistance. We've had reports of passengers being charged a whopping $260 for wheelchair assistance, which in many cases amounts to more than the cost of the ticket.

As you can see, the ACAA affords travelers using U.S. airlines at least a minimum level of protection—a protection that is not found on many foreign air carriers. Now, you may hear from time to time that the ACAA also applies to non-U.S. airlines. In fact, the Aviation Investment and Reform Act of the 21st Century (AIR 21), which was signed into law on April 5, 2000, promised to extend portions of the ACAA to include non-U.S. air carriers. So, where are we now with this "promise"? That depends on who you ask.

According to a Department of Transportation (DOT) spokesperson, "For now, foreign airlines have been put on notice that AIR 21 exists and they are strongly encouraged to comply with the spirit of the law." On the other hand, many travel professionals doubt the feasibility of enforcing this regulation. Says one East Coast travel agent who specializes in accessible travel, "How can you enforce something without any specific regulations? Even when the regulations are set, I think it will be very difficult for travelers to enforce a U.S. law on foreign soil, especially if they don't speak the language."

Time will tell how much protection AIR 21 will offer. For now, the best advice is to proceed with caution and operate on the assumption that only U.S. carriers are required to abide by the ACAA.

The ACAA is a pretty straightforward piece of legislation; that is, until you get to the gray area of *codeshare flights*. A codeshare is a marketing agreement between two airlines, in which one airline operates flights under the code of the other airline. Although not specifically addressed in the ACAA, in 1998, an interesting settlement transpired regarding a codeshare flight. The settlement stemmed from the following incident.

A wheelchair-user traveled unaccompanied from Seattle to New York on a United Airlines flight. He then tried to transfer to United flight 3516 to Frankfurt, Germany. This particular flight was a codeshare operated by Lufthansa Airlines. Lufthansa refused to board him, stating that he was a safety risk because he could not assist in his own evacuation in case of an emergency. Seeing that he had just traveled across the country by himself, and wheeled himself down the jetway unassisted, the passenger contended he could indeed assist with his own emergency evacuation. Still, he was refused boarding.

Under the terms of the settlement agreement, neither airline admitted any wrongdoing, but both agreed to cease and desist from future violations. United paid a fine of $3,000 and Lufthansa paid a fine of $1,000.

In another case, Continental Airlines was found to have violated the ACAA when its foreign partner, Alitalia, refused to sell a ticket to a wheelchair-user. This case arose when a Newark Alitalia ticket agent refused to sell an unaccompanied wheelchair-user a roundtrip ticket to Rome. Alitalia cited its long-standing policy that requires wheelchair-users to be accompanied by attendants on all flights over 3 hours long. Since the flight was a codeshare, operated on a Continental airplane and staffed by a Continental crew, the judge found in favor of the plaintiff and ruled against Continental Airlines.

The moral of the story is to be wary of codeshares. In practice, some foreign codeshare partners may still deny boarding to unaccompanied wheelchair-users. Granted, it's technically against the law, but it does happen, and it's the kind of thing that can really ruin your vacation.

The bottom line is, always err on the side of caution. At the risk of sounding ethnocentric, use a U.S.-based carrier whenever possible. That way, you know you're protected under the ACAA. (To be fair, Canada also has similar legislation called the Canadian Transportation Act.) Other than that, watch your step, especially in underdeveloped countries. I've heard more than one story from wheelers who were stranded in the Caribbean because a non-U.S. carrier refused to board them. Their only recourse was to purchase a higher-priced same day return ticket on a U.S. carrier; a very costly option. Don't let that happen to you.

Know Your Rights

BEFORE YOU PLAN your flight, you should learn your rights under the ACAA. Once you have an understanding of the regulations, you will also have a good idea of what to expect as far as access in the air is concerned. Education and consumer awareness are the essential first steps to getting the services you need.

To that end, a great resource is *New Horizons: Information for Air Travelers with a Disability*, a pocket-sized guide that explains your rights under the ACAA.

This Department of Transportation (DOT) publication details your rights, as covered under the ACAA. It's available for a $3 shipping and handling charge from the Paralyzed Veterans of America (item 2100-16). Call (888) 860-7244 to order your copy.

The guide is small enough to carry in your pocket or purse, and I highly recommend you take it with you when you travel. Somehow, people just tend to take you more seriously when you can actually point out the law in black and white. Plus, it's also a handy reference.

Of course, the ACAA has been amended a few times since its creation, so I also recommend reading both the seating amendment and the wheelchair damage amendment. Both amendments were published in the *Federal Register*—the seating amendment on March 4, 1998, and the wheelchair damage amendment on August 2, 1999. It wouldn't hurt to carry a copy of these documents with you either.

Know Your Aircraft

Do you know the difference between an EMB-120 and a 777-200? Well, you should learn if you plan to travel by air. I'm not implying that you should become an aeronautical engineer, but it really does help to know some of the basic differences between different types of airplanes.

Under the ACAA, U.S. airlines are required to provide prospective passengers with basic information about the accessibility of their facilities, services, and aircraft. Such information can include facts like the location of seats with movable aisle armrests, the locations and dimensions of storage facilities for mobility aids, and the availability of an onboard accessible lavatory. As you might expect, some airlines do a better job of providing this information than others.

For example, Continental Airlines has an excellent website (continental.com) that includes seating diagrams for all their aircraft, the location of the seats with movable armrests, and even the dimensions of the cargo bin doors on their commuter aircraft. You can also obtain most of this information by phone. Don't be shy about asking for it, and remember to ask for it *before* you book your flight.

Regarding the question about different planes, the big difference between the two is their size. The EMB-120 has 30 seats and the 777-200 has 383 seats. This is important, because most ACAA regulations regarding aircraft accessibility and boarding are referenced by aircraft size. Here are some important numbers; the following ACAA rules apply to planes ordered after April 5, 1990 or delivered after April 5, 1992:

* Planes with 30 or more seats must have moveable armrests on at least half the aisle seats, and airline employees are required to know the locations of those seats.
* Wide-body jets (those with two aisles) must have an accessible lavatory.
* Planes with more than 60 seats and an accessible lavatory must have an onboard wheelchair.
* Planes with 60 or more seats that do not have an accessible lavatory must carry an onboard wheelchair upon passenger request (48 hours advance notice required).
* And finally, planes with more than 100 seats must have priority space to carry at least one folding wheelchair in the cabin.

As far as boarding assistance goes, that also depends on the size of the aircraft. The ACAA mandates level boarding whenever possible on all aircraft with 30 or more seats. If level boarding is not possible, the airline is allowed to use a boarding device such as a lift, ramp, or stair climber. In aircraft with fewer than 30 seats, level boarding is not required. Airline personnel may use other mechanical boarding devices, as long as the passenger's physical limitations don't preclude using such devices.

Under no circumstances are airline personnel required to hand-carry a passenger on any aircraft with fewer than 30 seats. Airlines are required to maintain all lift devices, but even in the event of a mechanical breakdown, airline personnel are still not required to hand-carry passengers on any aircraft with fewer than 30 seats.

Additionally, a few aircraft are considered exempt from the boarding assistance requirements of the ACAA. These aircraft are the Fairchild Metro, the Jetstream 31, and Beech 1900 C and D models. Boarding assistance (lifts) are not required for these exempt aircraft. According to the DOT, using a lift could create a significant risk of damage to these aircraft. Disability rights advocates are currently fighting this exemption, but for now it's best to steer away from these exempt aircraft.

Boarding options can also vary, depending on the size of the airport. Not all airports have jetways that enable level boarding. Additionally, even airports that do have jetways may not have a level boarding option due to heavy traffic. This is a common occurrence at many large international airports. If all gates are being used, even a large plane will park out on the tarmac and passengers will deplane via boarding stairs. The passengers then are bussed to the terminal. It's always a good practice to ask what deplaning procedures are available at your destination airport, just so there won't be any surprises.

Can advance planning and aircraft research really make a difference when it comes to air travel? Well, the story of my friend Elaine comes to mind. Elaine is a rather heavy lady and she uses an equally heavy power wheelchair. Elaine booked a flight on a small (25 seat) aircraft. When she arrived at the airport check-in counter, the clerk asked Elaine if she could walk up a flight of stairs. Elaine informed the clerk that of course she could not. The clerk in turn told Elaine that she would not be able to board the flight. Elaine inquired as to why, and the clerk hemmed and hawed, but finally came out and told Elaine that she was too heavy for the lift, and too large to fit in the aisle chair. An argument ensued. Security was called. Things got ugly. In the end, the airline won out and Elaine had to reschedule her trip on a larger aircraft.

It was an unfortunate incident, but the airline was well within its rights under the ACAA. A 1996 amendment to the ACAA states that "on aircraft with less than 30 seats, if a passenger cannot get to a seat that he or she can use (i.e., they are not able to fit in the boarding chair used on narrow-aisle commuter aircraft or unable to walk through a narrow aisle to a seat), the air carrier is not required to provide boarding (lift) assistance, as it is futile."

Now, when Elaine makes flight arrangements, she asks the airline how they board nonambulatory passengers; and if they reply, "by lift," she then asks the weight capacity of the lift. She also asks for the width of the aisles and the boarding chair on smaller commuter aircraft. She then determines if she will be able to use the aircraft in question. Sometimes it takes two or three phone calls but Elaine vows never to make the same mistake again. She now realizes that a little advance research can save a lot of heartache and embarrassment. Live and learn.

Boarding Procedures

ALTHOUGH ELAINE'S STORY illustrates some of the problems you may encounter boarding a smaller commuter aircraft with a non-level entry, generally speaking boarding a larger aircraft from a level entry jetway is a pretty straightforward procedure. Of course, as always, a few potential trouble spots exist, so you need to know the standard boarding procedure to understand your rights under the ACAA.

First, you have to make it past the reservation agents. To be honest, these front-line employees could use better training on access issues. For example, one wheelchair-user reported that a reservation agent informed her that she could fly in her own wheelchair. The agent explained that their recently refurbished planes had removable bulkhead seats with wheelchair tie-downs. Fortunately, the passenger was travel savvy and knew the truth.

The next hurdle you'll likely encounter is at the check-in counter. If you arrive with your own wheelchair or scooter, the ticket agent may insist that you transfer to an airport wheelchair at this time. Here's where you need to be a little assertive and insist that you stay in your own wheelchair or scooter. It's your right under the ACAA to stay in your own wheelchair or scooter all the way up to the door of the aircraft. The one exception is if your wheelchair or scooter has a spillable battery. In that case, you must surrender it to the airline at least 1 hour in advance of the flight. In any case, I strongly suggest you keep your own wheelchair or scooter as long as you can, for a variety of reasons.

First, it's best to keep your own equipment with you as long as possible, because in theory, the less time the airlines have it, the less time they have to damage it. Second, as you may know, airport wheelchairs are not exactly what you would call comfortable, and you never know how long you will be stuck in one. It's not uncommon for flights to be delayed or canceled.

Finally, you will loose a lot of your freedom if you give up your equipment. Most airport wheelchairs come with a "wheelchair pusher," even if you can push yourself or if you are traveling with somebody who can push you. Your freedom (or lack of it) depends on the wheelchair pusher, and where he or she is allowed to take you.

So, by all means, stay in your own wheelchair or scooter as long as possible. Don't fall for the old "it's our procedure" line when the ticket agent tries to get you to transfer to an airport wheelchair. It very well may be their preferred procedure, but you do have the right to refuse, and you do have a choice.

By the time you make it to the gate, you would assume all of your information (like the fact that you are a wheelchair-user) would be entered correctly in the computer. But, that's not the way it works in real life. Don't be alarmed if the gate agent looks down at you in amazement and says something incredibly intelligent like, "Are you on this flight?" Don't let comments like that worry you. Things will be all sorted out by the time you board the aircraft.

At this point, you must remember to tell the gate agent that you would like to preboard the aircraft. This means that you board the aircraft before the rest of the passengers. Preboarding has a lot of advantages. It gives you time to get settled and change your seat if you find your assigned seat doesn't have a moveable aisle armrest. It also allows you first crack at the overhead storage compartments, and it gives you priority storage for your folding wheelchair in the onboard closet. The airlines can't force you to preboard, but it really is to your advantage to do so.

When it is time for you to preboard, you will be transferred from your own wheelchair to an aisle chair. This high-backed narrow chair has two or four small wheels, and you are belted in and rolled down the aisle to your seat. Upon request, you will be assigned a seat with a moveable aisle armrest. This makes transfers a lot easier, because you just flip up the armrest and slide over.

Airline personnel will help you transfer to your seat if needed; however, it's always best to tell them exactly how you would like to be transferred. Never assume they know anything, because they deal with a wide variety of passengers.

It's important to note that if an airline employee offers you boarding assistance that seems out of the ordinary, it's time to ask to speak to the Complaints Resolution Officer (CRO). For example, in 2003, the DOT responded to numerous customer complaints against Kansas-based Ryan International. Among other things, one complaint alleged that a passenger was actually strapped to a wooden office chair with clothing belts and carried off the plane! After an extensive investigation, the airline was fined $400,000 but was granted a $355,000 credit for the purchase of wheelchairs and ACAA training equipment.

Now, if you just need a wheelchair for distance, there are a few other things to consider. The airlines will supply you with an airport wheelchair (upon advance notice) at check-in. As I said earlier, the airport wheelchair usually comes with a mandatory wheelchair pusher. Under the ACAA, airlines are not supposed to segregate people with disabilities and put them in special boarding areas; however, this sometimes happens to people who use airport wheelchairs.

The airline rationale behind this is that they don't *force* people with disabilities to wait in special areas, but they do require all people who use airport wheelchairs to wait in a designated area. They say this is done to keep track of airport wheelchairs, and it is only done at certain airports. At other airports, the wheelchair pusher may not be allowed to let you stop anywhere, including the lavatory.

So, although this is a great service for people who cannot walk long distances, do be aware of the limitations. Best advice is to take some snack food and water with you, as you may not be able to stop and get anything to eat and drink. Also, if you connect from another flight, use the lavatory on the airplane before you land (if you are able).

If you travel with your own wheelchair, always ask for it to be brought directly to you at the gate. That way, you won't have to use an airport wheelchair to get to the baggage area or to your connecting flight. Generally speaking, airport wheelchairs are a good option for people who can't walk long distances, but they are a hindrance for people who travel with their own equipment.

And finally, let's talk about tipping. Is it appropriate to tip a skycap for wheelchair assistance? Some people claim you shouldn't tip for this service because under the law it's illegal to charge for a disability-related service. True, it is illegal to charge for wheelchair assistance, but a tip certainly isn't a mandatory charge. A tip is a way to show your appreciation for good service.

Granted, tipping is a personal matter, but it is customary to tip skycaps. That said, the appropriate tip for regular wheelchair assistance is $5, more if the skycap provides additional assistance. Again, tipping is a personal choice, but it's always nice to reward good service.

Seating

SEATING IS ANOTHER source of great confusion. Who is entitled to what type of a seat, and how do you actually get it? First off, let me debunk a popular myth. Wheelchair-users are not always guaranteed seating in bulkhead areas. Some airlines will seat you there, some will not—it is not a right given carte blanche to all wheelchair-users under the ACAA.

Seating is actually addressed in the 1998 amendment to the ACAA. In regards to bulkhead seating, this amendment requires air carriers to designate an adequate number of bulkhead seats as priority seating for individuals with a disability. These seats are required to be available to people who travel with a service animal or to people who have a fused (immovable) leg. Carriers can also assign bulkhead seats upon advance request to anybody with a disability who self-identifies himself as a person who needs this particular seating accommodation, providing those seats are not already assigned to other passengers.

Air carriers are not required to bump other passengers from bulkhead seats to accommodate passengers who do not meet the ACAA definition of disabled. In other words, only those passengers who have a service animal or a fused (immovable) leg qualify for priority bulkhead seating under the ACAA.

So, if you are a wheelchair-user (and you don't have a fused leg), you will be given a bulkhead seat only if one is available at the time of your request. Sometimes experienced travel agents can get bulkhead seats for their clients, sometimes they can't. Steer clear of any travel agent who guarantees you they will get you a bulkhead seat. There are no guarantees in life.

The best advice is to make your travel arrangements as early as possible. Additionally, some airlines give priority bulkhead seating to all passengers who have a disability. Call all the airlines in advance to learn their individual policies on this matter, and then do business with those that will give you the seating accommodations you need.

Of course, since this is an ACAA provision, it only applies to U.S. airlines. I've heard from a lot of people who have requested bulkhead seating on non-U.S. carriers only to be denied this accommodation. Some non-U.S. carriers even ask for medical documentation, and still deny the request. And of course, they are within their rights to do this, because they are not subject to the ACAA.

Moveable aisle armrests are another story though. The same 1998 ACAA amendment requires airlines to designate an adequate number of seats with moveable aisle armrests as priority seats for individuals with disabilities. These seats are required to be available to passengers who use an aisle chair to board the aircraft and who cannot readily transfer over a fixed armrest. Because there are a higher percentage of these seats, they are usually easier to get.

Confusion may still sometimes occur during boarding if some airline employees don't readily know the locations of these seats. It's usually not much of a problem, as the cabin crew will reassign you to another seat that does have a moveable armrest, even if they have to try to flip up every armrest on the airplane to find it. Another point to keep in mind is that bulkhead seats usually do not have moveable aisle armrests.

All seating accommodation requests must be made at least 24 hours in advance. If a requested accommodation is made less than 24 hours prior to the flight, the airline will do the best it can to accommodate the request, but it is not required to move any other passengers from their assigned seats. And of course, these seating provisions only apply to airlines that provide advance seating assignments.

Canada takes a slightly more stringent stand on bulkhead seating issues. On February 26, 2003, the Canadian Transportation Agency (CTA) ruled against Air France in a bulkhead seating complaint. As a result, Air France must give people with disabilities priority over able-bodied passengers for non-exit row bulkhead seats. Of course, this only applies to Air France's Canadian flights. The standard Air France policy of reserving bulkhead seating for families traveling with children still applies on all other Air France flights.

Another source of seating confusion (and frustration) are the highly prized exit row seats. The criteria for exit row seating is pretty well established. You must be able to operate the emergency door (which weighs 70 pounds), be able to understand and follow directions in English, be over 15 years old, and be able to assist crew members in an emergency.

That "be able to assist crew members in case of an emergency" qualification is somewhat open to interpretation by the airlines, but they are given this latitude under Federal Aviation Administration (FAA) regulations. Generally speaking, most airlines don't consider wheelchair users "able to assist in an emergency situation." The airlines are well within their rights to determine this as it's not an area covered under the ACAA. In fact it's an area exempt from the ACAA because it has to do with a safety issue. Safety issues are covered under FAA regulations. Final discretion in all safety matters is left up to the crew, and ultimately the captain.

Most wheelchair-users, or anybody who requires a wheelchair assist, won't intentionally be seated in an emergency exit row, but sometimes it happens. When it does, the cabin crew will simply reseat passengers who are inappropriately assigned to exit row seats.

The bigger problem with exit row seats is that some airlines insist that the center aisle of the bulkhead exit rows are also exit rows. I have known people who received their priority seating in bulkhead, only to be told by the cabin crew that they would not be able to sit there because it was an exit row. I find this reasoning somewhat absurd because the same airlines routinely seat families (with kids under 15) in this row. Still, some employees do believe that this is an exit row; so if you find yourself in this situation, ask to have the CRO resolve the matter. It is the quickest solution to this unfortunate situation.

And finally, a word about upgrades. Years ago, when fewer people traveled, wheelchair-users were routinely upgraded to first class. Today, those upgrades are few and far between, partly because more people are traveling, and partly because the airlines now regularly give those upgrades to their highest echelon frequent flyers. I shudder whenever I read a travelogue that even mentions a wheeler's first class upgrade. It's a great perk when it happens, but stories like that tend to create false expectations.

Don't count on getting an upgrade. If you absolutely need that extra room, then buy a business class or first class ticket. No provision in the ACAA (or anywhere) requires carriers to upgrade people with disabilities to first class. Now by all means, go ahead and ask for an upgrade at the gate, but don't be disappointed if you don't get it. My friend John has perhaps the best (or at least the most creative) upgrade technique around. John tries to "look as large as possible." Sometimes it works, but most of the time, John ends up in coach with the rest of us.

Attendants

UNDER THE ACAA, U.S. airlines cannot discriminate against a passenger solely because of a disability; however they can require some passengers to travel with an attendant. Which passengers? Well, according to the ACAA, "passengers who have a disability so severe that they can't assist with their own emergency evacuation." That's a pretty broad definition and truthfully sometimes it's a judgment call by the crew.

In practice, however, it generally applies to many quads, anybody with a visible cognitive disability, and some people with sensory disabilities. Of course, there are always exceptions to every rule, but the bottom line is, the final decision lies with the crew. In short, a U.S. air carrier can require a passenger to travel with an attendant, even if the passenger assures airline personnel that he can travel independently. However, the air carrier cannot charge for the transportation of that airline-required attendant.

That doesn't exactly mean that your personal care assistant (PCA) can travel for free though. Here's where it gets complicated: The air carrier can opt to designate an off-duty employee as your attendant, or they can even ask for a volunteer on the flight to be your attendant. Sounds good, right? Well, the big catch lies in the definition of an airline-required attendant.

Under the ACAA, an airline-required attendant is defined a person who will "provide assistance to the passenger in the event of an emergency evacuation." The airline-required attendant is not required to provide any type of personal service to the passenger; they just sit next to the passenger and, in the event of a water landing, well—you know the drill. In short, an airline-required attendant won't help you eat or use the toilet, but he will help you get off the plane if it crashes.

The bottom line is that U.S. airlines can require an attendant to travel with you, they can assign the attendant, and they can limit the duties of the attendant. Additionally, the airlines are not required to find an attendant for you if they deem you must travel with one for safety reasons. In this case, they can simply deny you passage.

So, what do you do if an airline tries to deny you passage because they feel you need to travel with an attendant? This emergency fix was recommended by my friend Doug: "Explain your situation to the person next to you in line and ask if they will agree to assist you in an emergency," says Doug. "You don't have to go into a lot of details, just explain that the airline won't let you fly unless you can find somebody who will agree to do that. Most people will readily agree. After you find somebody, inform the airline that you have your attendant. If they still say you can't fly, ask to speak to the CRO. I've tried it before, and it really works."

The good news is, if you do travel with your own attendant, U.S. airlines are required to provide adjacent seating for the two of you. That issue is clearly covered under the seating amendment of the ACAA.

When Nature Calls

WHAT DO YOU do when nature calls at 30,000 feet? That's a question I hear over and over again, as it's a major concern for first-time flyers. The toilet problem actually has many solutions, but they all take some sort of advance preparation. I also have to stress here that since everybody is different, what works for one person may not necessarily work for the next. Sometimes it takes a bit of fine tuning and adjustment to find a method that works best for you. With personal experience, you will be able to do this, but for now let me just outline your options.

One option is to travel on an aircraft with an accessible lavatory. All post-1992 wide body aircraft must have at least one accessible lavatory. All planes with an accessible lavatory must also carry an onboard wheelchair. Although this is the standard procedure, it's always best to request an onboard wheelchair when you make your reservations.

Be forewarned though: In most cases, the accessible aircraft lavatories are not the same models you'll find on the ground. According to the guidelines, an accessible aircraft lavatory must include a door lock, an accessible call button, and grab bars. No specifications delineate the height or placement of the grab bars or the toilet. In place of those specifications are performance standards.

In practice, most airlines interpret the regulations to mean that there should be enough room for a wheelchair-user to perform an unassisted front transfer to the toilet from the onboard wheelchair. Space is at a premium, and you won't find 5x5 turn-around spaces in onboard accessible lavatories. The roomiest onboard accessible lavatories are found on the newer wide-body jets.

My friend Carol has perhaps the most astute observation about the onboard accessible lavatories. Carol can walk a few steps, and she uses a scooter for distance. She sums it all up by saying, "Well, at least I never have to worry about falling down in the accessible lavatory on an airplane. There just isn't enough room to fall down."

Still, if you can use the onboard wheelchair and transfer independently, it is a good option. The flight attendants will help you use the onboard wheelchair, but their assistance ends once you reach the lavatory door.

How do you know if the aircraft you will be flying on has an accessible lavatory? This is one of the things the reservation agent should be able to tell you when you make your reservation. Actually, they may have to transfer you to another department, but the information is required (under the ACAA) to be available upon request.

Some travelers totally write off the onboard lavatory and wear a catheter instead. This is usually easier for men than women, because men can use a condom catheter whereas women have to use an internal catheter. If you don't normally use a catheter, the downside (for women) is that you have to arrange for somebody to remove the catheter when you get to your destination.

And, of course, if you are on a long flight, you also have to fig-

Figure 1.1.
Most accessible aircraft lavatories are considerably smaller than those on the ground. This lavatory, aboard an Air Canada Airbus 319, is classified as "accessible."

ure out a discreet way to empty your leg bag. I consider this a learned skill, as I have heard from many people who manage this feat under the cover of a blanket. You should practice this procedure before you leave home (with the blanket). Fortunately, most long flights have several movies, so the cabin is dark for a majority of the time, and darkness works in your favor.

I've also been told to make absolutely sure that your transfer container is leakproof, and that it has a very secure lid. I have heard about some unfortunate accidents where the lid came off the container while it was safely stowed in a duffel bag. This can be very embarrassing and quite difficult to explain to customs officials.

Of course, some people prefer a more personalized solution to the bathroom dilemma. By this I mean many people experiment with diets and vitamins, and limit their fluid intake. And in fact, many people swear by their personal pre-flight regime. I hesitate to recommend anything specifically, because it's such a personal choice. And as I said earlier, what works for one person may not work for the next. Suffice it to say that this is an option that you can investigate on your own. I just want to make you aware of all options, and I'm not really endorsing one over another.

I do recommend that you don't schedule things down to the last minute. Flights are often late or delayed, and sometimes it takes a long time to deplane. If you do cut it a bit close, it never hurts to wear a diaper for extra protection. I know it seems rather an archaic suggestion, but the extra protection may come in handy. And if you plan to go the diaper route, consider wearing two for extra protection, as leakage is a common problem.

Getting Off the Airplane

YOU WOULD THINK that getting off the plane would be a piece of cake, but here's another area where problems can develop. To nip things in the bud, remember to remind the flight attendant that you need your wheelchair brought to the gate when you land. This should be done about 30 minutes before landing, well before the flight attendants are busy scurrying through the cabin making last minute pre-landing preparations.

One good method is to make friends with a particular flight attendant. Introduce yourself to that flight attendant and learn his or her name. Address the flight attendant by name during the flight. Then, when you are ready to land, remind that flight attendant about your wheelchair. When you call the flight attendant by name, it puts more of a personal responsibility on him to follow through with your request. He realizes you know his name, and if something goes wrong, he knows he will be held personally responsible.

If you need an aisle chair to disembark, you must wait until the rest of the passengers deplane. At that point, the aisle chair will be brought to you, and you will be wheeled to the aircraft door, where your own wheelchair will be waiting for you. That's how it's supposed to work, but in practice sometimes it doesn't go that smoothly.

I've received countless reports from people who have waited an inordinate amount of time on an empty airplane. They waited for somebody to bring them an aisle chair, or for their own wheelchair to be brought up from the baggage compartment. Sometimes, the baggage handlers get confused and send the wheelchair to the baggage area, even though it has a gate tag.

There is really no excuse for people having to wait this long to deplane, but it does happen. So, don't plan your connections too tightly, and do hold the airline responsible if you miss your flight. Additionally, take nonstop direct flights whenever possible.

I've heard a few creative solutions to the deplaning problem but the best suggestion comes from my friend Dan. He takes his cell phone with him, calls the airline from his seat, and asks to speak to the CRO whenever there is a long delay in deplaning. Does it work? Well, it does seem to get some prompt action, but it really does nothing to solve the big problem.

The good news is, the DOT finally addressed this issue in 2002, when they fined Northwest Airlines for failing to provide accessible services for 250 passengers. The majority of those complaints were in regards to delayed deplaning. To be fair, all airlines are equally guilty of this, but when Northwest was hit with the fine, many of them at least looked at ways to resolve the problem. Hopefully, a workable solution will be soon found to this troubling problem, but for now don't be surprised if you encounter a deplaning delay.

Security Issues

IN THE WAKE of the September 11 tragedies, the FAA implemented a number of heightened security measures in airports across America. Although some of the measures have been lifted, they can be reinstated at any time. The most important thing to remember is, even in times of heightened security, all provisions of the ACAA still remain in effect.

Initially, the biggest concern for wheelchair-users was the elimination of curbside check-in. In times of heightened security, curbside check-in may be suddenly discontinued. Rest assured though, in the absence of curbside check-in, airline employees are available to assist passengers with disabilities. In fact, they are required to do this. This doesn't mean you are required to transfer to an airport wheelchair at curbside. Under the ACAA, you can still remain in your own wheelchair all the way up to the door of the aircraft (unless your wheelchair has spillable batteries).

Another area of concern is the prohibition of non-ticketed passengers beyond security checkpoints. Again, accommodations have been made for disabled passengers who travel with an aide, attendant, or companion. In such cases, the attendant should present photo identification at the check-in counter to receive a security checkpoint pass.

Another issue of concern involves gate checking assistive devices. According to a DOT spokesperson, during times of heightened security they routinely receive reports about air carriers who refuse to gate-check wheelchairs. Uneducated airline employees erroneously cite "security" as the reason for these denials. Remember, it's your right under the ACAA (providing you do not use spillable batteries) to stay in your own wheelchair all the way to gate. Don't let an airline employee talk you out of this right.

All passengers now face higher security measures and longer lines at airports; however, wheelchair-users can expect even closer scrutiny at all security checkpoints. Wheelchair-users and people who wear prosthetic devices are usually screened with a hand-held metal detector and patted down. Private screenings are available upon request.

Wheelchair-users should remember to stow their wheelchair repair tools in their checked baggage to avoid having them confiscated at security checkpoints. Assistive devices, such as canes, are permitted on board the aircraft after they are inspected. Syringes are also permitted, with medical documentation. Manual wheelchairs are still allowed to be stowed aboard the aircraft, provided they fall under the provisions of the ACAA.

The best advice is to allow plenty of extra time for security screening. Many airports suggest arriving a minimum of 2 hours early for domestic flights, while some airports even suggest arriving 3 hours early. Check with your departure airport for current recommendations. In the end, patience is really the keyword here; however, if you feel your needs as a passenger with a disability are not being adequately addressed, contact the CRO immediately.

Complaints Resolution Officer

I'VE ALREADY MENTIONED the CRO a few times in this chapter, so by now you should know this is the person you need to contact if you reach an impasse with front-line personnel. The CRO is a problem solver, specifically educated in traveler's rights and airline responsibilities under the ACAA. All U.S. airlines are required to have a CRO on duty 24 hours a day, so if you encounter a problem at any stage of game, from reservations to deplaning, this is the person to contact.

Of course, as I pointed out earlier, it really helps to know your rights when talking to the CRO. In other words, don't misquote the law and demand bulkhead seating or a first class upgrade. The CRO will help you resolve access problems and ultimately get you the services you need and are entitled to under the law. But, knowing the law is the first and all-important step in advocating for yourself. On the other hand, if airline personnel want you to transfer to an airline wheelchair at check-in, this is a good time to contact the CRO. The law is on your side, and the CRO will help to enforce it. The DOT operates a toll-free aviation consumer disability hotline at (866) 266-1368. Travelers are invited to call this hotline to obtain information and assistance if they should experience disability-related air service problems.

As far as air travel goes, the best survival tactic is to try to prevent problems before they happen. Of course, a lot of unknown variables factor into the accessibility equation, but you're ahead of the game if you confirm and reconfirm all your travel arrangements. I know this is a time-consuming process, and many people think it's an unfair burden to put on travelers with disabilities; but in reality it's the best way to head off potential disasters and help things go smoothly.

If you want to make a political statement, then go ahead and leave things to chance; but, if you actually want to take a vacation, remember to confirm and reconfirm all your travel arrangements. You can never be too careful, especially where access is concerned.

On a Wing and a Prayer | 2
Protecting Your Equipment

GETTING TO YOUR holiday destination with a minimum of muss and fuss can sometimes be a challenge. Getting your wheelchair or scooter to that same destination in one piece can be an even greater chore. No matter how hard travel is on people, it can be even harder on assistive devices. Generally speaking, passengers aren't stripped of their clothing and thrown into the cargo bin, a fate that many wheelchairs and scooters must routinely endure.

Unfortunately, equipment damage is still a top ranked problem for wheelers, but don't throw in the towel yet, because it's still possible to get your equipment to your final destination relatively unscathed. Of course, as with all aspects of travel, it takes a bit of planning and preparation. Although the whole process may seem rather daunting at first, after a few trips you'll have it down to a science, and then you'll be ready for just about anything.

Before we get into the nuts and bolts here (literally), I must share an anecdote with you. This unfortunate travel tale comes from a reader named Dan. It's about his first air travel experience as a wheeler, and it definitely gets my vote as the ultimate in wheelchair damage stories.

Dan uses a power wheelchair with gel cell batteries. Even though he could have gate-checked his wheelchair, he relented at check-in and transferred to an airport wheelchair. His plane was then delayed due to weather, and he ended up spending an extra hour in the uncomfortable airport wheelchair. But Dan saw past the pain, as he was really looking forward to his vacation. He remained optimistic.

To his delight, when boarding time came things went like clockwork. Dan was boarded first. He had no problems with the aisle chair, and his reserved seat had a moveable armrest. Things couldn't have gone any better. Dan sat back and stared out the window while the other passengers boarded. He was in a semi dream state when he noticed an unusual object out on the tarmac.

Upon closer examination, it appeared to be his wheelchair. Just as he was about to call the flight attendant, he noticed another object approaching the wheelchair—a 747 backing up out of the gate. He sat there speechless as he watched the jumbo jet crush his wheelchair. Ultimately, he canceled his trip. On the positive side, this incident happened while he was at home rather than while he was on the road.

Fortunately, Dan's experience is not the norm, but it does illustrate the importance of staying in your own wheelchair as long as possible. In Dan's case, the cargo handlers forgot to move Dan's wheelchair off the tarmac when his flight was delayed. In theory, if Dan had stayed in his own wheelchair up to the aircraft door, it would have been taken directly to the cargo bin instead of sitting on the tarmac. Now, Dan always turns down the airport wheelchair, no matter how hard the check-in agent tries to convince him otherwise.

Dan's story pretty much represents the worst case scenario. The only thing worse I can imagine is actually being *in* your wheelchair when a 747 backs over it. So when you encounter equipment damage problems, think about Dan. You'll be able to take some comfort in the fact that, no matter how bad things are, at least a jumbo jet didn't roll over your wheelchair.

Avoid the Cargo Bin

THE BEST WAY to protect your assistive device from damage (short of staying home) is to keep it out of the cargo bin. Let's look at things realistically. When you relinquish your wheelchair to the baggage handler, it really is a crap shoot. Face it: Nobody is going to take the same care with your wheelchair that you do, and most certainly not some baggage handler who has a schedule to keep. So where does that leave you? Some people have a choice in these matters, so the first step is to learn what can be carried in the passenger compartment and what must go in the cargo bin.

You can take canes and crutches on board most aircraft. You have to stow these items for takeoff and landing (for safety reasons), but you can get a flight attendant to retrieve them after you are airborne. You should make it a point to get your assistive device back after takeoff, as you will most likely need it if you want to move about the cabin. Additionally, if an emergency occurs, it would be a good idea to have it with you.

Walkers can sometimes be carried in the passenger compartment, depending on the dimensions of the walker and the availability of an onboard closet. Here's where knowing the dimensions of the onboard closet comes in handy, because you will then be able to determine if your walker will fit. Frankly, walkers don't fare very well in the cargo bin, so it's a good idea to invest in a folding walker that fits in the onboard closet.

Some manual wheelchairs will also fit in the onboard closet, depending on the size of the wheelchair and the dimensions of the onboard closet. Remember to take advantage of the preboarding privilege, as your assistive device gets priority space in the onboard closet only if you preboard the aircraft. Additionally, remember that the onboard closet is not large enough for two wheelchairs, so if you travel with another wheeler, one wheelchair will end up in the cargo bin.

Another solution is to invest in a folding power wheelchair or scooter. This is not really a good option for full-time wheelchair- or scooter-users, as the products on the market today lack the pep that wheelers are used to. However, if you only need a wheelchair for distance, this may be a good solution.

Amigo Mobility manufactures a lightweight folding scooter, the TravelMate, which weighs only 58 pounds including the battery pack. This travel scooter is best suited for slow walkers rather than full-time wheelchair-users. Additionally, when you take any assistive device on board an aircraft, remember it is not counted as carry-on luggage.

Of course, if you can't keep your wheelchair out of the cargo bin, it's a good idea to travel with an older wheelchair (if you have one). Some people travel with an old backup wheelchair. Another good solution is to rent a wheelchair or scooter at your destination. Obviously, this option only works for people who use a wheelchair or scooter for distance, but it is something to consider.

Care Vacations and Scoot Around North America can arrange for the rental of assistive devices throughout the United States and on most cruise ships. A premium fee is charged for this type of rental because these companies act as agents. Alternatively, a more economical solution is to make the rental arrangements directly with a medical supply company at your destination.

Onboard Wheelchair Storage

ALTHOUGH THE ONBOARD storage of assistive devices is mandated under the Air Carrier Access Act (ACAA) under certain conditions, it should be noted that most airlines have been fined or at least warned for noncompliance to this directive. Here are a few examples of violations the Department of Transportation (DOT) uncovered during a routine compliance review. These examples are not meant to single out certain airlines as violators, but merely to serve as examples of what happens in real life. They are also meant to show that the mandated onboard storage space is not always a closet.

* Southwest Airlines was found to be in violation of the ACAA for not providing space for the in-cabin storage of folding wheelchairs. Southwest claimed that storage space was available in the overhead bins, but agreed to retrofit their fleet of 737s to include a larger storage space. The DOT fined the airline $500,000 but gave them a $450,000 credit for the retrofit.
* America West Airlines was also found in violation of the wheel-

chair stowage provision of the ACAA. America West agreed to create storage space for one passenger wheelchair on the floor space between the last two rows of seats. It was fined $150,000 but given a $135,000 credit for costs associated with improving access.

* And finally, the DOT discovered that Jet Blue reservation agents were informing customers that folding wheelchairs could not be stored in the passenger compartment. Jet Blue subsequently admitted to the DOT that it did not have the required wheelchair storage space, but agreed to create such a space by stowing a wheelchair atop three passenger seats. The airline was fined $100,000 but granted a $90,000 credit to offset the cost of ACAA training.

As you can see, it's very important to learn the rules of the ACAA as they apply to onboard wheelchair storage. Don't be afraid to speak up when you feel your rights have been violated. Front-line employees don't always know or understand the rules under the ACAA, so sometimes you have to go up a few levels in order to get results.

Protection

IF IT IS impossible to keep your assistive device out of the cargo bin, a little preparation (and a few techniques) will help you protect your equipment. As I pointed out earlier, the best strategy is to stay in your own wheelchair as long as possible (remember Dan). If your chair has gel cell batteries this is pretty easy because gel cell batteries don't have to be removed and packed separately. Gel cell batteries are merely disconnected and the terminals are wrapped, which is a fairly simple procedure.

On the other hand, if your wheelchair doesn't have gel cell batteries, the entire battery is removed and packed in a protective container. This can be a time-consuming procedure. Under the ACAA, you must surrender your wheelchair to the airline at least 1 hour prior to departure if you have spillable batteries. This means you have to use an airport wheelchair for at least an hour. You might want to consider changing to gel cell batteries if they are compatible with your wheelchair. This simple change will save you a lot of time and trouble.

You will be asked about the specifics of your batteries when you check in for your flight. If you have gel cell batteries, make sure they are clearly marked so that they won't be inadvertently removed. If you don't have any labeling on your batteries, check with a local medical supply house, because they usually carry appropriate labels.

You should also learn how to reconnect your batteries. Although your assistive device is supposed to be returned to you with the batteries reconnected, sometimes this just doesn't happen. Knowing how to reconnect your batteries will save you time and frustration.

Many wheelchairs can be transported in the cargo bin without being disassembled, but that of course also depends on the aircraft type. Here's where knowing the dimensions of the aircraft, especially the width of the cargo door, comes in handy. For example, let's compare two aircraft; the EMB 145, which has 50 seats, and the ATR 42-500, which has 46 seats.

Although both aircraft have approximately the same passenger capacity, the dimensions of their cargo doors vary drastically. The EMB 145 has a 39-inch cargo door, whereas the ATR 42-500 has a 54-inch cargo door. So, the EMB 145 might not be the ideal choice for a large wheelchair.

Even if your only choice is the EMB 145, it would help to know in advance that your wheelchair was going to be disassembled for transport. This knowledge also gives you the flexibility to shop around and perhaps find a larger aircraft. Sometimes this is the best bet, even if you have to drive to another gateway city.

One of the best things you can do to protect your assistive device is to attach assembly and disassembly directions to your wheelchair or scooter. This sounds like a fairly simple task, but many people overlook it because they assume their assistive device will not be disassembled for transport. True, it may not be required to be disassembled under ideal conditions, but it never hurts to have instructions attached.

You are not encouraging baggage handlers to disassemble your assistive device by attaching instructions; you are merely giving them the proper instructions should it become necessary. Actually, most baggage handlers prefer not to disassemble assistive devices, because it's just more work for them. But sometimes due to the volume of cargo, it is necessary, even on the most accessible aircraft.

Instructions should be written clearly and simply in both English and Spanish. If possible, also use numbered illustrations or simple drawings to illustrate the assembly and disassembly procedure. Laminate the instructions and attach them securely to your assistive device. It also helps to talk to the baggage handlers to tell them exactly how to handle your chair, although this is not always possible. Clear assembly and disassembly instructions will help protect your assistive device. Many people even leave these instructions attached to their wheelchair or scooter all the time, because it saves preparation time when it's time to travel.

Remove any loose or protruding parts from your wheelchair or scooter. This includes items like mirrors, cushions, and leg rests. Put them in a duffel bag and carry them on the aircraft. Do not check them! Wheelchair parts fall under the category of assistive devices and are not counted as carry-on luggage.

Remember, something may be piled on top of your wheelchair in the cargo bin. If your wheelchair or scooter becomes a projectile object, loose or protruding parts may break upon impact. Additionally, remember to let a bit of air out of your tires and to carry-on all gel cushions. Most cargo bins are not pressurized. It's also a good idea to carry a compact bicycle pump with you so you can reinflate your tires when you reach your destination.

You will also need to protect your joystick if it's not possible to easily remove it. A plastic cup and packing tape works well for this purpose.

It's equally important to protect your controller. Says one frequent traveler, "I discovered that the very sturdy cardboard tubes that carpets are rolled on makes a great controller protective device. I scrounged an empty tube (some places call them cores) from the carpet store, then used a hacksaw to cut off the right length to slide over my controller. It works great."

Says another traveler, "My controller unplugs easily so I just take it off (along with the entire armrest), stuff it in a duffel bag, and carry it on with me."

And one veteran road warrior swears by his tried and true method. "I carry a spare joystick and controller when I travel," he says. "This is easy to do with an Invacare chair because all of the parts swap out. I stick some Velcro to the bottom of the spare controller. If I break down, I just peel and stick my spare controller to the top of the battery box, disconnect the wires from the busted one and connect them to my backup. I do the same thing with my joystick."

Many people come up with creative ways to protect their wheelchairs during transit. My friend Karen devised the following cheap and easy technique. "I travel fairly often and use an electric wheelchair," she says. "I carry on all removable parts and wrap the entire base of the chair with plastic cling wrap. This helps prevent scratches and dings. It also encapsulates the wires so nothing gets unplugged." I like Karen's method. It's simple, and the only out-of-pocket expense is for a roll or two of plastic cling wrap.

Says frequent-flyer Mike, "I've found that bubble wrap (which you can buy at an office supply store) works well in protecting my wheelchair from damage. I just take some to the airport with me and then, before I turn my wheelchair over to the airline, I pad the areas most likely to sustain damage. I also take some tape with me so I can secure the bubble wrap. So far, it works pretty good."

Other travelers go a bit further (and spend a bit more money) in their quest to limit wheelchair damage. In fact, Gloria even went as far as to build her own transport crate. "I was tired of the airlines damaging my son's wheelchair, so I had a crate-building company build a protective container for transport," she says. "They built a crate that has four locking caster wheels, handles, and a side door with a moveable ramp. All the major airlines have accepted the crate so far, although I do have to make advance arrangements for it. Now the crate comes back beat up but the wheelchair remains undamaged."

Gloria is on the right track: In fact, the Haseltine Corporation manufactures and sells protective containers specifically for wheelchair air transport. These containers are constructed out of rigid molded plastic. There are two models of the Haseltine Flyer, one for folding manual wheelchairs and another for power wheelchairs and scooters.

Model 504-A is designed for folding wheelchairs and consists of a polyethylene container with foam padding and internal straps to hold accessories in place. It is also available with wheels. The larger 504-C model is designed for rigid motorized chairs and scooters. The Haseltine Flyers are priced from $325 to $675, depending on the model.

The downside is that you have to arrange for storage of the con-

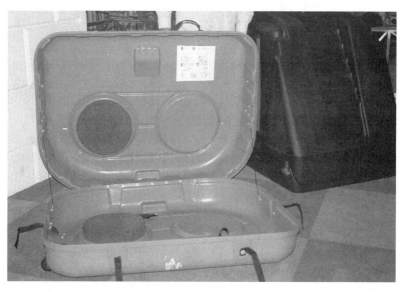

Figure 2.1.
The Haseltine Corporation manufacturers a variety of protective containers for wheelchair air transport. This is model 504-A, for folding wheelchairs.

tainer at your destination. Contact your airline in advance for more information on this matter. The Haseltine containers have been tested by several airlines, but so far no airline has purchased any. On the other hand, travelers are starting to realize the advantages of the Haseltine Flyer, and they are the primary market. We can only hope that the airlines will one day follow suit.

And finally, do remember to take a kit of basic tools with you when you travel. You will need these to prepare your assistive device for transport. Additionally, a tool kit will enable you to make quick repairs on the road, which will save you time and money. Your tool kit should include items such as a small screwdriver with interchangeable bits, a crescent wrench, a couple of Allen wrenches, a small roll of electrical tape, a few lengths of electrical wire, an assortment of electrical connectors, and a variety of nuts, bolts, and washers. Your own tool kit will of course depend on your particular equipment. If you use a scooter, don't forget to pack a spare key in your emergency tool kit. You never know when you will need it.

When Protection Isn't Enough

SOMETIMES, NO MATTER how hard you try, the inevitable happens. Your wheelchair is damaged in transit. You need to be prepared for this. The first thing you should do is learn what the ACAA says about airline liability for damage to assistive devices.

The ACAA originally limited airline liability for damage to assistive devices to $2,500. Due to public pressure and the rising incidence of wheelchair damage by the airlines, the DOT eliminated this cap on August 2, 1999. The new rule governing airline damage to assistive devices became effective on September 1, 1999.

The new rule lifted the previous cap, established guidelines for valuation, and permitted recovery for consequential damages. Under the new rule, airlines are responsible for all repairs to damaged devices; however if the devices are lost or damaged beyond repair, the airlines are only responsible for the original purchase price. For example, if you paid $3,000 for your wheelchair 10 years ago, but it would cost $5,500 to replace it today, you can only expect to recover the original purchase price ($3,000) if your wheelchair is damaged beyond repair. You are responsible for the additional $2,500 it would cost to replace your wheelchair.

Travelers are cautioned to know both the purchase price and the replacement cost of their assistive devices and to be aware of the difference between these two figures. If the difference is substantial, you may want to carry additional insurance with a high deductible to cover this gap.

Airlines are also required to pay for consequential damages, such as wheelchair rentals and unrefundable tickets, tours, or deposits. Please be aware that these rules only apply to U.S.-based carriers. The current compensation cap for international flights is still $9.07/lb. (covered under the Warsaw Convention). Know your rights and the value of your equipment before you fly and make sure you have adequate insurance coverage to cover your assistive devices.

It's also important to remember to report any damage to your wheelchair or scooter immediately. In most cases, this means before you leave the airport. Admittedly, some internal damage is hard to detect immediately, but it is important to report it as soon as you become aware of it. Even though you may be in the middle of a holiday, you need to take time out to file a claim with the airline if you expect to recover your damages. The airline may deny a claim if they feel it is not filed in a timely manner. Additionally, under the ACAA, airlines are not required to respond to complaints that are more than 45 days old.

This seems like a very simple task, but it amazes me how many people don't understand the importance of timeliness in this matter. For example, one lady I talked to at a health fair last year told me about some damage done to her scooter on a recent airline flight. When I inquired about her definition of recent, she matter-of-factly replied, "About 8 months ago. Should I file a claim?" Unfortunately this is not an isolated incident. If you had an automobile accident, and you waited 8 months to report the damage, do you think your insurance company would pay the claim? Most likely they wouldn't. And neither will the airlines. Report all damage (no matter how small it seems) immediately.

Finally, no matter how bad things seem (even if your wheelchair is returned to you in pieces), don't panic. I know this is easier said than done, but I would like to illustrate the importance of this point with a story about my friend John. John is a pretty well-seasoned traveler, but every now and then life throws him a few curves.

On a recent trip to the Bahamas, John's wheelchair was literally returned to him in pieces. John relates his humbling experience, "First they brought out the frame, then they kept bringing out smaller and smaller pieces," he says. "I didn't even know my wheelchair had that many pieces. Actually, I didn't care about the wheelchair, as I travel with my old backup klunker, but I didn't want to ruin my long-anticipated holiday. I just blew a fuse and started cussing and screaming. I was quite a sight right there in the middle of the airport."

"The embarrassing thing was that the baggage handler had my wheelchair back together in about 2 minutes. Apparently, this was standard procedure. I wheeled out with my tail tucked between my legs. On the positive side, I didn't even think about renting a car there. I figured if they could assemble my wheelchair that quickly, they could do wonders stripping a car."

Loaners

ALTHOUGH YOUR TOOL kit will allow you to make quick repairs on the road, if your wheelchair is badly damaged, you will have to relinquish the chair while it is being repaired. In the interim, you will need an appropriate loaner. But what is an appropriate loaner? That depends on who you ask, as some airline personnel have an interesting definition of appropriate. It's not that they are trying to pull a fast one on you, it's just that they really don't understand the difference between your Quickie and their E&J airport wheelchair.

Here's where a little patience comes in. Again, this is easier said than done, especially if you are tired and cranky. To advocate for yourself and to get what you define as an appropriate loaner wheelchair you need to calmly explain the facts of life to the airline personnel assigned to help you. You may even have to do this more than once, as you'll probably have to talk to a supervisor or another clerk. No matter how frustrating this is, it's the only way to get a wheelchair that adequately suits your needs.

If you have a highly specialized chair, you might even do some advance research and find an appropriate rental outlet at your destination (just in case). Whatever happens, keep your temper, and remember that the airlines are responsible for providing you with an appropriate loaner chair. In other words, if their E&J won't suit your needs, the airline has to foot the bill for an appropriate rental. Keep talking till they get it right.

Finally, if you don't get satisfaction from talking with front-line personnel, ask to speak to the Complaints Resolution Officer (CRO). The CRO will help you get the services you are entitled to, including an appropriate loaner chair.

Other Air Travel Issues 3

Beyond Wheelchairs

"I use therapeutic oxygen. Is it possible for me to travel by air?"

"I need to remain in a reclining position. What are my options for air travel?"

"I use a ventilator and want to travel by air. Is this possible? What advance arrangements do I need to make?"

"I've never traveled by air with my service animal. What can I expect? What are my rights?"

PEOPLE APPROACH ME with questions like these all the time. Admittedly, there are no pat answers to these questions. In fact, the answers usually depend on the individual circumstances of the traveler. These topics all fall into what I call the "beyond wheelchairs" category of air travel. In some instances, such as stretcher travel, special medical clearance is required. In other instances, such as travel with a service animal, travelers merely need to learn the rules and regulations, so they know what to expect. In all instances, in-depth research is usually required. So let's take a look at some of these special cases.

To be quite honest, I really dislike the word *special*, as it carries such bad connotations. It implies segregation, in this era of inclusion. Years ago, people were segregated into special programs, whereas today the goal is to include everybody in the same accessible program. Personal feelings aside, many airlines insist on using this archaic term to describe certain services or departments. For example, when you need information about travel with therapeutic oxygen, you usually contact the special services or special-needs department. So I hesitantly use the term *special* and use it only to direct you to the most appropriate airline department.

Oxygen

TRAVEL WITH THERAPEUTIC oxygen is not specifically covered under the Air Carrier Access Act (ACAA). By this I mean that U.S. airlines are not required to provide therapeutic oxygen services to their passengers. Each airline sets its own policy regarding therapeutic oxygen services. Currently, America West and Southwest Airlines do not accept passengers who travel with therapeutic oxygen. This exclusion is well within their legal rights, because travel with therapeutic oxygen is considered a safety issue and, as such, it is regulated by the Federal Aviation Administration (FAA). Of course, this statement usually prompts a lively discourse from therapeutic oxygen users.

The usual argument presented by therapeutic oxygen users is that their equipment is very safe and, as such, it should be allowed on all commercial aircraft. The FAA considers therapeutic oxygen a safety issue for two reasons. First, even though most people maintain their equipment in excellent working order, you never know when somebody could unintentionally bring damaged equipment on board. And second, an oxygen cylinder is an excellent place to conceal an explosive device; a device that could potentially go undetected by security. Plus, to be honest, some airlines just don't want to take the time to train their personnel or to make the proper arrangements.

Either way, the airlines are allowed to set their own policies on this matter, so your only choice is to deal with an airline that does provide therapeutic oxygen services. Before you decide which airline to travel with, call around and ask them all about their specific policies and procedures regarding therapeutic oxygen. Procedures vary between carriers, and they can change at any time. Please note that many non-U.S. carriers also accept passengers who use therapeutic oxygen.

Although different airlines have different procedures regarding therapeutic oxygen, they all prohibit passengers from using their own equipment on board. Passengers must use airline-supplied oxygen. The charge for this service usually runs between $50 and $150 per flight leg on most U.S. air carriers. It should be noted however that some non-U.S. airlines charge well over $1,000 for this service, so it pays to find out the price before your book your flight.

Oxygen services are charged per flight leg. A flight leg is defined as the time between one takeoff and one landing, so try to book a nonstop direct flight whenever possible. Most insurance policies do not cover in-flight oxygen, so check with your insurance carrier in advance. Even if your insurance carrier does cover in-flight oxygen, the airlines require payment in advance, and they won't accept an insurance assignment. You must pay the cost up front and seek reimbursement from your insurance company.

All U.S. airlines require a doctor's statement from passengers who intend to travel with therapeutic oxygen. Some airlines require the doctor to fill out specific forms, while others ask for a prescription. When making your travel arrangements, make sure to ask what kind of oxygen equipment is provided. Some airlines provide flow meters that can be adjusted from 2 to 8 liters, while others have flow meters with a low (2l) and a high (4l) setting.

Ask the airline if you need to bring your own mask or cannula. Some airlines provide them and some don't. It's also a good idea to take some empty tanks with you, so you can have them refilled at your destination. Airlines will allow you to carry empty tanks, but you must check them with your baggage. You cannot carry them on board the aircraft with you.

You will also need to make arrangements for oxygen services at your destination. Check with the airport to make sure they allow oxygen use in the terminal. Then check with your local oxygen supplier to see if they are affiliated with a national chain that can provide service to you at your destination. You must have the oxygen delivered to the airport, because you cannot use the in-flight oxygen in the terminal. Alternatively, you can have a friend or relative meet you at the airport with your oxygen supplies.

The price for airport delivery of oxygen varies, however since it's a labor intensive service, it's cheaper during regular business hours. You will pay a premium price for this service on weekends and in the evenings, so try to time your arrival accordingly.

Location also makes a difference, because oxygen services are cheaper at certain airports. For example, you will pay bargain prices for oxygen at Philadelphia, Denver, and Miami airports, but oxygen services at Boston, Washington D.C. (Dulles), and Minneapolis airports are among the most expensive in the nation.

In any case, it never hurts to call more than one supplier to get a competitive price. Many oxygen suppliers will not accept an insurance assignment for oxygen delivered to the airport, so be prepared to pay cash. You will also have to arrange for airport oxygen at your connecting airport, if you cannot arrange a direct flight.

It's extremely important to confirm and reconfirm all airline oxygen arrangements. This letter from a traveler explains what can happen if you don't:

"My husband has emphysema and needs to have oxygen on hand at all times," she writes. "We made arrangements with our travel agent to fly on Air France from Washington D.C. to Paris. I told the travel agent that my husband would need his own supply of oxygen on board, and she informed me my husband's doctor would have to contact the Air France physician. This was done.

"When we boarded the plane, there was no oxygen at our seat," she continues. "When I questioned the flight attendant, he asked to see my ticket. Several minutes later he informed me that our travel agent failed to follow up and order the oxygen after it was cleared by the Air France physician. We had to reschedule our trip because of this mistake.

"In retrospect, I should have followed up with my travel agent," she adds. "I thought it was a bit strange that we were not charged extra for our oxygen, but I just figured somebody forgot to enter the charge."

So be forewarned, if an extra charge for oxygen does not appear on your credit card statement, there is a good chance the oxygen hasn't actually been ordered. It never hurts to follow up, and in many cases it can even save a trip.

Finding an oxygen provider outside of the United States may be a little more difficult. Oxygen prescriptions written by U.S. doctors are not valid outside of the United States. Check with a foreign oxygen supplier to see if you need a prescription. If you do, sometimes the best bet is to work with a U.S. provider that has contracts with foreign oxygen providers. Your local oxygen supplier should be able to give you some good resources.

Another good resource for all therapeutic oxygen users is *Breathin' Easy*, by Jerry Gorby. Published annually, this handy guide includes over 2,500 updated listings for oxygen outlets in more than 100 countries. It also includes helpful tips for traveling by air, sea, or land with therapeutic oxygen.

The *Breathin' Easy* website (breathineasy.com) also features a chart that lists therapeutic oxygen policies for airlines around the world. This information includes advance notice requirements, charges, and flow-rates. Airlines that do not permit therapeutic oxygen are also listed.

Another good Internet resource is the All Go Here Airline Directory (everybody.co.uk/airindex.htm), a U.K.-based website that contains access information (including the availability of therapeutic oxygen services) for most major airlines around the world. Details are also included about the type of equipment provided and the amount of advance notice required.

The American Lung Association of San Diego and Imperial Counties publishes a good travel guide for people with chronic breathing problems. Filled with checklists, travel tips, and worldwide resources, the *Better Breathers Traveler* offers travel strategies for people with asthma, allergies, chronic obstructive pulmonary disease (COPD), or other breathing difficulties. Contact the American Lung Association of San Diego and Imperial Counties for pricing and ordering information.

Allergies

IS AN ALLERGY considered a disability? To be honest, there is no easy answer to that question. The Canadian Transportation Agency (CTA) has at least addressed it, however. The conclusion? A definite maybe.

This 2002 CTA ruling stems from seven complaints filed against Air Canada by passengers who had allergic reactions to dogs, cats, flowers, and paint. The allergic reactions in the individual cases were all different, and they ranged from sneezing and hives to respiratory distress and hearing loss.

The CTA concluded that an allergy, per se, is not a disability for the purposes of Part V of the Canadian Transportation Act. This jurisdictional ruling held that, while an allergy is not automatically considered a disability; some people with allergies may be considered disabled.

So what exactly does that mean? In short, it depends on the severity and intensity of the allergic reaction. The more intense the reaction, the greater likelihood the allergy will be considered a disability. This is something that will be decided on a case-by-case basis. If the allergy is considered a disability, then the accessibility provisions under the Canadian Transportation Act apply to that passenger.

The bottom line is, unless you have a severe life-threatening allergic reaction, your allergy is not considered a disability, and no special accommodations are warranted. And of course, this ruling only applies to Canadian airlines.

Ventilators

MOST U.S. AIR carriers accept vent-users as passengers, although only a few airlines provide onboard electricity for medical equipment. As you may have guessed, policies and procedures vary from airline to airline. Additionally, the availability of onboard electricity also depends on the aircraft type. A lot of restrictions are associated with the use of onboard electricity for medical equipment. Airline policies on this subject change frequently, so even if you travel often, check around with the different carriers for policy updates. Here's what a few U.S. carriers recently had to say about their current policies.

* Northwest Airlines. Generally speaking, ventilators can be plugged into the onboard electrical system, provided they are compatible and do not interfere with the aircraft's communication and navigation systems.
* Delta Air Lines. Ventilators may be used on flights that have onboard electrical outlets. These outlets are only at certain seat locations on some aircraft types, and the customer is responsible for providing any adapters.
* United Airlines. A number of the more common battery-powered devices are pre-approved for acceptance. All others must be cleared by United's medical and engineering staff. Passengers cannot plug in their equipment to the onboard power, but United can provide a special electrical hook up for some devices.

It goes without saying that you need to make your arrangements well in advance and reconfirm all arrangements at least 48 hours prior to travel. Always carry a backup battery and charger with you, because even if onboard power is available it can be dependent on the operational needs of the aircraft. Additionally, onboard electrical power is subject to power surges during hookup and disconnection from ground power.

Check around with the various carriers to see if they can provide onboard electricity for your equipment. If not, you might want to consider traveling under battery power. This option obviously depends on your equipment and on the length of your flight. It's not a possibility for everyone, but it may be worth your consideration.

If you do travel under battery power, take a backup battery and a charger with you on board the aircraft. That way, if you run low on battery power (and happen to be on the ground), you can have somebody get off the plane and recharge one battery for you. This method is especially useful if a delay in deplaning occurs. Above all, know the limitations of your equipment and don't plan things too tightly. Always allow for delays when making your calculations.

Make sure your equipment has gel cell batteries and that they are clearly marked. Wet cell (spillable) batteries are not allowed on board the aircraft. Your equipment must fit under the seat in front of you. If your equipment does not fit in this area, you may strap it to an adjoining seat, but you have to purchase the adjoining seat if you go this route.

No additional or special seating options are available for passengers who travel with a ventilator. You can always request an upgrade, but in this day and age, upgrades usually go to the top echelon of frequent flyers. It never hurts to ask, but don't depend on it. I know some vent-users who insist that they need to be seated in the first row of first class (when traveling on an economy class ticket). After a heated argument with ground personnel, they usually end up in coach. The airlines are not required by law to upgrade you, so if you request an upgrade, keep in mind that it's a request not a demand.

While in the terminal, keep your ventilator plugged into a wall receptacle until the last possible moment, so that your battery will have a 100% charge when you board the aircraft. Take along a 25- to 50-foot extension cord and an adapter to convert a three-pronged plug into a two-pronged plug. The control panels at the end of most jetways have an AC plug, so keep this in mind for emergency situations. Keep an eye open for these AC plugs when you board the plane, just in case a lengthy delay in boarding occurs.

Speaking of delays, what do you do if you experience a long delay on the tarmac? First, if you give yourself some extra time, you won't have this problem under usual circumstances. But unusual circumstances do occur, which are either weather- or traffic-related. So, what do you do if you end up sitting on the tarmac for an hour or more? Experienced vent-users say the best thing to do is to calmly explain the situation to the flight attendant. You need to stress that it is a matter of life and death, not merely a comfort issue. As silly as this sounds, some people just don't understand the concept of a ventilator. Be patient, and if your efforts fail, ask to speak to the CRO by radio.

Although it's not travel specific, a good resource for vent-users is the International Ventilator Users Network (IVUN). IVUN is a worldwide network of ventilator users and health professionals experienced in and committed to home care and long-term mechanical ventilation. IVUN publishes *Ventilator Assisted Living*, a quarterly newsletter, offering articles on family adjustments, equipment, techniques, medical topics, ethical issues, travel, and resources.

Stretchers

ALTHOUGH MOST PEOPLE consider stretcher travel a medical necessity rather than a vacation option, it may be the ideal solution if you are not able to sit upright or if you require additional head and neck support. To be clear here, I'm not talking about travel by a private air ambulance, but stretcher travel on a commercial air carrier. Many people don't even know this option is available and, although it's more costly than standard airfare, it's still much cheaper than an air ambulance.

Before you decide to travel by stretcher on a commercial airline, you should first rule out the possibility of first class travel. Although seat comfort varies from carrier to carrier, a first class seat might do the trick. The drawback to a first class seat is that it may not offer the needed head and neck support. No airline equipment offers additional neck support, but I've seen some homemade devices created by a few enterprising folks that all center around a neck pillow and chest straps. Additionally, even though first class seating offers more reclining room, all seats must be in an upright position for takeoff and landing. So, depending on your needs, this may work for you. It is the cheaper option, so it is worth ruling out before you decide to go the stretcher route.

Currently, Northwest Airlines is the only U.S. airline that provides stretcher service for people who must remain in a reclining position during the flight. Stretcher service is only available on select aircraft, including the Airbus 320; Boeing 757, 727-200, 747-200, and 747-400; and McDonnell Douglas D.C.-10-30 and D.C.-10-40 aircraft. The stretcher can hold up to 250 pounds and can accommodate a person up to 6'2". It is carried in the coach passenger compartment, and placement depends on the aircraft configuration. Existing seats are folded down and a stretcher frame is installed. Stretcher locations are as follows.

* A320   Rows 25, 26, 27   Seats ABC
* 727-200   Rows 5, 6, 7   Seats DEF
* 757   Rows 10, 11, 12   Seats ABC
* D.C.-10   Rows 10, 11, 12   Seats AB
* 747-100   Rows 31, 32, 33   Seats ABC
* 747-200   Rows 25, 26, 27   Seats ABC
* 747-400   Rows 29, 30, 31   Seats ABC

Companion seats are located nearby:

* A320
  * Seat 27C
  * Seat 7F
  * Seat 12C
* D.C.-10
  * Seat 10C
  * Seat 33C
  * Seat 27C
  * Seat 31C

Pricing for stretcher travel depends on both the aircraft and the destination. Passengers must also be delivered and picked up by ambulance. The ambulance fees are not included in the pricing. Passengers must arrange for ambulance transport separately. Here's a breakdown of the current pricing for stretcher travel on Northwest Airlines:

* Domestic.
  * A320/727/757: Four times the full first class fare.
  * D.C.-10, 747-200, 747-400: Six times the full coach fare.

* Transatlantic.
  * D.C.-10/747-200/747-200: Seven times the unrestricted economy fare.

* Transpacific.
  * D.C.-10/747-200/747-200: Nine times the unrestricted economy fare.

Under the ACAA, airlines may require a medical certificate from passengers who travel by stretcher. Northwest Airlines requires such documentation. The medical certificate is merely a written statement from the passenger's physician stating that the passenger is capable of completing the flight safely. The medical certificate should state that no extraordinary medical assistance will be required during the flight.

Northwest Airlines also requires stretcher passengers to sign a liability release prior to departure. All stretcher passengers are required to travel with an attendant or companion who can see to their needs during the flight. This is also permitted under the ACAA.

Reservations for stretcher travel must be made at least 48 hours in advance. Stretcher requests may be made through Northwest's domestic reservations at (800) 225-2525 or international reservations at (800) 447-4747. Northwest Airlines also has a helpful brochure, *Air Travel for People with Disabilities,* which is available by calling (800) 358-3100.

Service Animals

BY NOW, I'M sure you've heard the tale about the two ladies who boarded a U.S. Airways flight with their 350-pound pig in tow. They claimed porky was a service animal, and U.S. Airways employees bought their story and allowed the pig to ride in the first class cabin. Although much confusion surrounds the exact events that transpired during the flight, everybody agrees that the pig defecated on the jetway.

So, was the pig a service animal as defined under the ACAA? No, it wasn't. And not because it was a pig, or because it reportedly took four people to wheel it aboard the aircraft. It's not considered a service animal because it did not behave appropriately on board the aircraft. What is appropriate behavior? Well, it isn't (as one passenger reported) "running loose through the aircraft, and squealing loudly." Enough of the fairy tales. Let's look at what the ACAA has to say regarding real service animals.

Under the ACAA, U.S. airlines must allow service animals to accompany on board the aircraft any qualified person with a disability. This applies to any guide dog, signal dog, or any other animal trained to provide assistance to a person with a disability. This rule only applies to service animals while they are traveling with a person with a disability. For example, if a nondisabled animal trainer needed to transport a service animal by air, the service animal would be subject to the airline's general regulations regarding the carriage of animals. In other words, the service animal would not necessarily have the right to accompany the trainer in the cabin.

On May 9, 2003, the Department of Transportation (DOT) amended the ACAA to expand the definition of a service animal to also include emotional support animals. Airline employees are permitted to require documentation from passengers traveling with emotional support animals. The required documentation includes a letter from a mental health professional stating that the passenger has a mental health-related disability. The letter must state that the emotional support animal must accompany the passenger to ensure the passenger's mental health or to physically assist the passenger. The letter must be less than 1 year old, and be on letterhead from a mental health professional who is currently treating the passenger. The emotional support animal must behave appropriately to be considered a service animal.

According the DOT, these revisions were necessary to stop passengers from using the service animal provision to bring pets into the passenger cabin. The new guidelines were published in the *Federal Register* on May 9, 2003.

Assuming that a qualified service animal is traveling with a person with a disability, the service animal is allowed to accompany that individual everywhere on the aircraft. People who travel with a service animal are entitled to bulkhead seating if they desire, but they are not required to sit in the bulkhead section. They may choose a non-bulkhead seat if they prefer. The service animal must not obstruct the aisle or any other area that is required by FAA safety rules to remain unobstructed. If no space in the cabin can accommodate the animal without causing such an obstruction, the animal is not permitted to travel in the cabin.

Most of the time, service animals have no problems traveling on commercial air carriers. The exception might be on some smaller aircraft, where there may not be enough room for the animal to sit at the owner's feet without protruding out into the aisle. If a small aircraft is your only choice, ask for the seating dimensions (before you make your reservations) so that you can determine if enough room exists for your service animal to sit at your feet.

Of course, it is the owner's responsibility to make sure that her animal acts appropriately while on the aircraft. This is usually not much of a problem, because service animals are highly trained to act appropriately in public situations. If the service animal exhibits inappropriate behavior such as growling, barking, or running up and down the aisle, the airlines are not required to treat it as a service animal.

Airline personnel are trained to mitigate the effects of such behavior. For example, if a service animal barks, they might first suggest a muzzle to try to solve the problem. If mitigation doesn't work, they do have the right to require that the service animal travel in the cargo bin. Generally speaking, a properly trained service animal should have no problems traveling on a commercial air carrier.

One subject that comes up a lot when talking about service animals and air travel is cleaning and damage fees. Are they legal? The ACAA prohibits special charges such as deposits or surcharges for accommodations made for passengers with a disability. However, an airline can charge a passenger with a disability for damage done by their service animal, as long as it's the policy of the airline to charge nondisabled passengers for the same type of damage.

For example, if the airline regularly charges nondisabled passengers for cleaning and repair to damaged seats, they can also charge a person traveling with a service animal for similar damages. Again, a properly trained service animal should have no problems, but it's always a good idea to know your rights.

Of course, bathroom facilities are always a matter of concern, and the obvious question is how do you handle this situation while you are en route with your service animal? According to my well traveled friend Connie, a definite procedure applies. "Basically, you have to take connecting flights, and leave enough time in between flights for a doggy pit stop," says Connie.

"The airline needs to be advised that you are traveling with a service animal and that you will need assistance at the connecting airport to walk your dog," she explains. "There are computer codes the airlines use for passengers traveling with service animals. There isn't a specific code that addresses the doggy potty stop issue, so you need to ask the reservation clerk to note this in the remarks section. Of course, you also need to check back to make sure this has been done. Even after all that hassle, sometimes they still don't get it right. Don't panic, just ask to be guided to the appropriate area when you disembark."

Another issue of concern to people who travel with a service animal is the whole security screening process. What is the best way to train or prepare your service animal for the wanding procedure at the security checkpoint? One traveler suggests this method:

"I familiarized Oscar (my service animal) with the screening procedure by using a cordless telephone as a practice wand," she says. "After he was comfortable with it, I got a friend to do it. Then I got several strangers to go through the same procedure until Oscar was totally desensitized to it. When it finally came time for us to go through airport security, we didn't have any problems at all. Oscar was so used to the procedure, he didn't even bat an eye. He's an old pro at it now."

Finally, be sure to inquire in advance about any restrictions or special procedures for importing animals at your destination. Some countries impose strict quarantines on incoming animals, and most of these quarantines do not exclude service animals.

As of December 11, 2002, the United Kingdom lifted quarantine restrictions on dogs and cats entering the United Kingdom from the United States and Canada. It should be noted however, that a number of restrictions still apply to animals entering the United Kingdom from the United States. Some of these restrictions make it difficult or impossible for service animals to accompany their owners.

To bypass the 6-month U.K. quarantine, animals must have a microchip implanted, be tested and vaccinated for rabies, arrive on an approved air route, and travel in an approved container in the hold of the aircraft. The container is required to be sealed with a special seal, and the animal is not allowed to leave the container until it clears customs. There is no exemption for service animals. All animals must travel in the hold of the aircraft.

For more information about approved procedures and routes visit www.defra.gov.uk/animalh/quarantine/index.htm or call the PETS Travel Scheme Helpline at +44 (0) 870-241-1710.

The United States is not free from restrictions either. Hawaii lifted their strict quarantine in 1998 (actually it's a settlement to a lawsuit); however, Hawaii-bound service animals still face some entry restrictions. The terms of the settlement apply only to residents of the United States who have guide dogs trained at schools belonging to the U.S. Council Guide Dog Schools. The settlement allows these animals to enter Hawaii without quarantine, providing they adhere to a required program of vaccinations, exams, titers, and microchip identification. For details on the procedures, contact Guide Dog Users Inc.

The Pets Welcome Database (petswelcome.com/milkbone /quarmap.html) is another helpful resource for service animal travel. Even though this online database is geared towards pets, some of the information may also be useful to people who have service animals. This worldwide database includes information about a number of animal quarantines, embargoes, restrictions, and policies.

It's important to note that some countries have restrictions on pets, but not on working dogs, and the Pets Welcome Database only applies to pets. It's best to use this database as a general guide. Contact the consulate of your destination country for the most accurate and updated information regarding service animal quarantines and policies.

Getting Around on the Ground | 4

ACCESSIBLE GROUND TRANSPORTATION is one of the most important components of any trip because without it, you can literally fall flat on your face. You can also be stuck at the airport, trapped at your hotel, or segregated and separated from the rest of your party. The availability of accessible ground transportation can literally make or break a trip. It's also one of the major components of *seamless travel*, a term I coined many years ago while researching a story on San Diego.

Seamless travel is defined as "travel without any gaps in accessible services or facilities." Quite simply, it means you can get from the airport, train, or bus station to your accessible accommodations. And it means once you get there, you won't have to sit in your hotel room because the tourist attractions or public facilities are not accessible. If you're talking about cruises, seamless travel means that cruise ships, as well as shore excursions and transfers should all be accessible. Obviously, we have a long way to go in making seamless travel a reality; however, I believe it's a very viable goal.

Until seamless travel becomes a reality, it pays to thoroughly investigate your accessible ground transportation options before you leave home. This will not only save you a lot of time and trouble, but in some cases it will also save you money.

Airport Transportation

BECAUSE MANY PEOPLE travel by air, finding accessible airport transportation is a top priority. Your options vary depending on your destination, and in most cases even on your arrival time. You can do some advance research, but it's not a foolproof system. The best advice I can give you is to do your research, know your options, and make advance arrangements whenever possible—and be prepared for unexpected delays.

If you are staying at a hotel, find out if they offer courtesy airport transportation. Under the Americans with Disabilities Act (ADA), hotels that offer courtesy transportation must also provide accessible transportation free of charge. The catch is that most front desk personnel don't know this fact; so you have to know your rights and learn how to advocate for yourself. I shudder to think how many people are charged for this service because they don't know that it must be provided free of charge. In fact, that's exactly what (almost) happened to my friend Dana.

When Dana first made her hotel reservation, she inquired about airport transfers. The clerk told her that they did have a courtesy shuttle, but it wasn't accessible. Before Dana had a chance to express her disappointment, the clerk chimed in and said he could make arrangements for her with a local accessible transportation company. Dana was relieved that somebody else could take care of the details. The clerk called her back later and told her that everything had been arranged and even gave her a confirmation number. He also told Dana that it would cost $25.

At first, this seemed fine to Dana. Of course, she blew a gasket when I told her that, legally speaking, the hotel could not charge her for this service. She immediately called the manager and registered a complaint. The manager apologized profusely and told her that of course there would be no charge for her airport transfers.

Remember, if a property offers free airport transfers, they must also provide accessible airport transfers at no charge. Additionally, they cannot charge guests for this service, even if they have to contract it out. Don't let hotels off the hook on this issue, and if you run into problems (like Dana did), ask to speak to the manager. Management is usually well educated on ADA matters.

Many cab companies now have at least some accessible vehicles in their fleet. If you are staying at a hotel, you may be able to glean a little information about the local cab companies from the desk clerk. Call the companies directly and ask if they operate any accessible vehicles. If not, ask if they know of any local companies that do have accessible vehicles.

Be sure to specify your needs when talking to a cab company. Some cab companies operate ramp-equipped vans, while others consider a cab with a large trunk an accessible vehicle. If you can travel with a folding wheelchair, it greatly increases your accessible ground transportation options. If this is the case, you can use a standard taxi as long as your wheelchair fits in the trunk. It's also a good idea to carry a transfer board with you.

You may be able to make advance arrangements for an accessible cab. This policy varies, and most companies only accept reservations 24 to 48 hours in advance.

If a cab won't suit your needs, find out if any airport transportation companies serve the area. Again, some of these companies do have accessible vehicles. The service varies from company

Figure 4.1.
Many large cities now have accessible taxis. This is a ramp-equipped accessible taxi in San Francisco.

to company. The good news about airport transportation companies is that you can always book them in advance. The bad news is that sometimes they show up without the accessible vehicle.

My friend John travels with his Hoyer lift and uses airport transportation companies frequently. John reports that there seems to be no consistency in service, because even national companies are locally managed. Sometimes John has a great experience, and sometimes it's the pits. The best strategy is to call and reconfirm your reservation at least 24 hours in advance and, of course, remind the company that you do need an accessible vehicle.

Super Shuttle is usually a good airport transportation option if it is available in your city. Granted, there were some access problems with this company in the 1990s, but as the result of a 2002 ADA settlement, Super Shuttle added more accessible vehicles to their fleet. Now, you can even make reservations for accessible transportation on their website at supershuttle.com. It's important to note that all accessible services require at least 24 hours advance notice.

Of course, accessible airport transportation is far from flawless. For example, take Paula and Mike's recent experience at Miami International Airport (MIA). Paula and Mike planned ahead and made reservations with a shuttle company for accessible airport transfers. Upon arrival at MIA, Paula called the company as instructed. She was told a vehicle was on the way. Two hours later Paula and Mike were still waiting.

The problem? Well, it seems the shuttle driver had never driven the accessible vehicle, so he wasn't aware of the extra clearance required for the high-top van. Somehow, he managed to wedge the vehicle under a pedestrian overcrossing at MIA. He did manage to extricate the van, but in the interim he also attracted the attention of the police, the National Guard, and a good number of curious onlookers. Suffice it to say that, in this day and age of heightened security, the police took a while to sort out the matter. And of course the shuttle company had no other accessible vehicles to dispatch. Three hours after they touched down at MIA, Paula and Mike finally made it to their hotel.

So, what's a traveler to do? Plan ahead and be aware of the weakest link. Always have a back up plan when accessible transportation is involved. Ask yourself, "What will I do if the transportation is late, or doesn't show up at all?" Never schedule tight connections when accessible ground transportation is involved.

Public transportation is another option, although I tend to shy away from buses. There's nothing worse than riding on a crowded bus after a long plane trip. Plus, buses are at the mercy of traffic, and if you hit it at the wrong time of day, a 15-minute trip can easily turn into a 45-minute ordeal. Find out if there is a local rail or metro station at the airport, and if it stops close to your hotel. Contact the public transportation authority to find out if it is accessible.

Many airports have great metro service. I personally recommend taking the metro from Ronald Regan Airport in Washington, D.C. It's convenient, accessible, and very affordable. If you arrive late at night, however, I'd stick to private transportation. It's never a good idea to wander around a large city, suitcase in tow, after dark.

One of the big drawbacks to metro systems is that most of the stations are located underground. Access is usually by elevator; however, most elevators are routinely down for maintenance at one time or another. Many transit systems have a hotline you can call for an updated status report on the working (or nonworking) elevators. It's a good idea to get this number in advance and then call it just before you hop on the metro. It could save you a lot of time and trouble. It's nice to know if the elevators at your destination station are operational before you get on the train.

Finding accessible airport transportation is sometimes just a matter of whittling down your options. Contact the local Convention and Visitors Bureau (CVB) and find out what airport transportation options exist. Then, inquire directly with the individual providers to find out if they offer any accessible transportation. Most CVBs don't know a lot about accessibility, but they can usually provide you with a long list of transportation providers.

Additionally, a few CVBs now publish access guides. These

access guides describe the accessibility of all tourist services, including airport transportation. Hopefully, in the coming years, more CVBs will realize the importance of providing accurate access information. Until then, it never hurts to ask.

No matter what type of transportation you choose, it's a good idea to take a cell phone with you when you travel. It comes in handy when you're curbside, waiting for that long-delayed hotel shuttle. It sure beats trekking back to the terminal in search of a phone. Shop around and find a cellular plan that allows you to make long distance calls at no extra charge, and one that doesn't add roaming charges for calls made out of your home area.

Public Transportation

MOST PEOPLE REQUIRE some form of transportation once they get to their destination; however, many travelers rely on public transportation. When choosing your hotel try to find one that is close to many of the attractions you wish to see. Additionally, remember to pick a hotel that is close to the bus and metro stops, because utilizing public transportation will save you money. Of course, you will have to do some pre-trip research to find out what types of accessible public transportation are available.

The good news is that access on U.S. public transportation is really improving. In fact, many options that were entirely out of the question 5 years ago are nicely accessible today. For example, Memphis, San Antonio, St. Petersburg, and New Orleans now operate lift-equipped trolley cars. It's a fun and economical way to see the city.

One of the best resources for accessible transportation is the Project Action Accessible Transportation Database. Created by the Easter Seals Society, this online database lists accessible transportation throughout the United States, including taxis, buses, hotel shuttles, and airport transportation. Access this site, free of charge, at projectaction.org. I have to say that this database contains the most accurate information on the subject.

Figure 4.2. Lift-equipped trolley cars, like this one in St. Petersburg, are now available in many U.S. cities.

A few other accessible transportation guides are out there, but I've reviewed most of them and found them all to be lacking in accuracy. Plus, some of them are quite expensive. My advice is to save your money and use the Project Action Database. If you don't have Internet access, you can connect to the Internet at your local library.

When you search the Project Action Database, you will be able to get contact information for the public transportation authority in your destination city. This is very important information, as you can glean specific access information from the local public transportation authority. The volume and detail of the information varies from city to city, but some public transportation authorities even produce access guides.

Such is the case with the San Francisco Municipal Railway (Muni), one of the public transportation authorities serving the Bay Area. Muni operates the local bus and rail routes and publishes the excellent *Muni Access Guide,* which describes their accessible services. Many other public transportation authorities publish print access guides. Don't be afraid to ask. Additionally, most public transportation authorities have some sort of access information online.

The European Conference of Ministers of Transport (ECMT) also has some helpful accessible transportation resources on their website at www.oecd.org/cem/topics/handicaps/travel.htm. The listings are grouped by geographical region, and they include access information on planes, trains, buses, and paratransit services around the world. It's a good place to go for European resources.

Another great resource is the local Center for Independent Living (CIL). These nationwide centers go by a variety of names, including Independent Living Center (ILC), Resources for Independent Living (RIL), and Independent Living Resources (ILR). The one thing they all have in common is that they provide resources, advocacy, and support for people with disabilities who

Figure 4.3.
In many metropolitan areas, public transportation provides a convenient and economical transportation option. This is the accessible San Diego Trolley (light rail).

want to live independently.

The focus of each CIL differs, and some are better than others. Still, accessible public transportation is a big issue for people with disabilities, so many CILs have information on this subject. Many people working in the CILs rely on accessible public transportation, so you may get some helpful first-hand information. Again, it depends on the CIL, and in some cases even the contact person, but it can be a valuable resource, so I encourage people to give it a try whenever possible.

TIRR publishes the most accurate CIL directory, through their Independent Living Research Utilization (ILRU) program. ILRU was established in 1977, to serve as a national center for information, training, research, and technical assistance for independent living. ILRU's Directory of Independent Living Programs is a comprehensive listing of over 400 programs providing independent living services in the United States and Canada. The directory costs $10 and can be obtained in many formats. For more information contact TIRR at (713) 520-0232 or visit www.bcm.tmc.edu/ilru/ilru-directory.html.

Rental Vehicles

ADMITTEDLY, PUBLIC TRANSPORTATION is not for everybody. Some people just like the convenience of driving their own vehicle. People who want this convenience can either take their personal vehicle on a road trip, or rent a vehicle at their destination. Either way, it's best to investigate the availability and pricing of parking at your destination before you make this decision. In some cities, like San Francisco, parking is expensive and pretty much nonexistent.

And although most cities in the United States honor parking placards from other states, New York City is the exception to this rule. Unless you have a local New York City parking placard, expect to be cited or towed (or both) if you park in a designated accessible space in the Big Apple.

Most rental car agencies offer a variety of adaptive equipment for rental cars. Depending on the location, 24 to 48 hours notice is required for the installation of hand controls and spinner knobs. Because there are a wide variety of manufacturers of adaptive equipment, there can be a bit of confusion when it comes to getting the proper equipment installed.

A good tip is to take a picture of the adaptive equipment you need and then fax, mail, or e-mail a photo to the rental car agency, so that they will know exactly what you need. They can give the photo to their mechanic to ensure that the proper device is installed. It's always a good idea to deal directly with the local franchise, to make sure that your adaptive equipment request is treated appropriately.

Even a simple request like "hand controls" can cause some confusion. Such was the case with my friend Patty, who had driven her own hand control-equipped van for many years. Patty is a bilateral above the knee amputee, and she uses either a manual or power wheelchair when she travels. Because she was traveling with her 13-year-old son, she thought it would be a good idea to take her manual wheelchair and rent a sports utility vehicle (SUV) with hand controls. She figured that she could drive the vehicle, while her son could fold up her wheelchair and stow it in the back. In theory it was a great idea, but in practice it didn't work out very well.

When Patty arrived at the rental facility she could not get into the SUV because the hand controls protruded out near the bottom. Her own hand controls protrude out at the top, allowing her easy access. She ended up renting a more expensive van because the hand controls just wouldn't work for her. In retrospect, she thinks she could have avoided this situation by asking the rental car company to send her a photo of the hand controls, because she clearly knows what styles work for her. She also says that renting the SUV wasn't really a good idea, because there wasn't enough space for her on the driver's side.

It pays to know what vehicle will suit your needs and then stick to that choice even if a rental agent tries to talk you into an upgrade. Unfortunately, my friend Darryl learned that lesson the hard way.

Darryl recounts his rental car experience in Southeastern Maine in the following excerpt from his trip diary.

"I reserved a Ford Contour, which would have suited our needs fine, but I let the Hertz agent talk us into upgrading to a Ford Explorer," writes Darryl. "As roomy as it looks, the Explorer is really a pretty poor choice for someone in a wheelchair. It was very tight inside, with no maneuvering room. The doors didn't open very wide and the cargo area didn't hold very much. My son's manual wheelchair barely fit in the back, and left little room for anything else. Plus, I can't count the number of times I hit my back on the door trying to help my son transfer. Oh well, live and learn."

There are some limits on what types of services and equipment rental car agencies are required to offer. Title III of the ADA states that rental car companies must remove barriers that prevent people with disabilities from using rental cars, whenever doing so is readily achievable. This covers most adaptive equipment like hand controls and, in most cases, spinner knobs.

Rental car agencies have long held that some types of mounting hardware used to attach spinner knobs can cause damage to steering wheels. According to the Department of Justice, rental car agencies are not required to install spinner knobs if they damage the vehicle. It all boils down to the type of vehicle and mounting hardware, so if you need a spinner knob on a specific vehicle model, make sure to state this at the time you make your reservation. Theoretically, this should give the rental agency time to make alternate arrangements.

Of course, the biggest complaint about most rental car agencies is that they do not rent accessible vans. Congress specifically stated in the ADA that companies are not required to retrofit vehicles by installing hydraulically powered or other lifts. Moreover, companies that are in the business of renting vehicles are not required to purchase or lease lift-equipped vehicles.

A few car agencies have affiliate agreements with accessible van rental companies that allow them to provide accessible vans to their customers. The drawback is that these vans are expensive, with the average rental rate near $100 per day. It never hurts to ask, but remember that rental car agencies are not required to provide accessible vans.

In addition to adaptive equipment, all car rental facilities in the United States are required to make their facilities accessible. In fact, the May 2000 settlement of *Giacopini v. Hertz Corporation* mandates improved access at Hertz facilities. Under the terms of the settlement, Hertz is required to provide accessible transportation (shuttle buses) between airport terminals and Hertz off-site rental facilities. Additionally, Hertz must modify all their public facilities to conform with current ADA Accessibility Guidelines (ADAAG). Although this ADA settlement only covers Hertz facilities, under the ADA, all rental car agencies are required to provide this level of access in their U.S. facilities.

Getting to your rental car from the airport can sometimes be a challenge. Although airport locations are required to have accessible shuttle buses, in reality sometimes this just doesn't happen. Fortunately, many companies realize the need for this service, and others have been required to upgrade their fleet as the result of legal action. As a result of a 2003 ADA settlement, Alamo Rent-A-Car and National Car Rental both agreed to provide at least one lift-equipped shuttle bus at each of their airport locations. So, if you're looking for an accessible rental car shuttle, these two companies are a good place to start.

Some people who want to skip the fuss and muss at the rental car counter take their own hand controls with them when they travel. I have to say that although this method does appear to streamline the process, some definite drawbacks apply. First, many car rental companies will not let you install your own hand controls. Furthermore, if you have an accident with self-installed hand controls, you won't be covered under most insurance policies.

Still, some people claim that it's the greatest thing since sliced bread. I can't really endorse this method because it leaves you open to liability in case of an accident. If you are going to try it, however, do remember the following story.

My friend Bob always takes his hand controls with him when he travels. In fact, he's really quite smug about it, bragging all the time about how much money he saves, and how he always has the equipment he needs. That is, until his recent trip to London. It seems that Bob forgot that people drive on the "other side of the road" in England. Suffice it to say that his U.S. hand controls would not work on the British cars. He ended up renting a very expensive accessible van. Bob's not quite so smug any more. Watch out for the same thing in Australia and New Zealand.

Now, a few words about rental vehicles in Europe. Although practices vary from country to country, with a little research, you can find a car rental company that will install hand controls for you. It's usually easier to find a car with hand controls than an accessible van. The most updated resource on adapted rental cars in Europe can be found on the Internet at users.actcom.co.il/~swfm/. It's a private website and includes a lot of Europe resources.

Additionally, don't forget to pack your parking placard, if your travel plans include renting a car in Europe. In 1997, the ECMT passed Resolution No. 97/4, on Reciprocal Recognition of Parking Badges for Persons with Mobility Handicaps. As of Jan. 1, 1999, travelers from associate countries, including the United States and Canada, are also included in this resolution. The resolution requires permit holders to "display a document that shows the international symbol for persons with disabilities, as well as the name of the holder of the document," to receive reciprocal parking privileges in ECMT countries.

Another option is to rent an accessible van. For many people, this is the only vehicle that meets their needs, while for others it seems a wasted expense. Basically it's just a matter of personal preference and need. It's good to know that there are many companies that specialize in renting accessible vans throughout the world, however.

The best database of accessible rental van companies is on our own Emerging Horizons website at EmergingHorizons.com. Years ago, I realized the need for this information, and I decided to provide it online as a community service. I update the website every 2 to 3 weeks, and I'm constantly adding new links to our travel resources. This should be your first stop if you are in search of a rental van.

Paratransit

ALTHOUGH PARATRANSIT SERVICES are available in many communities across the United States, it's not exactly the ideal option for most travelers. This door-to-door accessible transportation service is used by disabled residents who cannot access their local public transportation systems. In other words, paratransit services are available in places where the public transportation system is not yet fully accessible.

Generally speaking, paratransit fares are comparable to bus fares, and the service operates the same hours as public transportation. So what's the big drawback for travelers? Advance reservations are required for all paratransit services, and priority is usually given to local residents who need transportation to medical appointments. You may need to make reservations as far as a week in advance, and delays and cancellations are commonplace. Additionally, most paratransit companies will not provide airport transportation.

So, although some people recommend paratransit as an economical choice for traveling wheelers, it's not really a viable option unless you plan to spend several months at your holiday destination. In that case, check with the paratransit authority well in advance to see what you need to do to get paratransit certification at your destination. Some paratransit authorities have reciprocal arrangements with those in other cities, while others require that you submit a lengthy application. Additionally, some paratransit services plainly state that they cannot provide services to visitors.

Tour Vehicles

ALTHOUGH TECHNICALLY NOT ground transportation, many people use city tours for at least a brief overview of their destination. Many types of city tours are available, and access varies among the different options.

The good news is that, as of October 2002, many bus-type tours (those that operate in over-the-road buses) are required to offer an accessible option. There are exceptions to this rule, but according to DOT regulations, tour operators who use over-the-road buses are required to provide accessible (lift-equipped) transportation upon 48 hours advance notice. Additionally, they cannot charge more for their accessible services.

For now, it's nice to know that there are some accessible options around the country. I give high marks to San Diego Trolley Tours for purchasing a lift-equipped tour vehicle. Their accessible vehicle looks like an old fashioned trolley car, with the lift cleverly concealed beneath the vehicle. Advance notice is required to make sure you get a tour on the accessible vehicle, but they have done a great job making their tours accessible.

Just because a tour operator owns an accessible vehicle doesn't necessarily mean they can actually provide accessible transportation. While visiting a Missouri tourist attraction, I flagged down a bus and asked the driver if they had an accessible tour. "Well," he replied, "we used to have an accessible tour, but Joe was the only driver trained to operate the accessible bus. After Joe quit, they just parked the bus."

Other tour operators have been more imaginative in making their tours accessible. For example, one innovative Baltimore tour operator does not have any accessible tour vehicles, so she offers wheelchair-users the option of using their own vehicles for the tour. This option won't work for everyone, but it's an excellent example of a small business working to make their services more accessible. Don't be afraid to ask about accessible options. You never know what the answer will be.

Recreational Vehicles (RVs)

ALTHOUGH MOST PEOPLE don't really consider RVs ground transportation, some people use them for both transportation and lodging. Many RVers consider this lifestyle to be especially conducive to people with disabilities because you don't have to worry about accessible hotels, restaurants, or restrooms. Still, it's not a worry-free existence.

RVers have to worry about accessible campgrounds and facilities, and of course they have to choose a RV that meets their needs. Since it's a major expense, many experts advise renting a RV before you purchase one. A few dealers across the nation (and even around the world) rent accessible RVs. For a complete list of those dealers, check out the travel resources on EmergingHorizons.com.

Another great online resource for RVers is Hope Sykes' Enabled RVer (maxpages.com/enabledrver). Hope's website includes lots of resources about accessible RVing and information about equipment, rights, destinations, and resources.

Finally, if you want to get the skinny on the accessible facilities at RV parks across the United States, check out the online database compiled by the Handicapped Travel Club (handicappedtravelclub.com). The parks are evaluated by members, and they are listed by state. Each listing contains a short description, along with access details. This database is continually updated, and new parks are added as members visit them and complete access surveys.

We Will Ride | 5
Bus Travel

ALTHOUGH MANY PEOPLE tend to discount over-the-road (OTR) bus transportation as a viable leisure travel option, in reality it's one of the only transportation links to many rural U.S. towns. Indeed, it's also a very economical and (sometimes) flexible way to travel. Additionally, it's a great way to see the country while leaving the driving to somebody else. So, what's the scoop on accessible OTR bus transportation in the United States? To properly answer that question, we must first look at the history that surrounds this issue.

History

IN TRUTH, THE struggle for access to OTR buses predates the passage of the Americans with Disabilities Act (ADA). In fact, many grass-roots disability activists fought long and hard for the access we enjoy today. At the top of the list of freedom fighters is ADAPT, the granddaddy of the disability rights organizations. Over the past two decades ADAPT has organized demonstrations, educated the public, and lobbied legislators to protect the civil rights of people with disabilities. One of those rights includes the right to ride on a bus without being carried on board like a piece of luggage. Besides being very dangerous, this practice is also incredibly degrading.

In 1997, ADAPT members made a series of Greyhound test rides throughout the country. Greyhound refused passage to 32% of the test riders. Of those who were permitted to ride, 35% were hand-carried on and off the bus, and 25% of the 68% that were permitted to ride were dropped or otherwise injured being "helped" on and off the bus. Keep in mind that these test rides were performed after the passage of the ADA, at a time when OTR buses were supposed to be accessible.

Personally, I find it ironic that people compare the disability rights movement to the civil rights movement because, unlike Rosa Parks, many of the people fighting for the rights of people with disabilities couldn't even get on board the bus. In any case, ADAPT fought the long hard fight, before and after the ADA was passed.

Access to OTR buses was officially mandated in the ADA, although it was still an uphill battle to achieve appropriate (lift) access. The ADA gave OTR bus companies an additional 7 years before they had to buy accessible vehicles. Greyhound claimed that it was too expensive to provide lift access to their buses and that hand-carrying nonambulatory passengers on board was an acceptable alternative. Obviously, the disability community strongly disagreed with Greyhound's definition of "appropriate" access.

Finally, on September 28, 1998, the Access Board published the final guidelines for access to OTR buses. ADAPT won the battle because, among other things, the final rule states that hand-carrying passengers on board a bus is not considered appropriate access. Coincidentally, just prior to passage of the final rule, Greyhound replaced a large portion of their fleet with inaccessible buses. This move outraged the disability community and won Greyhound the moniker of "the dirty dog" among disability rights activists.

Furthermore, shortly after the final rule was issued, the American Bus Association sought legal intervention to overturn the rule. The case was originally heard in Washington D.C. District Court (*American Bus Association, Inc. v. Rodney E. Slater*), and was later appealed in Federal Appeals Court. The initial decision upheld the rule in its entirety; however, on November 14, 2000, the appellate court ruled to delete section 37.199 of the rule.

The deleted section required monetary compensation for the denial of accessible services. On March 8, 2001, the DOT amended the final ADA OTR bus rule to reflect this change. It should be noted that this change does not affect ADA accessibility requirements for OTR buses, nor does it prevent people from seeking judicial remedies under the ADA.

The Rule

SO, WHAT DOES the final rule say? For starters, it requires OTR bus companies to provide service in an accessible bus upon 48 hours advance notice. As soon as the final rule was released, Greyhound announced that it would make all 4,000 stops on its nationwide bus system accessible to wheelchair-users one full year ahead of the official compliance deadline. Of course, this didn't come to pass, and it wasn't until April 2000 that passengers could actually book space in advance on an accessible bus.

Today, passengers who require accessible services should call Greyhound's ADA Assist Line at (800) 752-4841 at least 48 hours prior to their departure. If you're not able to make advance arrangements, Greyhound claims they will still make every reasonable effort to accommodate passengers without delaying their bus departure schedules. In other words, they will do what they can if you just show up, so it's best to make advance arrangements, especially around holidays and peak travel periods.

Under the new rule, it's also considered discrimination for any OTR bus company to deny transportation to a person with a disability, or to require a passenger to reschedule their trip in order to receive accessible transportation. Greyhound does not prohibit passengers with disabilities from traveling alone unless they require assistance with personal services.

Greyhound also provides personal care assistants (PCAs) with free passage, when they travel with a person with a disability. A free one-way ticket is issued to the PCA at the time of travel. If the PCA requires a round trip ticket, another one-way ticket must be picked up at the time of the return trip.

Unfortunately, the new rule stopped short of requiring accessible lavatories on board OTR buses. This fact was further emphasized by Sherman Qualls, Greyhound's Director of ADA Compliance. Mr. Qualls was a speaker at a travel conference I attended, and he proceeded to detail how Greyhound has gone out of their way to make their services accessible, because as Mr. Qualls said, "It's just the right thing to do."

Mr. Qualls talked about how Greyhound "goes the distance to make travel a pleasant and convenient experience for passengers with disabilities." He explained that Greyhound provided all these services for people with disabilities out of the kindness of their corporate heart. In short, he said they wanted to serve this market.

I looked around at the crowd, which appeared to be falling for this fairy tale, hook, line, and sinker. Then, there was a question from the back of the room, "Does Greyhound have accessible bathrooms on their buses?" asked a travel agent. The answer was a curt, "No, we're not required to do that under the ADA." Mr. Qualls then went on to berate the unfairness of ADA and to explain how much this regulatory legislation was costing Greyhound. So much for "serving the market" and "doing the right thing!"

In any case, even though OTR bus companies are not required to provide accessible onboard lavatories, the new rule does require them to provide passengers with disabilities boarding assistance at rest stops. Adequate time must also be allocated for these passengers to use the restroom facilities. This rule applies at all stops that are least 15 minutes long; so if you need to use the facilities at a rest stop, be sure to inform the driver.

Even though the new rule allows passengers to travel safely in their own wheelchairs, you still must be aware of the liability limitations for damage to assistive devices. Greyhound's liability for damage to anything carried in the baggage compartment is only $250 per item. This includes wheelchairs and other assistive devices.

This amount won't go very far if there is any substantial damage to your assistive device, so be sure you have adequate insurance coverage. Check your existing insurance policies first to see if you are covered, then ask your insurance agent about low-cost options for additional coverage. In the long run, it's better to be safe than sorry.

One of the best provisions in the rule for OTR buses addresses the future. The rule requires OTR bus companies to install lifts on 50% of their fleets by 2006, and on 100% of their fleets by 2012. According to Sherman Qualls, in 2000, Greyhound already had 95 lift-equipped buses in their fleet. Each lift-equipped bus has two tie-down positions for passengers who wish to remain in their own wheelchairs. Mr. Qualls also assured me that more accessible buses are on order. I look forward to the future and hope that Greyhound will indeed be able to abide by the final rule.

Personal Stories

OF COURSE NOTHING speaks out better than personal experience, so here are a few anecdotes from real life Greyhound travelers. Is Greyhound living up to its end of the accessibility deal? You be the judge.

From Pennsylvania

I had a wonderful ride on a Greyhound bus from Harrisburg to Pittsburgh on May 19, 2000. Making the reservation was not a smooth process, and it left me with great doubt as to whether or not I would actually get a bus with a lift. To add a margin of safety, I made a special trip down to the bus station to physically buy a ticket the night before. The next day, I was pleasantly surprised, as my bus actually had a lift! There were two wheelchair sites, side by side. It took a small army of about 10 bus employees to figure out how to use the lift and tie down my wheelchair properly. Due to the space required for my wheelchair, six regular seats were folded or were otherwise unusable. However, those seats were still sold, so the passengers had to sit or stand in the aisle. But the driver was jolly and so were the passengers, and in the end I had a gorgeous ride through the heart of Pennsylvania.

From Texas

We were scheduled to leave Dallas, Texas at 11:00 PM on September 26,1999. I checked in with the station master, who told me the bus was late. She also said an employee would help me board the bus when it arrived. We went outside and waited by the double doors for the bus. The bus pulled in, and the driver approached me. I told him I was an ADA passenger and would need some assistance boarding the bus. His reply was "Cracker, the line is over there and you are not getting on my bus." I immediately reported this to the station master. She instructed another employee to go and help me board the bus. The driver saw us coming and got back in his bus and drove off. He still had the baggage doors open, and some of the passengers were chasing the half-full bus. Needless to say, I didn't get on that bus!

From Washington

I took the Dirty Dog from Seattle to Portland on July 2, 2000. I notified the ADA line almost 72 hours before departure and received confirmation the following day. I got to the terminal a half hour before departure, and the accessible bus wasn't there. The terminal manager came out and said he had my trip on the board, but it had somehow been ignored by the mechanics. He sent the driver back to pick up another bus, so we left Seattle about 25 minutes late. I couldn't believe I actually rode on Greyhound and (at long last) I wasn't treated like carry-on baggage.

Charter and Tour Companies

TECHNICALLY, THE FINAL RULE applies to more than just Greyhound buses; in fact, its implementation dramatically reshaped the travel industry. Indeed, the rule makes U.S. travel more accessible even if you never step foot on a Greyhound bus. Why? Because the rule also addresses charter bus services and day tours.

As of October 2002, all tour operators are required to provide accessible services (with 48 hours notice) if they operate their tours in OTR buses. In this case, accessible services means either a lift-equipped bus or a separate ramped or lift-equipped van. An OTR bus is defined as a bus with an elevated passenger deck located over a baggage compartment. This rule also applies to any other private demand-responsive transit service provider.

This does not mean that all the small charter and tour companies must purchase accessible buses; they must, however, be able to provide them on 48 hours notice. The rule states that companies can do this by renting or leasing accessible vehicles. Additionally, disabled passengers cannot be charged extra, even if the charter company has to spend more money to provide accessible vehicles. The cost can, however, be passed on to all passengers in the form of higher prices.

The accessible vehicle does not have to be a bus, and many charter companies may opt to rent a lift-equipped van for this purpose. The choice is up to them, as long as they provide accessible transportation. Hand-carrying passengers on board is not considered appropriate under any circumstances.

This regulation ultimately makes charter tours and day tours more accessible. For example, if you want to take the bargain gambling bus tour to Reno or Lake Tahoe, all you have to do is give the charter company 48 hours notice.

It's important to note that all tour company reservation deadlines still apply. For example, if a tour company requires 30 days advance notice for reservations, then accessible reservations must also be made 30 days in advance.

Some tour companies like Gray Line of New Orleans have already added accessible vehicles to their fleet. Although the Gray Line city tour is considered a staple for Big Easy visitors, until 2003, you could only join this tour if you could walk a few steps and transfer to a coach seat. All that has changed now, thanks to the full implementation of the final regulations. Today, lift-equipped bus service is available for the Gray Line New Orleans Super City Tour, and you can remain in your own wheelchair for the entire tour.

Ultimately, package tours within the United States will be also more accessible, as tour operators are now required to provide accessible bus transportation on charter tours. Thus, people with mobility disabilities will have more choices and won't only be limited to booking tours with specialty tour operators. In the years to come, more mainstream tour operators will be required to provide accessible tours, which means more choices will be available.

In the long run, this rule will make tours and travel more accessible. In the short run, people with disabilities will most likely have to become skilled at self advocacy in order to get these services. The most effective plan of action is to learn the rule, and then speak up for your rights.

All Aboard | 6
Train Travel

TRAIN TRAVEL IS much more than just a mode of transportation. Throughout time, "riding the rails" has been portrayed as an exciting and romantic way to travel. Whether you choose the Orient Express or the Northeast Express, train travel has many advantages. It's a great way to enjoy the countryside in relative comfort and, if you travel on a rail pass, it's also very economical. As with everything else, train accessibility varies throughout the world. With that in mind, let's take a look at some of the major rail systems throughout the world and see how they stack up access-wise.

Amtrak—United States

AMTRAK, THE U.S. passenger rail carrier, operates routes throughout the country and even to (a few) portions of Canada. Access varies, depending on the route and the train, but all Amtrak trains have at least one accessible coach car. Amtrak passengers can either travel in their own wheelchair or opt to transfer to a coach seat. All trains have wheelchair spaces, although no lock-downs are provided on intercity trains. Some cars only have one wheelchair space, and no cars have more than two wheelchair spaces. Inquire about the specifics when you make your reservation.

Power wheelchairs (if not in use) can be carried as checked baggage, and manual wheelchairs can either be stowed in the passenger car or carried as checked baggage. Amtrak can accommodate scooters and wheelchairs (in the passenger compartment) up to 30 inches wide by 48 inches long, and with a maximum passenger-occupied weight of up to 600 pounds.

All wheelchair spaces, seats, and even some special cars are for the exclusive use of people with disabilities (and their travel companions). In reality, Amtrak employees selectively enforce this priority seating policy. I've seen conductors tell able-bodied passengers they had to move because the seats were reserved for people with disabilities; however I've also seen employees treat wheelchair spaces as overflow luggage storage compartments. Again, it depends on the employee, the train, and the route.

Many trains have accessible bathrooms, but the configuration varies depending on the train. Make sure to inquire about bathroom accessibility when you make your reservation. Don't be afraid to ask for the dimensions and measurements of the onboard bath-

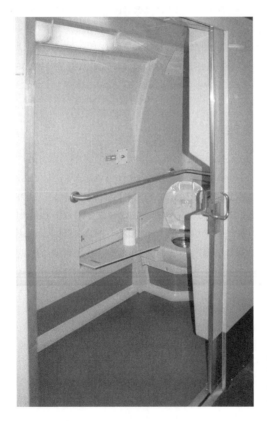

Figure 6.1.
Accessible bathrooms vary from train to train. Here's one on Amtrak's Northeast Direct train.

room, as size varies from train to train. Most onboard bathrooms are smaller than their land versions, so don't expect to find features like a 5-foot turning radius in the stall. They are accessible to a large majority of the population, but it's always best to ask for measurements in advance, so that you won't encounter any unexpected surprises.

Amtrak offers two types of accessible sleeping accommodations: the Superliner and the Viewliner accessible bedrooms. The Superliner accessible bedroom has two berths, an accessible bathroom, and it takes up the entire width of the car. The accessible bathroom has a privacy curtain, grab bars, and a 5-foot turning radius. The whole compartment measures 9'5" by 6'6".

The Viewliner accessible bedroom can accommodate three passengers, but it's more comfortable with only two passengers. It measures 7'1" by 6'8" and features two berths, a sofa, and an accessible bathroom.

One accessible bedroom is available in each sleeping car, and the availability and type depends on the route. Advance reservations are a must, as these accessible bedrooms go fast. Under a 1998 Department of Justice (DOJ) settlement, only passengers with a mobility disability can reserve an accessible bedroom up until 14 days prior to the departure date from the train's city of origin.

Amtrak employees will assist you in a variety of ways during your journey. Meal service is available to all passengers with disabilities. You may order from the menu and have the attendant deliver your food to your seat or bedroom. On some long-distance routes, wheelchair-users may transfer to and from the lounge cars at appropriate stops. Assistance with these transfers is available upon request. Amtrak employees will also assist you with reasonable food preparation tasks, such as opening packages and cutting meat. Additionally, onboard staff will help you board and leave the train and assist you in reaching the accessible bathroom.

Of course, boarding options vary depending on the train and the station, but all Amtrak stations offer at least one accessible boarding option. Some stations have raised platforms, and wheelchair-users can roll right on to the train. Be careful at stations with raised platforms, because many times a substantial gap is present between the train and the platform. Many stations have bridge plates that can be put down to eliminate this problem. Make sure to ask an employee about this option.

Not all stations have raised platforms, but many boarding options are available for these stations. Some trains have onboard wheelchair ramps or wheelchair lifts, and most stations also have manual lifts. So, even if there is a mechanical failure of the onboard lift, the manual lift at the station can be used in an emergency. At some stations, manual lifts are the only option for boarding wheelchair-users.

Passengers may carry therapeutic oxygen on Amtrak trains, with a few restrictions. Oxygen tanks and associated equipment must not exceed 75 pounds per tank for a two-tank system, or 20 pounds per tank for a six-tank system. One passenger can carry a

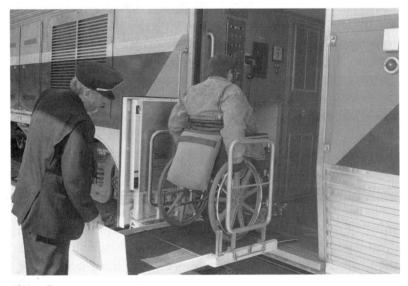

Figure 6.2.
Some trains, like this one on Amtrak's Capitol Corridor route, feature onboard lifts for wheelchair boarding.

maximum of two 75-pound tanks or six 20-pound tanks. If your oxygen equipment requires the use of onboard power, you must carry at least a 12-hour backup supply of oxygen that does not require the use of onboard power. You may have to carry more than one battery to meet this requirement.

All oxygen tanks must be secured while on board, and wheels must be removed for the duration of the trip. You must notify the reservation agent that you will be carrying therapeutic oxygen so that appropriate arrangements can be made. It's recommended that you estimate your total travel time, and then carry 20% more oxygen to make sure you have an adequate supply.

For safety reasons, oxygen tanks are not permitted in any cars that have a smoking area, although you can keep them in the enclosed area of a private sleeping room. In this case, you must keep the door closed and refrain from smoking for the duration of the trip.

Under a 1998 DOJ settlement, Amtrak implemented a number of discounts for passengers with mobility disabilities. All passengers with disabilities get a 15% discount off the published fare. Additionally, an adult companion (16 years or older) may accompany a passenger with a mobility disability at 15% off the published fare. Passengers with mobility disabilities also get 30% off the published fares for accessible bedrooms.

To obtain these discounted fares, call (800) 872-7245 and mention the discounts available for passengers with mobility disabilities. To receive the discount, you are required to provide written documentation of your disability at the ticket counter and when boarding the train. These discounts are not available on the Internet.

Another DOJ settlement addresses the Amtrak Thruway buses used in California. On several California Amtrak routes, transportation is provided by a combination of bus and rail service. Under this September 2000 settlement, all Thruway buses were required to install improved securement and restraint features. Thruway bus operators also expanded and standardized the training provided to drivers and maintenance personnel to help ensure that access features remain in working order.

Amtrak publishes an *Access Amtrak* print guide for passengers with disabilities. Call Amtrak's Office of Access at (877) 268-7252 to receive your free copy. Access-related questions can also be addressed at this number. Alternative formats of *Access Amtrak* are available in Braille, large print, audio tape, and on diskette. Amtrak also posts updated access information on their website at amtrak.com.

And although it's not disability specific, John Pitt's *USA by Rail*, presents a good overview of U.S. rail routes. This handy resource lists and describes rail routes throughout America. It is available through The Globe Pequot Press.

VIA Rail—Canada

WITH THE EXCEPTION of a few Amtrak routes, rail service in Canada is operated by VIA Rail, the Canadian national rail carrier. Most VIA Rail trains are wheelchair-accessible, except for some trains running between London and Sarina, Ontario. Accessibility varies throughout the system and depends on the specific route and equipment.

The most accessible VIA Rail passenger coaches are the LRC VIA 1 first-class coaches. Each first-class coach has wheelchair tie-downs and an accessible bathroom. The accessible bathroom has grab bars and a sliding door with an entry width of 35 inches.

Some standard coach cars also come equipped with tie-downs and an accessible bathroom. The major difference between these two types of coach cars is the door width between the cars. On the LRC VIA 1 first-class cars, the width is 28 inches, whereas on the standard coach cars it is only 25 inches. The standard VIA Rail coach cars come equipped with reduce-a-width tools, which are used to help manual wheelchairs fit through the smaller doorways.

VIA Rail's Renaissance rail cars also offer a high degree of access. Designed in the 1990s, these cars were built to offer fast overnight train service between France and England. VIA Rail purchased them in 2000, and refurbished them to include accessible features.

VIA Rail added an accessible suite with wide doors and a wheelchair tie-down in each Renaissance service car, modified the economy washrooms, installed companion seats for the economy-class wheelchair tie-down spaces, and added more moveable armrests to the economy-class cars. These accessible Renaissance cars are used on the overnight train between Montreal and Toronto, on all trains between Montreal and Quebec City, and on certain trains between Montreal and Ottawa and Montreal and Halifax.

Most VIA Rail stations do not have raised boarding platforms, so wheelchair-users are boarded either with the use of a station lift or with the help of VIA Rail personnel. On some routes, passengers must provide their own boarding assistance. Contact VIA Rail in advance to find out if boarding assistance is available on a particular route.

VIA Rail uses a Washington Chair to board wheelchair-users who cannot stay in their own wheelchairs. This narrow chair has no arms and small wheels and is very similar to the aisle chairs used on airplanes. Wheelers are transferred to the Washington Chair for boarding, and then transferred to their seat. Once on board the train, wheelchair-users must use the Washington Chair to move about the train or to use the bathroom. VIA Rail personnel are available to assist passengers with the Washington Chair en route.

Folding manual wheelchairs can be stored in the coach cars. VIA Rail also accepts wheelchairs as checked baggage, as long as the owner travels by rail in at least one direction. In most cases, power wheelchairs cannot exceed 150 pounds, be wider than 32 inches, or longer or higher than 72 inches. In some cases, VIA Rail will accept power wheelchairs as baggage if the total weight does not exceed 250 pounds. This applies only as long as the origination and destination stations have the proper facilities to load and unload them. Check with VIA Rail in advance for specifics on station equipment.

On transcontinental trains, passengers who cannot access the dining car or snack counters may have their meals served in their compartment. Make sure to inform a VIA Rail employee if you require this service. Some VIA Rail sleeping cars can also accommodate stretchers. A minimum of 48 hours advance notice is required for stretcher travel.

Passengers who use therapeutic oxygen are allowed to bring their own equipment aboard, but they must give VIA Rail 48 hours advance notice. VIA Rail can provide voltage regulators on certain trains, but passengers are required to provide adequate battery backup for their equipment.

Advance notice (usually 48 hours) is required for accessible services on VIA Rail. Passengers must be able to attend to their own personal needs for the duration of the trip. VIA Rail employees are not required to assist passengers with eating, medical, or personal hygiene tasks. Passengers who cannot attend to their own personal care must be accompanied by an escort. VIA Rail provides free economy-class passage to required escorts.

For more information on VIA Rail service, call (888) 842-7245 or visit viarail.ca.

BritRail—United Kingdom

BRITRAIL, THE NATIONAL rail network of the United Kingdom, is made up of over two dozen regional rail carriers. These regional carriers provide rail service to Scotland, Wales, and England. To complement this regional service, high-speed Eurostar trains travel under the English Channel to connect the United Kingdom with continental Europe. Under the provisions of the Disability Discrimination Act of 1995, all these regional rail companies are required to provide service to passengers with disabilities. Access varies from do-able to excellent, depending on the route you choose.

The first step in planning a BritRail trip is to determine where your journey will begin. Although this sounds like simplistic advice, it's really quite useful because the rail company that services your departure station is responsible for access arrangements throughout your entire rail journey. This applies even if you travel on several other regional rail companies throughout your trip.

Contact National Rail Enquiries in the United Kingdom at +44 8457 484 950 or visit nationalrail.co.uk to find out what regional rail company services your departure station. Ask for the phone number or website of the local rail company and contact them directly to make the arrangements for your entire rail journey.

According to the BritRail public relations department, you can make accessible arrangements directly with BritRail; however, in practice this method doesn't really work. My friend Carol tried this method while she was planning her recent trip to Britain. Carol says of her experience, "When I called BritRail here in the United States, none of the agents could answer my questions regarding access, or make the appropriate arrangements for me. In fact they hadn't the foggiest idea of what to do with me, or even where to begin. Unfortunately, I got similar results on all my inquires directly to BritRail. I got the best results when I dealt directly with the regional rail companies."

In truth, BritRail's primary function is to sell rail passes to overseas travelers. These rail passes are good for unlimited train travel over a specific period of time, and they can be a great bargain if you plan to do a lot of train travel. So, plan your route, check out the access, and then calculate your fares. If a rail pass proves to be a bargain, then buy it directly from BritRail before you leave home. Don't rely on BritRail for access information, because you will literally be left waiting at the station.

Although access varies from one regional rail company to the next, some general guidelines hold true throughout the system. Generally, you will find the best access in the manned stations in the larger cities. Access to the rural stations varies widely, and in some cases wheelchair-users even have to be carried up steps. Accessible ground transportation is also more difficult to find in the smaller rural stations.

Remember to ask a lot of questions regarding station access when you make your reservations. The best method is to ask the employee to describe the station access, rather than to just ask if it is accessible. Even if they say the station is accessible, it's always good to follow up with, "How many steps are there?" You'll be surprised at how many times the answer will be, "Only two."

The maximum width for wheelchairs is 26.5 inches and the maximum length is 47 inches aboard BritRail trains. None of the regional rail companies will officially carry scooters; however, says Carol of her recent BritRail trip, "Nothing was ever said to me about my scooter, and my feeling is that scooter-users should be OK if your scooter measures less than the maximum allowable wheelchair. You must be able to maneuver in tight quarters. If you primarily use your scooter for distance, don't try it, as accessing many of the wheelchair spots requires some tight turns."

You should confirm your reservation and access arrangements at least 24 hours in advance and even further ahead in peak travel seasons. And always allow plenty of time for connections.

Eurostar service to continental Europe is a great deal, as wheelchair-users get to ride in first class while paying coach fares. Two designated seating areas are available for wheelchair-users (and their companions) in first class coaches 9 and 10. Wheelchair-users are allowed to stay in their own chairs in these seating areas. It should be noted that the boarding gangway is 29.5 inches wide. Accessible toilets are also located in coaches 9 and 10. These toilets have doorways that are 27.5 inches wide.

It's great to travel on the Eurostar, as you can be in Paris in just under 3 hours. Says my friend Mark of his Eurostar Experience, "It was a smashing 3-hour trip, and even though I didn't get the free meal, I could access the toilet. It's a great deal for wheelers."

For more information about accessible services on Eurostar trains, call +44 1233 617 575 or visit eurostar.co.uk.

Although not entirely rail-related, the *Smooth Ride Guide* to the United Kingdom is an excellent resource. In addition to contact information for the various regional rail companies, this handy guide contains detailed accessibility information on hotels and attractions throughout the United Kingdom. It's available for $16 (plus $9 shipping and handling) from Smooth Ride Guides at +44 1279-777 966. I highly recommend it!

Europe—Eurail

EUROPEAN RAIL TRAVEL has long been touted as a very economical way to see Europe. Economy aside, it can also be a very accessible. I do stress "can be," because advance planning is essential. You will, however, be well rewarded for your research efforts, because with proper planning you can choose the most accessible Eurail routes and avoid taking those not-so-accessible trans-European commuter flights. Additionally, you can save money by purchasing a Eurail pass before you leave home.

Like BritRail, the Eurail network is made up of many regional carriers. These regional carriers are usually country specific, but some long-distance trains do cross borders. Also included in the Eurail network are some regional ferry and bus routes that connect the train network. So, when planning your Eurail vacation, make certain you investigate access on all modes of transportation along your route.

As you can imagine, access varies throughout Europe; however, regional carriers in Finland, France, Germany, Italy, the Netherlands, Spain, Sweden, and Switzerland all officially offer some type of access. Even in those countries, the access varies depending on the route. Remember, your rail travels don't necessarily have to be limited to those countries, because some long-distance trains cross borders.

The best bet is to contact the regional carrier directly. Although several outlets sell rail passes in the United States, these offices have very little knowledge of the true accessibility of the trains. You need to contact the regional carrier directly to find out the access details.

For example, even though it is possible to travel by rail in Italy, in most cases power wheelchairs can only be carried in baggage cars. So, although most rail pass outlets can tell you that Italian trains provide "disabled access," most are unaware of specific access details. Contact rail pass offices for information on rail passes, and contact the regional carriers for detailed access information. It's also important to specify what type of access you require and what type of an assistive device you use when making your inquiry, as some trains can only accommodate manual wheelchairs.

Rail passes are very economical, but it's important to note that there are many different types. Most passes are valid for unlimited travel within a certain time frame. Some passes cover only one country, some cover a combination of countries, and some cover the entire network. Plan your route before you purchase a rail pass, because the economy of a rail pass is directly dependent on your needs.

Even though not all trains are officially accessible, some are doable. It really depends on your ability and attitude. My friend Jack spent several weeks riding the rails in Europe last year. Jack is in his mid-twenties, loves to travel, and is in pretty good physical shape. He traveled throughout Europe with his friend Tim. Although he had a great time, he readily admits there were a few "incidents."

Here's his recollection of one of the more memorable glitches of his trip: "I had a great time in Europe, although some of the trains I took didn't exactly have roll-on access," says Jack. "At several stations, Tim had to pick me up and carry me on the train, and then go back and get my wheelchair. This worked OK, except for one time in Germany when the train left the station before Tim had a chance to load my wheelchair. At the time, I was hysterical. We both just kept shouting 'rollstuhl,' which is the German word for wheelchair. I thought I'd never see my Quickie again. It all worked out OK, and eventually I was reunited with my wheelchair, but it was a very stressful situation."

But don't let Jack's rollstuhl experience dissuade you from train travel in Europe. Some trains have excellent facilities. For example, the French rail carrier SNCF has designated wheelchair spaces on all non-TGV mainline trains. These spaces are located in first-class compartments, but wheelchair-users who purchase second-class tickets are able to reserve them at no extra charge. It works much like the system on the Eurostar trains. Advance reservations are a must for this and many other access arrangements. Contact SNCF for specific information.

Most rail pass offices should be able to give you contact information for the regional rail carriers. You can also search the Internet under "Eurail" for general information on the Eurail network and rail pass retailers.

Australia—Rail Australia

RAIL AUSTRALIA PROVIDES support to the international market for the major tourist-orientated passenger rail operators in Australia. These include Queensland Rail, which operates passenger rail service in Queensland; Countrylink, which is based in New South Wales; and the Great Southern Railway, which is based in South Australia and includes the world famous Indian Pacific route.

Access varies depending on the route. Not all trains have wheelchair spaces, so wheelchair-users may have to use a boarding chair and then transfer to their seat. The best station access is generally found at the larger city terminals, although even the Alice Springs station now has a lift.

The XP trains operated by Countrylink are nicely accessible. The XP trains operate on the Sydney to Brisbane, Sydney to Melbourne, and Sydney to Dubbo routes. One car per train has a wheelchair space, lock-down straps, and an accessible toilet. These features allow wheelchair-users to remain in their own wheelchairs for the duration of the trip.

Another route with nicely accessible facilities is the Indian Pacific transcontinental train. The Indian Pacific, which connects Sydney and Perth, is one of the world's longest train routes (4,352 km). The accessible Pullmans Cabin has ample room to maneuver a wheelchair and an accessible toilet and shower. It features an armchair plus a three-seater lounge that converts to an upper and lower sleeping berth at night. A special wheelchair, which can fit in the corridors, is also available on the Indian Pacific route. It's a great way to see the varied landscape of Australia, because the train travels from the Blue Mountains to the Nullarbor Plains.

A variety of money-saving rail passes are also available through Rail Australia. Contact Rail Australia for specific access information or for contact information for regional rail providers. Rail Australia can be reached at +61-8-217-4321 or www.railaustralia.com.au.

Rail Tours

RAIL TOURS ARE another train travel option, but to be honest, many of them are not accessible. Most of these all-inclusive tours are operated by private tour companies, and the basic premise is that you travel along a specific route and sleep either on board or at a hotel along the way. Meals and side excursions are usually included, and many of these tours feature onboard guides who point out the

Figure 6.3.
Rocky Mountaineer Railtours uses this station lift for wheelchair boarding in Vancouver.

scenic highlights along the way. In short, it's an all-inclusive land and rail package.

Many of these rail tours are operated in historic trains, which makes access difficult. And, let's face it, even the most accessible sleeping compartments are compact at best. The good news is that Rocky Mountaineer Railtours (RMR) operates one accessible rail tour through the Canadian Rockies. This multiday, all daylight excursion includes all onboard meals, ground transportation, and lodging.

Due to the availability of accessible services along the Vancouver to Calgary Kicking Horse Route, RMR is able to work with local suppliers to create a very accessible travel experience. That includes accessible hotel rooms with roll-in showers and ramp-equipped transportation to and from the stations.

Boarding the RMR Gold Leaf dome cars is via a platform lift, and access on board is pretty good. A spiral staircase to the upper level has handrails on both sides. Alternatively, a small elevator is available for wheelchair-users. The elevator measures 2'10" by 4' so to use it, you must transfer to an aisle chair.

The doorways and aisles are too narrow for wheelchairs, so you must transfer to your assigned seat for the rail journey. The Gold Leaf seats do not have flip up armrests, but plenty of legroom is available; you can just pull the aisle chair up in front of the seat. Wheelchair-users are seated close to the elevator, and an onboard aisle chair is available for use during the trip.

The bathrooms are located downstairs. The accessible bathroom has a large double-door entry and grab bars near the toilet. Not enough room is available for a lateral transfer to the toilet, but it is larger than the standard bathroom.

The Gold Leaf cars work for many people; however, you must inform RMR about your specific access needs when you make your reservations. All access needs are flagged in the manifest, and most requests require advance preparations. It's one of the few accessible rail tours around, and it's a great way to see the scenic Canadian Rockies. For more information, contact RMR at (800) 665-7245 or visit rockymountaineer.com.

Finding the Right Room | 7

I F I'VE HEARD it once, I've heard it a thousand times, "I reserved an accessible room and when I got there I couldn't even get into the bathroom." Of course, there are many variations on that theme, but it all boils down to the same issue: appropriate access. What is appropriate access? That varies from person to person, because what's adequate for one person may not necessarily meet the needs of another person. That's what makes finding the right hotel room such a challenge, because not only are people's needs different, but so are access standards.

What Is Accessible?

HOW CAN YOU tell if a property has accessible rooms? The first thing you have to do is define the word accessible. That's a tall order. Truth be told, the experts have been trying to do that for years. The bottom line is, there's no one uniform definition of accessible. Many properties have developed their own access criteria, but even these standards vary widely from property to property. It's definitely not what you would call uniform.

It would be great if an accessible room at Hotel X in St. Paul was exactly the same as an accessible room at Hotel Y in Amarillo, but that's just not the way it works. Even that little blue wheelchair pictogram can have many meanings, depending on how and where it's displayed.

For example, in California (where I live) if you see that blue wheelchair pictogram posted at the entrance to a hotel, it means that the entrance to that hotel is accessible. It doesn't necessarily mean anything else within that property is accessible. It may or may not be. Basically, it's a crap shoot. The same pictogram is often prominently featured in advertisements for hotels and motels. What does it mean? Well, that depends on the property.

Generally speaking, there's no uniform criteria or any standardized usage of the international accessibility pictogram. In fact, two properties right next door to one another may have different accessibility criteria, yet both may also proudly display that pictogram. You may ask, "How can this be possible in the United States, where we have access laws such as the Americans with Disabilities Act (ADA)?" To answer that question, you need to understand a few things about the ADA, so let's take a brief look at how the ADA addresses accessibility in the lodging industry.

Properties constructed after January 26, 1992, are subject to the new construction guidelines of the ADA. Under this criteria, new properties are required to have a minimum number of accessible rooms, which ranges from 2% to 4% of the number of total rooms, depending on the size of the property. This criteria also specifically defines access features required in the accessible rooms. The inclusion of some of these access features, however, also depends on the size of the property.

For example, if a property has 51 or more rooms, it must have a minimum number of rooms with roll-in showers. Again, this depends on the total number of rooms, and it ranges between 2% to 4% of the number of total rooms. Properties with less than 51 rooms are not required to have any rooms with roll-in showers, although they still must have a minimum number of accessible guest rooms. So, an accessible guest room does not always have a roll-in shower. This only applies to new construction, not to remodeled properties.

Properties constructed before January 26, 1992, are subject to different guidelines under the ADA. The ADA states that these existing facilities are required to remove architectural barriers when it is readily achievable. *Readily achievable* is further defined as being easy to accomplish and carry out without much difficulty or expense. So as you can see, the definition of readily achievable is open to interpretation, because cost and difficulty are sometimes relative terms.

In fact, what might be readily achievable for a large hotel chain would not necessarily be readily achievable for a small owner-operated motel. So, two properties next door to one another could in fact have ADA compliant rooms with completely different access features. It's pretty easy to do, especially when you bring the readily achievable concept into the picture.

Additionally, some cities and states have local access codes, and where two laws conflict, the more stringent of the two applies. Sometimes it's the ADA, sometimes it is not. And then you have historic buildings, which may or may not be subject to access standards. Indeed, sometimes it takes an attorney to decide exactly how the ADA applies to public accommodations.

If you take only one thing away from this chapter, remember this: Never just ask for an accessible room, because there isn't a universal standard for accessible rooms, even within the United States. The terms *accessible* or *ADA compliant* are meaningless unless you understand how the property defines them. To do that, you have to learn to ask a lot of questions.

Ask the Right Questions

TO GET ACCURATE answers to your questions, you need to ask the right people. Always call the property directly, rather than calling the central reservation number. Sometimes access improvements at a local property are not entered in the central reservation database. Reservation agents at the property are usually able to give you more updated and detailed access information. They are more familiar with the property. In fact, many properties include a tour of the rooms and public areas, as part of their reservation agent training program.

We've already determined that you should never just call up a property, ask for an accessible room, book it, and then hang up.

Many reservation clerks assume that their accessible rooms are a one-size-fits-all solution for every traveler. The results are disastrous, and many novice travelers end up in ADA compliant rooms that don't meet their needs.

Most likely, your conversation with the reservation agent will go something like this. After you say you need an accessible room, the reservation agent will tell you that they have ADA-compliant rooms. "Great," you reply. But you're not out of the woods yet. Your next step is to ask the reservation agent to describe that ADA-compliant room.

Ask the reservation agent to describe the access features of the room. Try to refrain from asking the reservation agent yes or no questions. For example, instead of asking if there is a roll-in shower in the bathroom, ask the agent to describe the bathroom. Additionally, be especially careful about asking yes or no questions in Asian countries, as many customer service employees consider it rude to answer a question (any question) with a no. If a particular access feature is important to you (such as an open frame bed), make sure you specifically inquire about that feature. Never assume anything.

As noted earlier, it's also very important to understand that a roll-in shower is not a standard feature in every accessible room. If you need a roll-in shower, you need to specifically request one, instead of just saying you need an accessible room. Sometimes a roll-in shower is also called a wheel-in shower or a no-hob shower. Terminology varies around the world.

Of course, even when you call the property directly, you can still be in for some surprises. I remember one time I called a hotel and asked if they had any accessible rooms with roll-in showers. Not a hard question, right? Well, apparently the reservation agent was new, or just didn't understand the question, or was having a really bad day. After talking with me for about 10 minutes she put me on hold and vowed to find an answer to my perplexing question. After another 5 minutes, she came back on the line and breathlessly replied, "We have kits that we can put in the shower so that deaf people can use the shower." Then she shouted, "Are you deaf?"

Which brings me to my next point. Trust your instincts. If you think you are talking with a flake, hang up and start over. Reservation agents have a high turnover rate. The good ones go on to better jobs, and the bad ones either get fired or keep at it. So if the reservation agent makes no sense at all, or if you get bad vibes, or if you think they don't understand what you are asking, don't take any chances. You're probably right in your assessment of the situation. Just say, thank you, hang up, and start over, either with that property or with your next pick.

If, for some reason, the reservation clerk seems competent, but is just having problems describing the room, ask if they have ever been in the room. If the reply is no, then ask to speak to somebody who has been in the room. If the reservation agent doesn't seem to know who to talk with, ask to speak to somebody in house-keeping. Nobody knows the rooms better than the housekeeping staff, because they have to clean them each and every day.

Don't be afraid to ask for specific measurements. If door width is a concern, ask for that measurement. Don't forget about the door width of the interior (bathroom) doors too. Dennis Ciesielski of Menomonie, Wisconsin came up with a good procedure for finding out the specifics about important measurements. After inquiring about the details of an accessible room, he then asks the clerk to fax him a floorplan (with measurements) of the room. How's it working? So far, Dennis reports that all of his requests have been fulfilled. He also adds, "Perhaps if people asked for floorplans more often, properties would have this information readily available." So when in doubt about measurements, ask the reservation agent to fax you a floor plan of the accessible room.

Sometimes you need to employ a little creativity when making your lodging arrangements. For example, if you need some specific equipment in your room, and the reservation agent doesn't seem to understand the difference between a shower chair and a pool chair, then try this little technique. When the conversation reaches an impasse, try communicating your needs with a photograph.

Snap a photo of your assistive device and fax it to the property. If you don't have a camera, then look through a medical supply catalogue or search the Internet to find a photo of the type of equipment you require. Then fax the photo to the hotel, or take it to your travel agent to illustrate your needs. Remember, a picture is worth a thousand words.

Finally, always request a written confirmation notice that includes the specifics of your reserved accessible room. Bring this confirmation notice with you when you check into the hotel. Additionally, I always ask for the name of the reservation agent; in fact I even ask them to spell it, for emphasis. Sometimes when people know you have their name, they tend to do a better job, because they feel more accountable. It's not a 100% guarantee, but it takes so little time, and the benefits far outweigh the effort.

Beds

NO MATTER HOW you slice it, choosing a bed that's right for you is a very personal decision. Let's face it, most of us put a lot of time and effort into shopping around for the perfect bed at home. Unfortunately, that's not the case with hotels. Granted, they do try to make their guests as comfortable as possible, but other factors sometimes rate a higher consideration when it comes to furniture purchases. In fact, most hotel furniture is purchased in bulk. That in itself is not horrible, but when you look at it from an access point of view, it may cause problems for some travelers. Especially when you talk about beds. All beds are not created equal, and some are just more accessible than others.

One of the biggest points of contention about hotel beds centers around open frame versus platform beds. Indeed, it's a pretty controversial issue even within the disability community. Some people need open frame beds so that they can use a Hoyer-type lift. Others claim that the open frame beds used in hotels are too high for independent transfers. It's an individual preference, and there is no right or wrong answer. The point to remember is, if this is an issue for you, it's important to inquire about bed types when you make your reservation.

That said, the reservation agent will probably give you the wrong answer at least 50% of the time. So what do you do when you arrive and discover the hotel only has platform beds, when you need an open frame bed? The first step would of course be to call the front desk and see if they have any rooms with open frame beds. If not, then explain your problem and ask if they can send up somebody from the engineering staff to remedy your problem.

Some people come up with their own do-it-yourself solution. "We can't use platform beds because we need to use a lift when traveling," says one traveler. "When we have been unable to get a room without an open frame bed, we placed wood blocks made from 6-inch squares of lumber at the four corners of the bed. They raised the bed enough to use the lift. Of course, they are heavy, so not very practical except for driving trips."

It should also be noted at this point that most hotels do not provide Hoyer-type or track lifts. A few Las Vegas hotels are exceptions. The best option is to arrange to rent one at your destination. Most medical supply houses will pick up and deliver them to your hotel if you make advance arrangements.

Alternatively, you can purchase a portable travel lift. The Take-Along Lift (www.takealonglifts.com) is an ideal choice, because it only weighs about 50 pounds and is easy to wheel through an airport.

Another hotel bed issue involves roll away beds and cots. "Cots or roll away beds are often much too low for a transfer back into the wheelchair," say savvy traveler Sharon Myers. "I found a simple solution by asking the hotel engineer to bring another mattress and place it on top of the cot or roll away bed. It brings the level up and makes for a much easier transfer."

If you need a hospital bed, you need to make arrangements with a hospital supply company to have one delivered to your hotel room. Some travelers have also found a creative solution to this problem.

Says frequent-traveler Ann, "I need to sleep with my head elevated, but I've often found it difficult and expensive to get a hospital bed delivered to my hotel room. My solution is to contact a furniture rental company and rent a recliner. It's usually a lot cheaper (and easier) than renting a hospital bed. However, I always remember to first ask the hotel if they have a recliner they can put in my room. Sometimes they do, and then I get it for free. Of course, this won't work for everybody, but I'm very comfortable sleeping in a recliner."

And then there is the problem with bed firmness. "The first thing we worry about when staying at a hotel is the bed," says Robert. "Most of the time it's as hard as a rock. This means my wife would have to turn me three or four times a night to prevent skin problems. Since this is not much of a vacation for her, we tried an Aero Bed on our last trip. We purchased one for under $100 and placed it on top of the hotel bed. Then she transferred me on to the bed and we inflated it with the electric pump. Whenever my wife woke up during the night she just let some air out of the bed. We were able to get through the night with only one turn and sometimes none at all, and I didn't develop any skin problems."

The best advice I can pass on about hotel beds is to ask about the height when you make your reservation. This is especially important in properties that offer a Victorian ambiance (read high beds), however it can save you a lot of time, trouble, and frustration no matter where you stay. It only takes a few minutes, and it's a good way to head off a potential problem.

Shower Chairs

A LOT OF confusion exists about hotel shower chairs or benches. It would be nice if there was some sort of standardization of this equipment from one property to the next, but that's just not the way it works. I've seen everything from plastic pool chairs to padded shower chairs—and lots of stuff in between.

If you need a shower chair, it's best to find out what specific type of shower chair the hotel has. When you make your reservation, ask if they have a shower bench or a shower chair, if it has arms, and if it is padded. You might also want to find out the make and model of the shower chair. Most likely, somebody will have to call you back with that information, but it could save you a bathroom accident in the long run.

Of course, it's always a good idea to be prepared in case an unsafe or inadequate chair is provided. "When I'm faced with an adequate roll-in shower but one that doesn't have a suitable bench or a bench at all, I have found this works for me," says Sharon Myers. "I take along a thin plastic poncho. After transferring onto the bed, I cover my chair with the poncho, transfer back into my wheelchair and roll inside the shower and proceed with taking a shower as usual. Sometimes, I've even placed the shower curtain beneath me and it works fine. I never tell the manager because it wouldn't encourage them to get a proper bench."

Many roll-in shower enclosures have built-in shower benches, but the fixed height can be a problem for some wheelchair-users. One frequent traveler offers this suggestion. "If the bench is too low, I usually fold up three to five bath towels and set them on the bench. This usually raises the level enough for an easy transfer. It's very important to remember to wet the towels before you transfer, as wet towels won't slip but dry ones can be a real safety hazard."

Additionally, if you need a roll-in shower chair or a commode chair, you are probably going to have to provide that yourself, because it is beyond the scope of the equipment that most properties provide. A number of portable shower chairs are on the market, but Nuprodx (nuprodx.com) makes one that can be converted to a roll-in shower chair or a commode chair. It breaks down for transport, and it's made out of lightweight aircraft aluminum. It's lightweight yet very sturdy, and a good choice if you plan to travel a lot.

Emergency Fix-it Kit

LET'S NOT FORGET about those little access features that make rooms more comfortable and useable, like lever handles, lowered clothing hooks, properly placed grab bars, and accessible bedside lamps. Although these items are mandated in the ADA, they are often overlooked by the lodging industry. So what's a traveler to do? Many people carry an emergency fix-it kit to overcome these access obstacles.

Faucets and doorknobs without lever handles can create problems for many people. Fortunately, this oversight is fairly easy to remedy. Great Grips (greatgrips.com) sells accessible faucet and door grips that simply slip over the existing hardware. These grips all have a mini-lever and, although they may require a little assistance to install (ask hotel personnel if traveling alone), it sure beats fighting with inaccessible hardware. Leveron also manufactures an economical doorknob adapter with a large lever. It is available online and at many medical supply houses.

Another problem lies in the grab bar area. Although most properties have grab bars in their accessible bathrooms, sometimes they aren't exactly positioned correctly. I've seen a number of baffling grab bar configurations, but most commonly they are too high or too low or simply on the wrong side of the shower or toilet.

One way to overcome this problem is to carry along a few Port-A-Bars (grabitonline.com). These portable grab bars are available in two sizes, and they attach to the wall with vacuum cups. They are lightweight and easy to pack, yet very sturdy. They are especially useful if you require grab bars on a specific side or at a specific height.

And then there are those bothersome bedside lamps. When was the last time you could actually operate one from the bed? In most cases, they require a good deal of manual dexterity. Other times they are simply out of reach. Apparently, I'm not the only person bothered by this problem, because a good number of adaptive solutions are available.

Lamp Commander is at the top of the list. This plug-in, voice-controlled switch lets you turn a lamp on and off with a simple voice command. Manufactured by Salton Inc., this compact device is easy to use. You just plug Lamp Commander in the wall outlet and plug a lamp into the Lamp Commander unit. To operate the lamp, simply say "Lamp Commander On" or "Lamp Commander Off". It sells for about $20 and can be found at most Target, Wal-Mart, Sears, and JC Penney stores.

A number of other lamp solutions can be found at most hardware and home improvement stores. If you have problems operating those awkward switches on bedside lamps, take a touch lamp control switch with you. This portable device turns an ordinary lamp into a touch control lamp. Just screw the adapter into the light socket of any metal lamp. Alternatively, shop around for a lamp switch adapter that works for you. These devices are available in many sizes and shapes but they all fit over the existing lamp switches and make them easier to turn.

And finally, my favorite hardware store item is a simple suction cup hook. This inexpensive and lightweight device is the perfect solution for those out-of-reach bathroom robe hooks.

Block That Room

HAVE YOU EVER arrived at a hotel, reservation in hand, and discovered your accessible room had been given to another guest? Well, you're not alone. More and more travelers are learning that a reservation by itself doesn't necessarily guarantee an accessible room upon arrival. So, what's a traveler to do? Basically, you need to learn how to separate the wheat from the chaff so that you can become an effective self advocate. In order to do this, you need to get the inside scoop on some lodging industry practices.

First, you need to understand a little bit about hotel reservation systems. The ability to reserve an accessible room depends directly on the type of reservation software used by a specific property. Generally speaking, the older reservation software doesn't give reservation agents the flexibility to reserve a specific room. In this case, a reservation for an accessible room is treated as a request, and it's entered as free text into the reservation system. In other words, a specific accessible room cannot be reserved.

Fortunately, many hotel chains updated their reservation software in order to be Y2K compliant. Most of the new reservation software allows properties to reserve a specific room, but only to the extent that the properties have defined their specific room types in the computer system. So, in most cases, if a hotel has flagged their accessible rooms, the new software can reserve a specific accessible room.

The only way to determine if a property can reserve an accessible room is to ask, but be careful how you phrase your query. Many people ask if the property will guarantee the room. This is the wrong terminology, because in hotel-speak *guarantee* means to secure with a credit card deposit. In other words, your room rate and reservation will be guaranteed with your credit card. This locks in your rate, and assures you that a room (any room) will be there for you, even if you arrive late. It does not ensure that your room will be accessible. The correct way to phrase your request is, "Can you block that accessible room for me?" In hotel terminology, block means to reserve a specific room for a specific guest.

Of course, even if you ask the right questions, you may still go through a lot of properties before you get the appropriate responses. Basically, it's a numbers game. You just have to keep calling until you find a property that doesn't hem and haw about blocking accessible rooms. The best way to speed up your search is to begin with properties that have a better than average chance of answering your query affirmatively. Here are a few places to start:

Microtel CEO Mike Levin claims their company will block accessible rooms upon reservation. Although there is no written policy on this matter, in practice Microtel seems to follow through on Levin's promise.

Motel 6 claims it will block accessible rooms. In practice, accessible rooms are blocked; however, some guests have complained that many of the older (pre-1992) Motel 6 properties lack appropriate access.

Hampton Inns has been very proactive about blocking accessible rooms. This is not a system-wide policy, so make sure to inquire directly with the specific property.

Under the terms of a 1996 Department of Justice (DOJ) settlement, all Marriott Courtyard properties are required to block their accessible rooms.

All BASS Properties (Holiday Inn, Crowne Plaza, and Staybridge Suites) are required to block their accessible rooms under the terms of a 1998 DOJ settlement.

Unfortunately, it takes extra time to locate properties that block accessible rooms. There seems to be no way around that, but perhaps in the years to come, more properties will adopt this as a standard practice. Until then, shop around, and remember—even the most accessible room in the world is useless unless it's actually available when you arrive.

No (Accessible) Room at the Inn

OF COURSE, SOMETIMES even when you do everything right, you can still run into problems. What do you do then? What do you do when you arrive at a property and find out they don't have the appropriate room for you, even though you have a confirmed reservation?

If the property doesn't have any accessible rooms left, they must find you appropriate lodging at another hotel. Sometimes this is acceptable and sometimes it is not. For example if you chose a hotel because of its location, you might also want to ask for a transportation allowance. If it's really a big inconvenience to you, ask for a voucher for free stay on a future visit.

These are both reasonable requests. Do not, however, ask the property to foot the bill for your entire vacation. This is not considered a reasonable request, and in most cases, management won't even address your problem if you ask for something they view as being totally unreasonable.

In most cases, the solution is open to discussion. In truth, there is no one right procedure for getting the best resolution, because it all depends on your own personal style. To illustrate this point, let me tell you a true story, about how three people handled the same problem in three completely different ways. The players in this little drama are Carol, John, and James. The scene was the check-in counter of an upscale business hotel on the first day of a disability conference. All three players held a confirmed reservation for a specific type of accessible room. They all arrived at different times, only to find that their confirmed room type was not available. Here's how they each handled it.

Carol was the first to arrive. Her reservation was for an accessible smoking room with a tub and shower. The desk clerk explained to Carol that the only accessible rooms left were nonsmoking rooms. This was not acceptable to Carol. She quoted the law, calmly explained her needs, and patiently reasoned with the clerk. In the end, the clerk handed her an astray and told her to ignore the no smoking signs in the room. Problem solved. As a nonsmoker, I cringe when I consider the resolution, but as a disability rights advocate, I applaud Carol's victory.

John was the next to arrive. He was accompanied by Phil, his personal care attendant. John's reservation was for an accessible room, with two beds and a roll-in shower. No accessible rooms with two beds were available. Now John is a very astute businessman, with a no-nonsense approach to life. After reviewing the law with the clerk, John quipped that he had no intention of sleeping in the same bed with Phil. He added that he was very tired, and that if they didn't provide him with an appropriate room, he would sleep on the sofa in the lobby. Of course John added, "I sleep in the nude." Problem solved. In short order, the clerk found an appropriate room for John and Phil.

No accessible rooms were left by the time James arrived. However, this good-looking, 20-something young man didn't let that stop him. He effortlessly explained the law, and slowly won over the clerk with his charm. His southern accent didn't hurt matters either. James ended up with the accessible penthouse suite.

Who's the best problem-solver? In truth, there's no winner, because they all achieved equally appropriate results. What's the most effective advocacy style? It's the one that works best for you.

The first step is to learn the rules, know the law, and understand your rights. Then find your style, fine-tune it, and add it to your advocacy toolbox. It may take some time, and a bit of trial and error, so be flexible until you find a style that works for you. It's not an exact science, but it is effective. It's the way to get results.

In Case of Fire

IN THIS DAY and age, it just pays to be prepared. What if the fire alarm goes off in your hotel in the middle of the night? What should you do? Should you evacuate (if you are able), or should you wait until emergency personnel come and get you? A lot of questions go through your mind while that emergency alarm is ringing. Rest assured though, most hotels already have a plan of action in place.

The first thing you should do is try to remain calm. The security staff keeps a record of all guests who require emergency evacuation assistance. If you don't have a visible physical disability, yet require emergency evacuation assistance, inform the desk clerk of this at check in. Your name will then be added to the list.

When you get to your room, remember to look on the back of the door for the map that shows the emergency evacuation routes. Familiarize yourself with this map and go out and actually follow the route to the exit.

If an emergency alarm sounds, the best rule of thumb is to remain in your room unless you are specifically told to evacuate. If evacuation is necessary, you will be notified by intercom or telephone. The security staff should know within 3 to 5 minutes after the alarm sounds if evacuation is imminent. If immediate evacuation is necessary, security staff should be at your room within 60 to 90 seconds to provide assistance. If you do not hear from the hotel staff, then call the front desk to inquire about the situation and to remind them you may need assistance.

If you smell smoke, place wet towels beneath the door and stay in your room as long as you feel safe. If you do leave the room, stay low to the ground, beneath the layer of smoke, and head for the area of emergency refuge (usually the stairwell). Although the stairwell might not seem like it offers much protection, it is pressurized and can withstand intense heat. Emergency rescue personnel are also trained to look for people in the area of emergency refuge.

Additionally, it's a good idea to carry a pocket-size flashlight with you. I keep one in my suitcase at all times. You don't want to be left in the dark in the event of an emergency.

Inns and B&Bs

ALTHOUGH MANY PEOPLE overlook small inns and B&Bs when searching for accessible lodgings, some of these owner-operated properties are in fact nicely accessible. Under the law, many of the

Figure 7.1.
Many small inns are nicely accessible. This is the bathroom of Mae's Room at the Redbud Inn in Murphys, California.

smaller properties aren't required to be accessible if they're owner-occupied. On the other hand, many are accessible, either because of need or design.

For example, if one of the owners or a family member is disabled, then it's quite likely that their property will be accessible. Additionally, many of these small property owners don't want to lose any wedding business, so they've made their properties accessible. They want to be able to accommodate all the friends and relatives of the wedding party. Smart business people don't want to have to turn business away, and indeed the B&B business is very competitive.

Additionally, some designs just lend themselves better to access than others. For example, many older homes have nice hardwood floors and wide double doors. In short, it never hurts to ask about access, but be sure to ask the clerk to describe the access features.

One advantage to staying at a small inn or B&B is that the owners are very familiar with their rooms, and most can describe them down to the smallest detail. Additionally, many small inns and B&Bs have the ability to reserve specific rooms. In fact, it's standard practice at many B&Bs to reserve a specific room for each guest. So, if you reserve an accessible room, you can rest assured that it will be available when you arrive.

A great source of access information on small inns and B&Bs is InnSeekers. You can search this online database for wheelchair-accessible properties in the location of your choice. Visit innseekers.com to access this free database.

Hostels

HOSTELS ARE ANOTHER often overlooked accessible lodging option. Although hostelling first gained popularity in the 1970s, as an inexpensive way for young people to see the world, today most hostels are open to travelers of all ages. The one exception is in Bavaria, Germany, were the age limit is 26.

Traditionally, hostels provide inexpensive lodging in dormitory-style bedrooms, with separate quarters for males and females. Today, many hostels also have private family rooms that can be reserved in advance. Most hostels still have kitchens, and all have storage areas and public rooms. Some hostels even have swimming pools, barbecues, and hot tubs. A wide variety of hostel accommodations are available throughout the world, and many hostels have accessible facilities.

Hostelling has many advantages. The major perk is big savings on lodging costs, as nightly hostel rates run between $10 to $35 per person. Rates vary depending on the location and the amenities of the property, so expect to pay more in the larger cities and less in the country. Another advantage to hostelling is that you can meet other travelers. And finally, cooking your meals can cut down on food costs.

Figure 7.2.
Hostels are an often overlooked accessible lodging option. This accessible bathroom is in a New Zealand hostel.

As far as access goes, most hostel proprietors are very familiar with the access features of their property. I've also found that they are incredibly honest about the access, because they don't want guests to be disappointed when they arrive.

Hostelling International (HI) maintains a worldwide database of hostels. Although membership is not required to stay in a HI hostel, members get a discount. Members also receive a print copy of the HI hostel directory. The HI directory is also available online at hiayh.org.

Accessible hostels are noted on the website, but access details are not listed. Contact the property directly to find out about specific access details. For more information about hostels, contact Hostelling International at (202) 783-6161. And don't just limit yourself to hostels in the United States, because I've seem some wonderfully accessible hostels around the world.

Home Exchange

HOME EXCHANGING IS not a new idea; in fact, it's been a popular practice in Europe for decades. Today, this money-saving vacation option is gaining popularity in North America. The good news is that home exchanging is the ideal solution for people who need accessible holiday accommodations. In fact, it kills two birds with one stone, as home exchanging is an accessible and affordable holiday option.

The principles behind home exchanging are pretty simple. The idea is to find somebody with a lifestyle similar to yours, in another part of the country or world. Then the two of you exchange homes. You both live in each other's house while you are on holiday. It's an even exchange, so both exchangees pocket the money they would have spent on other lodging arrangements.

The benefits of home exchanging are obvious. If you have made some accessibility modifications to your own home, then it just makes sense to find another person like you, who has made similar modifications to his home. One of the best resources for accessible home exchange listings is the Vacation Home Swap Bulletin Board (www.independentliving.org/vacex/index.html). This Internet resource is operated by the Institute on Independent Living in Stockholm, Sweden, and contains accessible home exchange listings from around the world. Visitors can browse through the listings, do a keyword search, or add their own home to the growing collection. There is no charge to view or post listings on this bulletin board.

The number of home exchange listing services is also growing. These vary by size and service, but most charge a fee for their services. Some sell print directories, some offer Internet access, and some offer a combination of both services. Even though many of these listing services have an accessible homes section, in reality most homes listed in these sections are not very accessible. Remember, people have different definitions of accessible, and to some people an accessible home is one that has a wide front door. Truly, the best source of accessible homes is the Vacation Home Swap Bulletin Board. Plus, it's also free!!

Many people feel funny about having a stranger live in their home. Indeed, caution should be used when screening a potential home exchange partner. In fact, many people turn to friends and relatives as home exchange partners. Some people post notices on school and work bulletin boards, and some people even meet exchange partners through friends. There are no rules here, and you can be as creative as you want. Do what is most comfortable for you.

In any case, consider a home exchange for your next holiday. This tried and true European idea offers big monetary savings, plus the comfort and freedom of real accessibility.

Taking the Kids | 8

LET'S FACE IT, we all start out life on wheels. In fact, most parents are quite adept at wheeling around their young charges in strollers and baby carriages. It's pretty easy to do when they are small. But what about when they get bigger? Can you imagine wheeling around a teenager in a stroller? That uncut curb that was once easy to bump up is no longer a piece of cake with a teenager on board.

Although this example may be an oversimplification of the situation, it illustrates a very common problem. I've seen it played out time and time again as children get bigger and make that transition from stroller to wheelchair. Mom and dad can no longer lift them and those "few steps" that were once easily navigable in a stroller become impossible in a wheelchair.

It's usually at this point that I hear comments from parents such as, "We used to be able to travel when John was small, but now that he weighs 100 pounds we just can't do it anymore." Although I understand the frustration, that's not exactly a fair assessment of the situation. Travel is still possible, even with a child in a wheelchair.

The truth is that most parents don't give access much thought while their child is in a stroller. After all, why should they? A stroller fits through standard doorways, it's not too heavy to bump up a curb and, if worse comes to worst, they can always carry junior.

When a child graduates to a wheelchair, parents have to think about accessible rooms, toilets, and transportation for the first time. And when this happens, it takes more time to plan, organize, and actually execute a trip. Although this can be frustrating to many parents who traveled easily before, the good news is that family vacations don't have to end just because your child uses a wheelchair.

Car Trips

CAR TRIPS ARE A favorite family vacation option. It's just easier to travel by car when your kids are small. Let's face it, you take a lot of things with you when you travel with young children. That fact by itself makes the family vehicle (with plenty of room for luggage and extras) the ideal vacation transportation choice. Additionally, many toddlers aren't exactly ideal air passengers. They get bored easily, and it's hard to keep them entertained on long flights. On the other hand, a road trip allows you the flexibility to make as many stops as you need along the way to relieve that boredom, plus you can pack along all those favorite toys without having to worry about airline baggage restrictions.

Car trips also present an especially attractive option for wheeler kids. As one mom says, "My son can't fly anymore because he can't really sit in an airplane seat. He just doesn't have enough head and back support. He can only sit in his wheelchair. So now we travel by van and he stays in his own wheelchair. We can stop when we want, and he is safer and more comfortable this way. It's really a good solution."

Some families take it one step further and go camping. "We usually camp with our travel trailer," says another mom. "It is a great way to travel because we pull it with our lift van, so we have accessible transportation at our destination. Also, it is less expensive, and we can bring along any piece of equipment we think we might need, like bath chairs, potty chairs, or special bikes."

No matter which option you choose, finding accessible rest stops along the way is a vital component of any car trip. To be honest, it's kind of a hit-or-miss process, but you can improve your odds by seeking out fast food chains that look like they were built within the last 5 years. Most of these are built from cookie-cutter designs and, although the food may not be that nutritious, the restrooms are well done access-wise and they are fairly standard from location to location. (The exception, of course, are older restaurants that have been retrofitted for access.)

Unfortunately, there aren't a lot of resources that list accessible rest stops. In fact, I only know of one. The Oregon Department of Transportation has a website (tripcheck.com/General/restareas .htm#hc) that lists accessible facilities available at rest areas throughout Oregon. It's organized by route number, and it's a very handy trip planning tool if you happen to be traveling in Oregon. Hopefully, other states will follow suit with similar resources in the near future.

If you're not towing your own accessible trailer with you, you'll also have to find accessible hotels for your car trip. This perhaps is the biggest adjustment parents need to make when their child transitions from a stroller to a wheelchair. Although some parents can manage with a nonaccessible room when their child is in a stroller, it's almost impossible with a wheelchair.

Wheelchairs are wider than strollers and nonaccessible rooms present many access obstacles, including narrow doorways and tiny bathrooms. Plan ahead and make a checklist of your access needs and make sure the hotel you choose can meet them. Even though it takes more time in the planning stage, booking an accessible room makes for a happier vacation in the long run.

Air Travel

AIR TRAVEL HAS its benefits too, but admittedly it's not for everyone. The major advantage to air travel is that it allows you to cover a long distance in a relatively short amount of time. The downside is that once you get off the airplane you need to find accessible transportation at your destination. This is sometimes hard to do; in fact, accessible ground transportation is the most often overlooked component of any trip.

Additionally, any time you travel by air, there is the very real possibility that the airline will damage your wheelchair. Granted nobody wants to have their wheelchair damaged, but for some people with highly specialized wheelchairs this fact by itself prevents them from flying. In short, it's just not worth the risk to some people. If your child falls into this category, realize it in the beginning and choose another mode of transportation. Air travel is not the idea choice for everyone.

But air travel works for many people. In fact, when your child is small enough to use a car seat, it's a good choice. Car seats can help with head and neck support in young children. But what about when they get too big for a car seat? Can you just make your own seating and support device? Not exactly.

To take a child restraint device on an airplane, it must be Federal Aviation Administration (FAA) approved. What makes the cut? Well, most car seats do, but home-made seating devices do not. Generally speaking, neck pillows, towels, and blankets are allowed, but one parent recently got a "30-inch piece of foam rubber needed for back support" nixed at the cabin door. The bottom line is, if your child is too big for a car seat and needs a lot of neck or trunk support, flying may not be an option.

Another option for lap infants is the Baby B'Air flight vest. This cotton garment fits over the child's head and is secured by straps under the arms and between the legs. After takeoff, a seat belt can be attached to the back of the vest to secure the child. The FAA does not allow any harness to attach directly to the parent but the Baby B'Air is designed to attach to the seat belt instead of body. Although this is only an option for lap babies, it may work for children who need some extra support, but who are not comfortable in a car seat. The company also promises a full refund if any airline refuses to let you use the vest. The major drawback is that the vest cannot be used during takeoff and landing.

Once you decide that air travel is for you, be sure to familiarize yourself with the Air Carrier Access Act (ACAA). (See Chapter 1 for more tips on air travel.) It's important to note that the same rules and regulations that apply to adults also apply to children. The best course of action is to familiarize yourself with your rights so that you will know what to expect before you hit the road.

Cruises

THE CRUISE INDUSTRY has drastically changed over the years. At one time, this all-inclusive travel option was only attractive to seniors. Today, cruising is a great family vacation idea, because many cruise lines have a plethora of special programs and activities for children of all ages, from toddlers to teens.

Cruising has many advantages. First, you can visit a number of destinations without having to pack and unpack at every stop. You just get off the ship. Second, with the increasing number of home ports, almost everyone can drive to an embarkation point. This means you can take that exotic vacation without having to get on an airplane. And finally, with the wide variety of onboard kid-centric programs, not only do kids have something interesting and educational to do, but their parents can also enjoy some much needed alone time. Everybody gets a vacation.

The key to a successful cruise lies in picking the right cruise line and the right ship. After all, you don't want to get stuck on a ship that only has limited wheelchair access or on a cruise line that isn't kid friendly. With that in mind, two cruise lines stand head-and-shoulders above the crowd, Royal Caribbean International (RCI) and Carnival Cruise Lines (CCL). Each line has a different personality, but both are a good family vacation option.

RCI offers the Adventure Ocean program. This complimentary program is open to kids between 3 and 17 years of age and is designed to blend educational activities with just plain fun. Kids participate in age-appropriate activities, learn about local customs, do science experiments, and make new friends. Special play areas are available for kids and a nightclub for teens is present on most RCI ships; however, the Adventure Ocean program is not always restricted to one area.

To participate, children must be 3 years old and potty-trained. They cannot wear diapers or pull ups. There are no exceptions to this rule, even for wheeler kids. Still, if your child is potty-trained, RCI is a great choice because their kids programs consistently get rave reviews, and most of their newer ships offer excellent access.

Camp Carnival is the kids program offered by CCL. This day program is open to kids between 2 and 15 years of age. Like the RCI program, children are divided by age group and supervised by specially trained youth counselors. They participate in a variety of activities from bingo and sponge painting to teen dinners and dance parties.

The main difference between the two programs lies in the potty-training policy. CCL has a more liberal policy, and they do not require children to be potty-trained to participate in the program; however, they do require parents to provide diapers and toiletries if their child is still in diapers. So, if your child wears diapers, CCL is the better choice.

No matter which cruise line you choose, always pick the newer ships because, generally speaking, they are more accessible. Talk with the special-needs department, find out about the specific features of the accessible cabins, and then book the one that best suits your needs. *Accessible* can mean a number of different things, so do your research and make sure the accessible cabin will really work for your child.

Destinations

IF YOU'D PREFER to stay on dry land during your holiday, rest assured that there are many accessible family-friendly choices. Generally speaking, you will find better access in large cities because most have some type of accessible public transportation and many even have accessible taxis. Your selection of hotels will also be bigger in a large city, which means you stand a better chance of finding an accessible room that suits your needs.

As far as tourist attractions go, look for aquariums, zoos, and museums for the best access. And although I'm not a big fan of theme parks, most have good access and many publish detailed access guides about their accessible facilities and services. It's a good idea to review the access guide before your visit, so that you know in advance which rides are accessible. Policies vary from park to park, but most parks have at least a few rides that are off-limits to wheel-chair-users. Knowing this in advance can help avoid disappointment.

Learning vacations are also a popular family travel choice and Washington D.C. tops the list of accessible and educational destinations. Most of the public buildings in the nation's capitol are accessible, but advance research is a must. Some venues (like the popular Smithsonian National Air and Space Museum) have barrier-free access at the front door, whereas others (like the White House) require advance arrangements for the accessible tour. As an added bonus, there is no admission charge to most Washington D.C. attractions.

If you'd like to stay closer to home, then plan a trip to your state capital. Government buildings usually have good access, and it's a great place for kids to learn how the state legislature works. Many state capitals also have large museums and other accessible tourist attractions.

Colonial Williamsburg is also a big hit with kids, especially when they are studying colonial history in school. Many of the buildings are accessible, and lots of hands-on activities and interpreters dressed in period costumes are available. Kids learn while they have fun. The Colonial Williamsburg Foundation publishes an excellent access guide that lists the accessible attractions and buildings. Best bet is to review the access guide before your visit so that you can plan your activities in advance.

If you'd like to explore the outdoors, consider visiting a national park. Access varies from park to park, but most parks at least have an accessible visitor center. Many parks also have short, accessible, interpretive trails and lodging facilities. Visit the National Parks Service website at nps.gov for access information.

And finally, don't forget factory tours. Many are free and most have at least partial access. Accessible kid favorites include the Basic Brown Bear Factory (San Francisco, CA), Jelly Belly Candy Company (Fairfield, CA), Kellogg's (Battle Creek, MI), Ben & Jerry's (Waterbury, VT), and The Crayola Factory (Easton, PA). A great resource for factory tours (including access details) is *Watch It Made in the USA* by Karen Axelrod and Bruce Brumberg.

Words of Wisdom

THE BEST ADVICE about kid-focused accessible travel comes from parents who have already hit the road. With that in mind, here are some words of wisdom from a few real life experts.

- "Try to find equipment that can do double duty. For instance, I buy a cheap beach chair every year and attach a seat belt to it. Then we use it to sit in sand, at the edge of the beach and also in the tub as a bath chair."
- "If accessible transportation looks like it's going to be an issue, we'll usually opt for a manual wheelchair that can fold up and go into the trunk of a rental car. If we're flying to a destination, I've got to be really comfortable that there will be great accessible transportation when I get there to be able to take the power wheelchair."
- "Allow tons of time. It will take three times as long to get something done! And don't forget to pack your patience and your sense of humor."
- "I always pack a little personal backpack for my daughter with a couple of favorite books and a Walkman. I also try to add several little things she hasn't seen before such as new books, a little art activity we can do together, a coloring book, or one of those little games with magnetic pieces that won't get away. She can't manipulate all of these things alone, but she enjoys making choices and playing games. She knows it's going to be fun to open the pack!"
- "Don't be spontaneous. Plan ahead for everything. The romantic notion of just packing a bag and heading off to some destination with no plans just doesn't work for someone who needs accommodations for their disability. You need to approach it like an invading army."

So You Want To Get Off the Ship? 9
Cruise Travel

CRUISE TRAVEL HAS long been touted as the most accessible vacation option by a plethora of self-proclaimed travel industry experts. In reality, cruises are only an appropriate option for some people. It's true that some of the newer ships are very accessible; however the same can't be said of the older ships. Additionally, very few shore excursions offer roll-on access. In short, it takes a good amount of advance planning and preparation to ensure adequate access on any cruise holiday.

So why does the travel industry continue to promote cruising as the most appropriate accessible travel choice? The answer to that is pretty simple: time and money. It takes a good deal of time and effort to package individual itineraries. Cruises already come in a nice neat package, so they are easy to sell. More important, in this day of dwindling commissions, cruise lines are still able to offer travel agents top dollar for selling their products. In short, it just makes sense to promote a product that puts money in your pocket.

Now, don't let me discourage you from taking a cruise, if that's truly your heart's desire. I'm just trying to give you a realistic look at the situation, so that you understand all your options. Many inexperienced travel agents present cruise travel as the only option for accessible travel, and that's really a great disservice to the traveling public. If you truly want to take a land tour, then don't let a travel agent talk you into a cruise. Of course, you should understand that some land tours also present access barriers.

It's truly a situation of buyer beware. Don't assume all cruises are accessible. And if you work with a travel agent, work with one who is well versed in accessible travel, not just in cruise travel.

No matter how luxurious the staterooms are or how decadent the food is, if you can't get off the ship. it's just a long boat ride. Now some people can live with that; in fact, some people love the idea of getting on a ship and being pampered. However, if you want more from your cruise experience—like being able to enjoy the ports—you have to jump in and do some research. Access doesn't magically materialize just because you choose to cruise. Additionally, if you plan to visit foreign ports of call, you must become familiar with access in that country.

Access on the Seas

THE DEPARTMENT OF Justice (DOJ) has long held that cruise ships are covered under Title III of the Americans with Disabilities Act (ADA). According to John L. Wodatch, Chief of the DOJ Disability Rights Section, the ADA also applies to foreign flag cruise ships that dock at U.S. ports, unless, as he says "there is a showing that the application of the ADA to a foreign flag cruise ship would conflict with an international convention to which the United States is a party." Seems pretty simple, right? Well, not exactly. That point is aptly illustrated by Tammy Steven's much publicized experience with Premier Cruise Lines.

Tammy's saga began in 1998, when she saw an advertisement for a four-day cruise aboard Premier's *SS Oceanic*. The cruise was priced at an affordable $349, so she contacted her travel agent for more details. Her travel agent was assured by Premier that the *SS Oceanic* was indeed wheelchair-accessible; however, a wheelchair-accessible cabin was not available for the $349 price tag. Still, Tammy wanted to cruise, so she booked the trip, paid extra for her wheelchair-accessible cabin, and looked forward to a relaxing cruise.

After the *SS Oceanic* set sail, Tammy discovered that her cabin was not wheelchair-accessible. To use the bathroom, Tammy's sister and mother had to physically pick her up and put her on the commode or set her in the shower. To say this was humiliating is a gross understatement. Tammy was also left with bruises all over her arms and legs from this procedure. To add insult to injury, Tammy further discovered that many of the ship's public areas were not wheelchair-accessible. Such was the birth of *Stevens v. Premier Cruises, Inc.*

The U.S. District Court ruled against Stevens on her original complaint. The judge found that Stevens didn't have the right standing (a legal technicality), and that the ADA does not apply to foreign flag cruise ships. The appellate court ruled that Stevens should have had the opportunity to amend her original pleading. The appellate court also found that Title III of the ADA does apply to cruise ships, including foreign flag carriers.

So, where do we stand today in regards to the ADA and cruise ship access? The appellate court ruling actually established case law on the subject, which is an important first step in any ADA matter. The problem is that the U.S. Access Board has not established any accessibility standards for passenger vessels (cruise ships). Hopefully, that will change in the next few years.

The Passenger Vessel Access Advisory Committee submitted its recommendations to the Access Board on December 18, 2000. The next step is the issuance of proposed regulations by the Access Board. This is followed by a public comment period. There is no timeline for the release of the draft regulations, but the status of the project is updated on the Access Board website at www.access-board.gov.

So in theory, yes, cruise ships that call on U.S. ports are covered under the ADA. However, since no accessibility standards currently exist, it's difficult to prevail in any ADA action involving cruise ship access. For now it's best to proceed with caution and remember to ask about specific access details and features before booking any cruise. As evidenced in the Stevens case, *wheelchair-accessible* can indeed have a very broad definition.

Service Animals

THE DOJ RULE regarding service animals is pretty explicit. It states that public accommodations must modify their policies, practices, or procedures to accommodate service animals. And, yes, this includes cruise ships that dock in U.S. ports. That's the short and easy part; the more difficult part is the documentation, preparation, and (of course) the paperwork.

It's important to realize that you can't just stroll on board a cruise ship with your service animal. You must inform the cruise line when you book your cruise that you will be traveling with a service animal. All cruise lines require a health certificate for service animals. You must present the health certificate at embarkation. Some cruise lines require additional forms.

Some ports of call require even further documentation, and as mentioned in Chapter 3, some countries impose quarantines on imported animals. If you dock at a country that has such a quarantine, your service animal will not be allowed off the ship. Make sure to find out about quarantines, restrictions, and all required documentation in advance. This simple step will save you a lot of heartache.

What are your options if you can't take your service animal ashore? Basically, you have two choices. You can stay on board while the ship is in port, or you can go ashore without your service animal. The latter is only a realistic option if you are traveling with an able-bodied companion. Still, it's something to consider if you really want to see the port.

Many cruise veterans also agree it's a good idea to let the cruise line know about the size of your service animal in advance, just so there will be no surprises. Some people prefer to describe the animal (including the weight) while some people opt to send a photo of the animal.

One of the biggest concerns about service animals and cruises is the toileting arrangements (for the service animal that is). Is there really a poop deck? Well, there will be the week you cruise!

Seriously, ask about the cruise line's toileting policy well in advance. It's also a good idea to get the policy in writing. Policies vary from cruise line to cruise line. Some cruise lines provide a wood box filled with mulch, while some provide Astroturf. On the other hand, some cruise lines require passengers to bring their own piddle pads.

I've also received reports from a few cruisers who just let their service animals piddle in the shower. Most cruise lines do not condone this action, so don't go this route unless you receive permission in advance. Contact the special-needs department to determine if this is an acceptable practice.

It's a good idea to get your dog used to non-grass toileting prior to your cruise. In regards to that issue, I'm reminded of my friend Karen's predicament when she took a cruise. Her service animal just wouldn't (or couldn't) do his business for days. Finally, her husband took the dog out for a vigorous run around the deck, just to shake things up a bit. It worked like a charm; doggy did his business but hubby was pooped (no pun intended). The moral of the story is that it pays to familiarize your dog with toileting conditions similar to what you'll find on the ship.

It also pays to be prepared for the unexpected. Learn how to deal with problems when they arise. One cruise passenger reported that he left his service animal in his cabin while he went ashore, only to discover his cabin steward refused to clean his cabin. Apparently, the cabin steward was afraid of dogs. If you have an incident such as this, report it to the purser, remind him it's an access issue, and request that appropriate accommodations be made. In the above case, an appropriate accommodation would have been to have another cabin steward clean the cabin.

Finally, a word of warning if you book a cruise and air package. Never rely on the cruise line to relay information about your service animal to the airline. Deal with the airline directly. Never trust the cruise line to make access arrangements with the airline. Always contact the airline directly to confirm all access arrangements.

Oxygen

DIFFERENT CRUISE LINES have different policies regarding the use of therapeutic oxygen. Some cruise lines allow it and some don't. In nearly all cases, a physician's statement is required for passengers who use therapeutic oxygen.

Some cruise lines may be able to arrange for the delivery of oxygen, but remember this is not a free service. You can also arrange for oxygen delivery on your own with one of the cruise line's approved suppliers. Contact the special services department for a list of approved suppliers. Make sure you bring enough oxygen to last for the duration of the trip. Alternatively, you can arrange for refills at the ports of call.

If you are driving to the port, you might want to consider bringing your own oxygen supplies. In most cases, this is the most economical option. Check with the special-needs department to see if any limitations apply to the types of equipment you can bring on board.

If you are flying to the port, make sure you also make arrangements with the airline for in-flight oxygen use. If your travel agent is making both your cruise and air arrangements, remind her that you will also need in-flight oxygen. This crucial step is often overlooked by many cruise travel agents.

Dialysis at Sea

SPECIAL ARRANGEMENTS CAN be made on some cruises for passengers who require dialysis. Although cruise ships do not have dialysis equipment routinely on board, a few tour operators organize special dialysis cruises. These tour operators make all the arrangements for dialysis equipment, supplies, and medical personnel. These cruise packages are not cheap, but many people enjoy having somebody else take care of all the details. The major drawback is that unless enough people sign up, these specialty cruises are usually canceled.

Some people opt to arrange dialysis on shore. This can be a risky (and sometimes expensive) plan of action, as evidenced by Linda's experience. "When I booked our seven-day Caribbean cruise, I carefully chose our itinerary so that I could arrange for dialysis at the U.S. ports of call, as our insurance only covers dialysis in the United States," says Linda. "When we boarded the ship we were informed of a last minute change of itinerary. Instead of docking at St. Thomas we docked at St. Maarten. That port change cost me $738, because dialysis on St. Maarten wasn't covered by my insurance."

Most cruise contracts state that the cruise line is not responsible for additional charges due to last-minute port changes. Although in Linda's case the port change happened before they boarded the ship, it's important to note that it can (and does) also happen while en route. Always have a backup plan if you opt to get dialysis ashore.

Two good online dialysis resources are Dialysis Finder (dialysisfinder.com) and Global Dialysis (globaldialysis.com). Dialysis Finder features a database that contains the locations of dialysis clinics around the world, while Global Dialysis is a U.K.-based web site with lots of information on dialysis travel.

Cruise Lines

YOU SHOULD TAKE several things into consideration when selecting a cruise line, including ship personality, fleet age, and passenger demographics—and last but not least, access and attitude. Some cruise lines have a more proactive approach to access than others. Ultimately, your decision will be largely based on personal tastes and budget; however, don't overlook the cruise line's overall attitude about access issues.

Royal Caribbean International (RCI) stands head-and-shoulders above the crowd as far as accessibility and attitude are concerned. In fact, according to RCI Executive Vice President, Adam Goldstein, "Royal Caribbean wants to be the preferred cruise line for people with disabilities."

RCI cemented their commitment to access by selecting a

respected member of the disability community to reign as Godmother of their final Voyager class vessel. On November 14, 2003, wheelchair athlete and disability advocate Jean Driscoll christened RCI's most accessible ship, the *Mariner of the Seas*. Says Mr. Goldstein, "The selection of Jean Driscoll as Godmother of *Mariner of the Seas*, is the reflection of our multi-year commitment to access."

Attitude kudos also go to Seattle-based American West Steamboat Company, for making their Columbia River cruises more accessible. Their *Queen of the West* and *Empress of the North* offer small-ship paddlewheel cruises in the Pacific Northwest. The *Empress of the North*, which also sails the Inside Passage to Alaska, is the newest ship and the most accessible choice.

Figure 9.1.
Royal Caribbean International installs extra access features such as automatic doors and pool and Jacuzzi lifts on many of their ships. This pool lift is aboard the *Adventure of the Seas*.

All shore excursions are included on American West Steamboat Company cruises. Their Columbia River shore excursions are all conducted on company-owned buses with wheelchair lifts and tie-downs. All bus drivers are trained on lift usage, and the cruise staff is ready to assist whenever needed. The crew also gets high ratings in the courtesy department, as they actually ask if you want assistance before they try to push or lift you.

Many cruise lines are changing their attitudes about access. For example, back in 2001, Norwegian Cruise Lines had a policy that prohibited passengers with a physical disability from traveling alone or with another passenger with a disability. They had to be accompanied by an able-bodied companion. This requirement is a thing of the past, although it's still suggested many times for safety reasons. Indeed, the world is coming around.

So shop around for a cruise line that meets your access needs and has a proactive attitude about access. Truthfully, the best tip-off that a cruise line actually wants your business is the fact that they have a dedicated access department that passengers can contact directly. Additionally, it's always a good sign when a cruise line has access information available on their website or in their collateral materials.

Ships

CHOOSING A CRUISE ship is analogous to choosing a hotel, because it's where you'll live, sleep, and play for the length of your holiday at sea. And although most cruise ships offer more amenities than hotels, they're of little use if you can't actually access them.

For example, some of the ships built in the early to mid 1990s have good access to most public areas, except for the spas. So, if you want to enjoy a facial or massage aboard these ships, you're out of luck. Remember to ask about access to *all* areas of the ship. Access can vary greatly from ship to ship, even on the same cruise line.

Generally speaking, the newer and larger ships offer the best access. Try to stay away from the older ships that have been refurbished; you'll find the best access on ships that were designed to be accessible, rather than on those that were retrofitted.

A good place to start your research is at The Cruise Ship Center, a nonprofit cruise portal at cruise2.com. Billed as a free platform for buyers and sellers of cruises, The Cruise Ship Center has scads of helpful information, including a list of accessible cabins. Cabin numbers of the accessible cabins are listed for many cruise ships, so it's a good place to bookmark. The downside is this list hasn't been updated for many years, and the newer ships are not listed. It will, however, give you access details about some of the older ships.

Once you've narrowed down your choices, contact the cruise lines directly regarding access on each specific ship. Ask to speak to the special-needs department or to an access specialist. This is the time to ask specific access questions about each ship.

It should be noted that, unofficially, some of the cruise lines' special-needs agents "prefer" not to talk to passengers directly. The reason given for this is that the passengers "bog down the special-needs agent with general cruise questions in addition to access questions." The general feeling seems to be that if the booking is later made through a travel agent, much of the information is duplicated.

No official policy exists regarding this, but be aware you may encounter resistance from some special-needs agents. If that happens, call back and speak to another agent. If you can't get the access answers you need before you book, take your business elsewhere. On the other hand, if you book with a bona fide accessible cruise specialist from the start, you won't need to talk to the special-needs department at all.

You should also be aware that if you book through a travel agent, most cruise lines will refer you back to that travel agent if you have questions or need changes. Some cruise lines will answer simple inquiries or verify that you have an accessible room reserved. If, however, you find your travel agent didn't request an accessible room, the cruise line will inform you that your travel agent is the only one who can make changes in your reservation.

When you contact the cruise line's special-needs department, remember to ask very specific questions. As with everything else, don't just ask if the ship is accessible, or if the ship has accessible cabins. Ask specific questions about the access features of the ship. Inquiries regarding physical access are generally broken down into three main categories: the cabins, the bathrooms in the cabins, and the public areas of the ship. Make a worksheet for each ship and record the answers of the access specialist.

One of the first things to ask the access specialist is if they have any accessible cabins on the ship in question. But don't stop there. Ask how wide the doorway clearance to the cabin is, and if there is a sill or lip at the threshold. Some ships still have sizable threshold lips called *coamings* (a marine term not in the vocabulary of most customer service agents). Ask about the square footage of the accessible cabin as compared with a standard cabin and request a detailed floor plan if available. Don't forget also to ask about the

Figure 9.2.
Accessible cabins, such as this one aboard the *Adventure of the Seas*, are usually larger than standard cabins in the same class.

width of the corridor outside your cabin. It really doesn't matter how wide your cabin doorway is if the outside corridor isn't wide enough for you to turn into the doorway.

If you use a power wheelchair or scooter, make sure the electrical supply on the ship is compatible with your battery charger. You may need to bring an electrical converter. Some cruise lines provide converters, but make sure (in advance) that it's compatible with your equipment.

Because usually only one or two electrical outlets are available per cabin, it's a good idea to pack an extension cord in case the outlet is out of reach of your wheelchair. Additionally, if you plan on plugging in more than two items, like a curling iron and a hair dryer, pack a power strip. It doesn't take up much room, and it makes life a lot easier.

You might also want to bring along a manual wheelchair, as a backup and to use in some of the more inaccessible ports. As accessible travel specialist Connie George says, "While a scooter or power chair typically gives you comfort and more independence in day-to-day life, it's the manual that can give you more comfort and independence in some ports." If you do bring a manual wheelchair, make sure there is enough room in your cabin to store your power wheelchair or scooter. You cannot leave your scooter outside your cabin, so make sure there is enough room for it in your cabin.

Next, you need to inquire about the bathroom in the accessible cabin. Ask for specific measurements, including the bathroom doorway clearance and the dimensions of the bathroom. Ask if there is a lip at the bathroom door. If so, ask if they provide a portable ramp. If a portable ramp is used, ask about the height of the bathroom lip. Do the math. A 1:12 grade means that you need 1 foot of ramp length for every inch of rise; so a 6-inch lip would require a 6-foot long ramp. Make sure there is enough room in the cabin to accommodate the ramp.

You also need to ask about the bathroom fixtures, including the toilet and shower. Ask if there are toilet grab bars installed on the wall. Some cruise lines provide a raised toilet seat with grab bars attached to the seat. Although this configuration is preferred by people who have difficulty standing, it's unsuitable for many wheelchair-users, as it makes lateral transfers impossible. Ask if the room has a roll-in shower or a tub/shower combination. If it has a roll-in shower, ask if there is a fold-down shower seat. If there is a tub/shower combination, ask if they provide a portable shower chair.

If you need any special equipment, such as a commode chair or a shower chair, ask if the cruise line can provide it. Provide a detailed description and even a photo of the type of equipment you need. Sometimes it's difficult to get the cruise lines to provide the proper equipment, so if you have very specific needs, it's best to bring your own equipment. In most cases, you can also make arrangements to have rental equipment, such as a Hoyer lift, delivered to

Figure 9.3.
Many accessible bathrooms, such as this one aboard the *Empress of the North*, feature roll-in showers and a full 5-foot turning radius.

the ship. Ask the special-needs department for a list of their approved suppliers.

Finally, you need to inquire about the public areas of the ship. Ask about the width of the doorways leading to the outside decks and if there are any sills (coamings) on the doorways. Ask if there are any sills or lips on the doorways of any of the public rooms, including the public restrooms. Ask about the wheelchair seating in the showroom or theater. Some cruise lines seat wheelchair-users in the back (behind the last row of fixed seating) and make no allowance for companion seating.

Ask if there is wheelchair access to all public areas of the ship, and inquire specifically about any area that is of particular interest to you. When you book your cruise, remember to request a table

Figure 9.4.
Make sure to find out if the public areas are accessible. This jogging track aboard the *Mariner of the Seas* offers good wheelchair access.

near the restaurant entrance, but out of the main traffic flow, because this will make for a more pleasant dining experience.

Accessible ground transportation is another important thing to consider. Unless you live in the port city, you will most likely arrive by air and require accessible ground transportation to and from the ship. If you purchase transfers from the cruise line, be sure to inform them that you need accessible transportation.

Under the ADA, if a cruise line provides transportation to or from a U.S. port, they must also provide an accessible option. Additionally, the cruise line cannot charge more for accessible transportation, even if it costs them more to provide this service. If the cruise line provides free transfers, they must also provide accessible transfers at no charge.

According to the DOJ, "The ADA requires a cruise line to remove barriers in the facilities that they own or operate—including at U.S. ports of call, on board ships (including guestrooms), and in transportation services." This also applies to foreign flag vessels that dock at U.S. ports.

You can also opt to make arrangements for transfers on your own. Some travel agents are able to arrange transfers for you, but only if you book your cruise through them. Make sure you work with a travel agent who understands all the intricacies of accessible travel.

If you do work with a travel agent, make sure that the cruise line debits your credit card directly. Why? Well, for one thing it protects you from the few unscrupulous agents who re-price cruises, doctor the tickets, and then don't pass on the savings to their clients. It's not all that common but it does happen. If you pay the cruise line directly, your agent won't be able to pocket any savings due you.

Also, if you pay the cruise line directly you'll be more protected from travel agencies that are on the edge. I've come across a few agencies that offer huge discounts for prepayment to them (rather than the cruise lines). In short, they lose money on the deal just to increase their cash flow.

It goes without saying that any business that's willing to do that may be in dire financial trouble. You don't want to be left holding the bag, so it's best to avoid any agency that relies on this method to keep afloat financially. Remember, it's standard practice in the industry to have the cruise lines charge your credit card directly. Steer clear of anybody who claims otherwise.

Booking an Accessible Stateroom

ONCE YOU'VE FOUND a ship that suits your needs, you still have to jump through a few hoops to actually reserve an accessible stateroom. Most cruise lines require some sort of doctor's statement that describes your disability. Some cruise lines have specific forms to fill out, and some ask you detailed questions about your access needs.

Because accessible rooms are limited, cruise lines want to make sure you actually need the accessible stateroom. In other words, if you use oxygen but do not use a wheelchair, then most likely you won't need a room with a roll-in shower. The goal is to make sure that limited resources are distributed to those who really need them. Try to bear this in mind when booking and realize you will most likely have to supply some sort of documentation of your disability.

Of course, some people believe it's really not fair to only require disabled passengers to provide a doctor's statement. The following story illustrates why this is necessary.

"One morning we had breakfast with the family who booked the accessible stateroom we needed (I'll just call them the Smiths)," says frequent cruiser Paul. "They were all able-bodied, and they confided in us that they had to lie about being disabled in order to get their cabin. After all, Mr. Smith said, 'It's the only cabin that could accommodate our family of four.' He added, 'I had to instruct our travel agent to lie to the cruise line and tell them that we were disabled. I told her that I'd take my business elsewhere if she didn't. She knows which side her bread is buttered on!'"

So, if you ever become frustrated with the paperwork or the documentation required to book an accessible stateroom, just remember the Smiths. Proper documentation is the only way the cruise lines can avoid this kind of flagrant abuse.

Getting On and Off the Ship

SHIP ACCESSIBILITY IS only part of the equation when it comes to cruising, because getting on and off the ship is another big concern. How does the whole embarkation and disembarkation process work, and how do you get on and off the ship at the ports of call?

To be honest, embarkation and disembarkation can be a real zoo. After all, the goal is to get thousands of passengers and their luggage on or off the ship in a matter of hours. So, if you have any kind of physical disability, make sure it is noted in your file, even if you do not need an accessible stateroom. Embarkation assistance can range from moving you quickly through the process to providing wheelchair assistance. If you can't stand for long periods

Figure 9.5.
There are a variety of ways to get on and off the ship. Some ports offer roll-on gangway access, but remember that's not always the case.

of time or if you use any type of assistive device, it's important to request embarkation assistance when you book your cruise.

Wheelchair assistance is also available during disembarkation. Different cruise lines have different procedures for disembarking people with mobility disabilities. Some cruise lines gather people needing assistance together in one area, whereas other lines let them disembark before the other passengers. If you need assistance during disembarkation, make your needs known to the purser when the disembarkation procedure is announced.

Although home ports generally offer roll-off access, that's not the case in every port of call. How do you get off the ship if you are in a wheelchair? Do you just roll down the gangway? Well, sometimes that's the case, but often it's a bit more complicated, as illustrated by the following comments from Bill, a first-time cruiser.

Says Bill of his cruise experience, "Last fall my wife and I cruised to Alaska on the *Crown Princess*. Although the ship was wonderfully accessible, and our cabin was complete with a roll-in shower, the ports themselves were lacking in accessibility. Many times I had to be carried off the ship in my wheelchair, by untrained personnel. At times I feared for my safety, not to mention the safety of my very expensive (and heavy) power wheelchair. I was also very embarrassed, as the rest of the passengers gathered around to see this 'spectacle.' I was told the ports were accessible and not informed that I would have to be carried off the ship in this fashion."

Bill brings up a few good points. How do you find out if the ports have roll-off access? How do you know if you will be carried off the ship? Are there any other options? Basically there isn't one pat answer here. Although many cruise lines advise people that the ports are accessible, this doesn't necessarily mean roll-off accessibility. As Princess Cruise Lines stated in reply to my inquiry on Bill's behalf, "Generally, most ports are accessible to 'roll-off' with some help from our crew." In plain English that means you may be carried off the ship.

To be fair, Alaska does experience some drastic tidal fluctuations, so what is accessible in the morning will not necessarily be accessible that same afternoon. Sometimes you can roll off, sometimes you will be carried off, sometimes cruise lines use a stair climber, and sometimes wheelchair-users can use the more level crew gangway.

Princess Cruise Lines also advertises a separate accessible gangway with a ratcheted device to get wheelchairs on and off the ship. Unfortunately, their employees seem hesitant to use this accessible boarding option.

"When I asked about the accessible gangway I was told it breaks down a lot and costs a lot to fix," says Loretta. "The crew said it was too much trouble for them to set up just for one person. So instead I was carried up and down, by people who didn't know what they were doing. It was unsafe and very embarrassing. Princess may have a special gangway, but getting the crew to use it is impossible."

And then there's the issue of tendering. Some ports are just not accessible to large ships, and sometimes even the larger ports are too crowded to allow all ships dockside access. In these cases, the ships must anchor offshore and tender their passengers to the docks. *Tendering* is the process of ferrying passengers by small boats, or tenders, from the cruise ship to the main dock. Most cruise lines can provide a list of tender ports, but depending on traffic and tide conditions, any port is a potential tender port.

Tendering is handled differently by the different cruise lines, but in most cases it involves hand-carrying wheelchair-users onto the tender. Indeed, sometimes tendering can be a white-knuckle experience, especially in rough seas. It should also be noted that some cruise lines will not tender power wheelchairs at all. This is another good reason to bring along a manual wheelchair for shore excursions.

Some ships have a more accessible method of tendering passengers. The Shore Tender Accessibility Project was first introduced on Holland America Lines in 2000. The system was designed by Cap Sante Marine, Inc. and includes a lift that runs on an inclined track from the top of the ship's gangway to the tender. A ramp on the tender then allows wheelchair-users to roll on board the tender. When the tender reaches the dock, a hydraulic leveling system adjusts for the height differences between the dock and the tender. This process gives wheelers roll-off access to the dock.

The downside to this process is that the lifts do not accommodate power chairs or scooters. They are only available for lightweight wheelchairs. Additionally, the lift must be reserved ahead of time, and sometimes wheelchair passengers are only tendered after the main rush of passengers.

In the end, how you get off the ship depends on the port, the incline and access of the gangway, and what the cruise line considers the safest procedure for the conditions. The final decision on the safest procedure always lies with the captain of the ship. If the captain deems it too dangerous to carry off a passenger, then so be it. Basically, roll-off access is a roll of the dice.

Shore Excursions

ALTHOUGH MANY CRUISE lines are pretty forthcoming with information about their official shore excursions, most are rather tight-lipped with information about port accessibility. They are even tighter lipped when it comes to information about the accessibility of their official shore excursions. At times, it seems like this information is a closely guarded state secret!!

For example, several years ago I contacted Princess Cruise Lines to inquire about the accessibility of their Alaska shore excursions. All I wanted to know was which shore excursions were accessible. It seemed a simple enough question. After dodging the issue for several months, Princess' official reply to my query was that this information would be available to me after I booked a cruise.

Basically, they told me that unless I booked a cruise they wouldn't even tell me if any of their shore excursions are accessible. That seemed unfair; after all, most people like to know what they are buying before they write out the check. To be fair, Princess isn't alone here. It's like pulling teeth to get any access information about shore excursions out of the cruise lines.

In truth, only a handful of accessible shore excursions are available, so be wary if a cruise line indicates that a specific shore excursion is accessible. Make sure to ask a lot of questions, especially about the availability of accessible transportation. I've had reports from travelers who booked accessible shore excursions only to discover that standard buses were part of the package. If you book an accessible tour, make sure a lift-equipped or ramped vehicle is used for transportation. In many cases, the tour operators expect you to climb up the stairs to the bus and transfer to a seat.

Replies from tour providers about their access deficits range from "it's only a few steps" to "once you get on the bus the rest of the tour is accessible." So, be forewarned that there is a very broad definition of accessible when it comes to shore excursions. Some tour providers assume that anybody in a wheelchair can walk at least a few steps, so what's accessible to them may not exactly be accessible to you.

Additionally, if you book a snorkeling or scuba shore excursion, it's important to double check with the tour operator to make sure you will be able to participate. One wheelchair-user reports this incident in Cozumel. "The catamaran operator told me I would not be allowed to snorkel, even after I produced my scuba certification card," says Steve. "He said it was company policy that people in wheelchairs could not snorkel. My shore excursion ended right there. I also had a hard time getting a refund from the cruise line."

So, what's a person to do when it comes to shore excursions? You have two options. One is to work with a travel agent who is experienced in accessible travel and have them plan your cruise and accessible shore excursions. The other option is to hit the books and plan your own accessible shore excursions. The one thing you shouldn't do is book your cruise on your own and then contact a travel agent to plan your accessible shore excursions.

Most shore excursions are conducted by local tour operators. The cruise lines charge these operators a hefty percentage in order to add them to their official shore excursion list. So, the tour operators have to raise their prices to make a go of it. The end result? You pay higher prices for official shore excursions. Additionally, if something goes wrong on the shore excursion, the cruise line passes the buck to the tour operator. The cruise line's defense is that they contract out this service so the tour operator is ultimately responsible for the service.

On the other hand, if you book a cruise line shore excursion and there is a delay getting back to the ship, they will wait for you. That's not true with independently booked shore excursions.

Granted, it's not always possible to book directly with the tour operator, especially if that tour operator also provides shore excursions for the cruise line. In most cases the cruise lines have exclusivity agreements with their shore tour providers. These agreements prohibit tour operators from accepting direct bookings from passengers. In most cases, this won't affect the smaller tour operators or specialty tours, so try to book directly whenever possible.

Additionally, cruise lines expect travel agents to peddle their shore excursions. It's not required, but certainly a good deal of pressure is put on agents to do this. This results in many travel agents pushing the official shore excursions, even if they aren't accessible. It's a buyer beware situation. If you are working with a travel agent who insists that all the shore excursions are accessible, ask for specific access details. Chances are they are just reciting cruise line rhetoric, and they don't fully understand the real meaning of accessible.

If you go it on your own, the best tool for finding information on accessible shore excursions is the Internet. If you don't have an Internet connection, try logging on at a library. The reason the Internet is such a good resource is that it allows you to connect directly with a local tour operator.

You'll also be able to get first-hand access information if you deal direct. E-mailing is a lot cheaper than faxing and phoning; and if you don't speak the native language, many free translation programs are available. On the downside, it's important to note that some local providers don't take credit cards, so it may be hard to get a refund if the appropriate services aren't provided.

There are many ways to find information on accessible shore excursions. Two of my favorite resources are Cruise Critic (cruise-critic.com) and Cruise Mates (cruisemates.com). Both these sites have message boards dedicated to accessible cruising, and they are good places to post questions about accessible shore options.

You can also do an Internet search under "accessible travel" and look for contacts in your port cities. Another good source of information can be disability organizations. Make a list of your port cities and post messages on travel bulletin boards for information on access. Search for destination-related resources and then find out if they have any access information. Contact tourist bureaus to see if they have any access information.

Many smaller tour companies are willing to work with tourists to create specialized tours. Seek out these local companies. Join e-mail lists, search disability web sites, and ask anybody and everybody if they have any information or contacts. You never know when one person may be the key to your search. It really is a numbers game—ask enough people and eventually you will get the answers you need. Be sure to allow plenty of time for your research, because results don't magically materialize overnight. Like anything else, you have to work at it.

Once you've found a local tour operator, be sure to allow some leeway when scheduling your tour. On many cruise lines, passengers booked on the official shore excursions get first crack at the tenders. Be sure to inform the tour operator of your need for flexibility with the time frame. Make sure this is understood before you book your tour. You should also make sure the tour operator will refund your money if the ship doesn't visit that port because of a last-minute change in itinerary or weather-related problems.

Another option is to find accessible transportation and see the port on your own. Sometimes this is a better solution if you feel you will be pressed for time. This way you can see the sights and go back to the ship at your leisure. Sometimes, this is the best option for short port stops.

Finally, common sense should prevail as far as pricing is concerned. I've received reports on some third-party agents who charge in excess of $1,000 per person per day for European shore tours. Granted, accessible transportation can get expensive in some parts of the world, but prices like that indicate a substantial mark up. Shop around for yourself. Chances are you will be able to find the same local operator and arrange the tour for a fraction of the price.

Destinations

JUST AS CRUISE ships vary in accessibility, so do destinations. Some destinations are simply more accessible than others. As far as cruising goes, Alaska is by far the most accessible destination. There are many reasons for this, including the fact that many of the tourist sites have been made accessible in order to comply with the ADA. A greater availability of accessible transportation is also available in Alaska. Some of the cruise lines even own accessible buses, which they use for some shore excursions.

Access information on Alaska is also readily available. First off, the language isn't a barrier. Second, you can directly contact many CILs and disability organizations. And third, it's pretty well touristed by wheelchair-users, so local businesses seem to be aware of access issues. Here are a few details on the Alaska port cities of Ketchikan, Juneau, and Skagway.

* Much of Ketchikan is built on a hillside, but Saxman Totem Park has limited accessibility for guests using wheelchairs or scooters. As one traveler puts it, "it's do-able for wheelchair-users, but it requires strong arms, or somebody to push your wheelchair." Also recommended is the Southeast Visitors Center, which is just a short walk from the dock. It features great accessibility and interesting displays, plus you can do it on your own. The whale watching tours are not accessible, even though some cruise lines indicate otherwise. The only

way to board the whale-watching boats is to be carried on board.

* Walking in Juneau also presents some difficulties, due to the steep hillsides. Accessible attractions include a dockside cultural center, which features Alaska native crafts, the Gastineau Fish Hatchery, and the spectacular (and very accessible) Mount Roberts Aerial Tramway. ERA Helicopters (800-843-1947) also offers accessible flightseeing tours over the nearby glaciers. Advance reservations are a must for this popular attraction.

* The town of Skagway is only about four blocks square, and it's not too strenuous for wheelchair-users. The White Horse Yukon Railroad is very accessible and offers dramatic scenery.

Figure 9.6.
The *Empress of the North* docked in Skagway, just a few level blocks from the accessible White Horse Yukon Railroad.

This is a must-see for train buffs. The railway has lifts for accessible boarding and wheelchair tie-downs.

Overall, Alaska is one of the most accessible cruise destinations; however be prepared for varied methods of ship disembarkation due to the fluctuating tides.

The Caribbean is another story altogether in regards to access. In short, access in the Caribbean is spotty but improving. Although accessible transportation is still limited in many places, it's available now in Bermuda, Puerto Rico, St. Thomas, St. Croix, Grand Cayman, Ocho Rios, and St. Vincent. Accessible tour and transportation providers are listed in the resource chapter. Be sure to make your arrangements for accessible transportation well in advance. Also, don't forget to contact the CILs as a resource in the U.S. Virgin Islands and Puerto Rico.

And then there's Europe. Although Europe isn't very good for

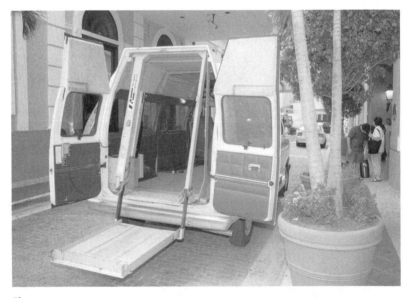

Figure 9.7.
Accessible city tours in lift-equipped vehicles are available through Anticipation Tours in San Juan, Puerto Rico.

access on large cruise ships, a wide variety of accessible options are available on the smaller river boats, barges, and canal boats. European ocean cruises just can't compare to Alaska cruises for overall accessibility. Two-time cruiser Tim sums it up best with comments about his *Crown Princess* cruise to Europe. "I really wanted to see Europe," he recalls, "but I was very disappointed with my Princess Cruise experience. They told me they had accessible shore excursions, but they didn't. It was a real struggle in every port. They did give me some access information, but it was very outdated. In retrospect, I would have been better off on a barge or river cruise. It was quite a disappointment, compared to my cruise experience in Alaska."

Rolling on the River

FROM BARGES TO river boats, river and canal cruising continues to grow in popularity throughout the world. In the United States, river cruising options range from barges to paddlewheel river boats, while in Europe self-drive barging holidays and canal narrowboats are very popular.

Because these river and canal cruises use smaller ships (actually boats), not as many accessible staterooms are available. But don't let that deter you from trying a river or canal cruise, because a number of nicely accessible options are still available. Here is a brief rundown of some of my favorites.

In the United States, The American West Steamship Company operates two paddlewheel river boats, the *Queen of the West* and the *Empress of the North*. Both boats cruise the Columbia River, while the *Empress of the North* also cruises Alaska's Inside Passage.

The *Queen of the West* has two accessible staterooms that are do-able for many wheelchair-users. These staterooms feature wide doorways and a level entry. The bathroom has a small roll-in shower, but it lacks a 5-foot turning radius. Although they are not barrier-free, these rooms will work for many slow walkers and part-time wheelchair-users.

The more accessible *Empress of the North* has two accessible staterooms with wide doorways, level thresholds, and adequate pathway access. The bathrooms in both staterooms are identical and each has a roll-in shower with a hand-held shower head, a fold-down shower seat, grab bars in the shower and around the toilet, and a full 5-foot turning radius.

Both ships feature elevator access to all decks and good access to the public areas. And both crews get high marks in the attitude department.

The Delta Queen Steamboat Company also offers one accessible option, the grand *American Queen*. This paddlewheel river boat (which has nine accessible staterooms) cruises the Mississippi River and features itineraries that focus on the history and culture of the area.

The accessible cabins are available in a broad range of categories and feature wide doorways, level thresholds, and good pathway

Figure 9.8.
The *River Explorer* offers a very accessible way to explore the rivers of America's heartland.

access. The accessible bathrooms have either a roll-in shower or a tub/shower combination. Access features include grab bars in the shower and toilet areas, lever handles, a 5-foot turning radius, and a hand-held shower.

And then there is the *River Explorer*, a barge that cruises the rivers of America's Heartland. Operated by River Barge Excursion Lines, this unique vessel has three wheelchair-accessible staterooms with roll-in showers.

Over in Europe, you can cruise the canals of Northwest England aboard *New Horizons*, an accessible narrowboat. *New Horizons* is operated by the Stockport Canalboat Trust, and is staffed with a skipper and volunteer crew. It features a boarding ramp and lift, plus wheelchair access throughout the boat.

The Lyneal Trust provides accessible canal boat holidays on the Llangollen Canal, from their base at the Lyneal Wharf (near Ellesmere). This U.K. charity operates two accessible canal boats, the *Shropshire Lass* and the *Shropshire Lad*. The *Shropshire Lass* is a 70-foot residential canal boat that sleeps eight, and the *Shropshire Lad* is a 45-foot canal boat designed for day trips.

Cruise the waterways of Ireland on the *Saoirse ar an Uisce* (Freedom on the Water). This fully equipped barge has central heating, a full galley, and a large bathroom and shower. This barge is accessible to wheelchair-users via a boarding ramp. Day cruises, which depart from Bell Harbor in Monasterevin, are available for groups and families. This is not a self-drive option.

The 110-passenger *MV Dresden* makes weekly cruises between Hamburg and Dresden on the Elbe River in Eastern Germany. There is one wheelchair-accessible cabin, with a roll-in shower. This riverboat was built in 1991, and refurbished in 1996. All public rooms are barrier-free, except for the gift shop and the beauty shop

Over in France, Croisieres Canal Boat offers the Triton 10.6, an accessible houseboat that sails on the canal du Midi in Southern France. It can sleep up to six people, and it features a hydraulic platform lift between the corridor, the pilot area, and the two front cabins. The bathroom has a continental-style shower, and one of the front bedrooms is big enough to accommodate a wheelchair. Level boarding is available via an adjustable gangway. This self-drive boat can be leased for the week or the half week

And finally, you might want to consider a French barge holiday. Le Boat, Inc. operates accessible barges on the Midi, Digoin, and Nivernais canals of France. If you prefer to leave the driving to somebody else, they also have a wheelchair accessible barge with full service and a crew (*La Reine Pedauque*). Says one veteran barger, "If you think a trip to Europe won't be accessible enough for you, then barging may be the way to go. Floating slowly through the canals of France was a very accessible and a totally enjoyable experience for me!"

When Things Go Wrong | 10

ANYBODY WHO TELLS you that your travels will be trouble-free is either a liar or a fool. There are no guarantees in life, and travel by its very nature is unpredictable. Numerous variables are involved on any given trip and, theoretically, something could go awry at any stage of the game. Add accessibility issues to this equation and your odds of experiencing a travel mishap greatly increase. I'm not trying to scare you or discourage you. I'm just trying to prepare you. Expect something to go wrong at some point in your travels. It may not happen on your first trip; it may not even happen on your second trip. But odds are it will happen. So the best defense is proper preparation.

One of the best ways to prepare for your trip is by playing a healthy game of "what if" before you depart. Ask yourself questions like "What if my wheelchair breaks while I'm on vacation?" Having some well thought out solutions to these what-if scenarios will come in very handy when disaster strikes. For example, a good solution to the previous what-if question is to gather the phone numbers of a few wheelchair repair shops in your destination city. Of course, it's easy to go overboard with the what-if game. Remember I said a *healthy* game of what-if. Sometimes it is a fine line between obsession and preparation.

So, what do you do when disaster strikes while you are on the road? Well, your immediate goal should be to solve the problem and salvage your vacation. Next, you should try to mitigate or prevent further damage. Sometimes these two goals overlap, and sometimes they conflict with one another. For example, if your wheelchair is damaged, your first priority should be to make it useable so you won't have to cancel the remaining portion of your trip. However, if using your chair as is could cause further damage, it's best to sacrifice a few days of your trip in order to get it properly repaired. In the end it's a judgment call on your part.

You will also have to learn how to effectively communicate your needs to customer service personnel. For example, if your power wheelchair is damaged, you will have to explain why a manual wheelchair is not an appropriate loaner to airline personnel. Try not to lose your temper, although admittedly that's difficult when dealing with morons. Threatening to sue or file a formal complaint at this point never really helps. It just creates an adversarial situation. Concentrate on maintaining your composure and try to calmly explain your needs. It also helps to explain the reasons behind your needs; in other words, tell the clerk why you can't use a manual chair. In the long run, this is usually the quickest way to an appropriate resolution. Sometimes this is easier said than done.

You may also want to address your financial loss at the time of the incident. Bear in mind, you may not get a final resolution to this matter, but at least you will have set the ball in motion. You may get an upgrade or some other minor perk for your troubles. Not that I'm implying that a first-class upgrade is payment enough for a mangled wheelchair, but if an upgrade is offered on the spot, take it. If you later learn your actual damages are substantial, you can address that problem when you get home.

Be sure to keep all documentation of your actual damages, such as extra hotel nights and airline cancellation charges. Many companies will reimburse you because it's a good public relations move. In any case, be realistic when you ask for compensation. If your trip was delayed for one day and you had to pay a $100 cancellation penalty to re-book your flight, don't ask for $1,500. You have a much better chance of receiving prompt compensation if your demands are realistic.

Save your official complaints for when you get home. Remember to collect documentation along the way, save receipts, and get names. You might also want to jot down the details of the incident while they're fresh in your mind. Then, go away on your vacation and try to enjoy yourself. I know this is easier said than done, but there's no sense ruining your trip over an unfortunate incident. Dwelling on the matter won't accomplish anything. When you get home, you can start the official complaint process. Most likely, there won't be a swift resolution to your official complaint and, in some cases, it won't even be acknowledged. After all, we are talking about government agencies here.

So why take the time to file an official complaint? In most cases this is the only way to enforce U.S. access laws and to effect change. Filing an official complaint is a very personal decision, but you must also realize that access won't improve until more people come forward and complain. Although many agencies don't respond to individual complaints, they do look at trends. So, if a particular business is getting a lot of the same type of complaints, there is a chance the enforcement agency will look into it. The first step in filing an official complaint is determining how and where to file it. This varies and depends on the nature of your complaint.

Air Travel

THE AIR CARRIER ACCESS ACT (ACAA) covers all aspects of airline travel on U.S.-based air carriers. The enforcement agency for the ACAA is the Department of Transportation (DOT). A common misconception shared by many people is that air travel is covered under the American with Disabilities Act (ADA). It is not. Air travel on U.S. carriers is addressed in the ACAA, which was established in 1986 and actually predates the ADA.

I stress this fact because you need to know the law in order to advocate for yourself. If you spout off to an airline employee that you are unhappy with their service and that you are going to file an ADA complaint, this will only prove your ignorance. The airlines know the rules better than most of us, so you need to be educated about the law to be taken seriously.

Although there is much debate about the effectiveness of the ACAA, it does offer some protection and many essential services to people with disabilities. One of the most useful mandates of the ACAA is the creation of the Complaints Resolution Officer (CRO). All U.S. carriers must have a CRO available 24 hours a day to specifically address alleged ACAA violations and to solve customer complaints.

The CRO is an airline employee specifically trained in airline duties and passenger rights under the ACAA. The CRO must be available either in person or by phone. If you encounter a problem en route in regards to a violation of the ACAA, and you can't solve the problem with front-line personnel, ask to speak to the CRO immediately. Bear in mind that the gate agent or ticket agent may not know who or what the CRO is, especially if they are new employees. In that case, just ask to speak to a supervisor. Anybody in a supervisory position should be very well educated on the role of the CRO.

Interestingly enough, CROs technically also have authority over third-party contractors. This is important to remember, because many airlines use third-party contractors as wheelchair pushers (in the airport) and for assisting nonambulatory passengers with boarding and deplaning. When a problem arises with one of these services, airline employees may claim there is nothing they can do because the service is provided by a third-party contractor.

According to section 382.9 of the ACAA, all airline contracts with third-party providers must include a clause that states, "contractor employers will comply with directives issued by CROs." So the next time you have a problem with a third-party contractor, make sure to point out this often overlooked section of the ACAA to the CRO.

You can also file a written complaint with the airline after you return home. This is your best (and sometimes only) route to monetary compensation for damages. Watch your deadlines here though, as airlines are not required to respond to complaints postmarked more than 45 days after the violation. For complaints filed in a timely manner, the airline must respond in 30 days. You also have the right to file an official complaint with the DOT at any time. Additionally, you can just skip the airline and go right to the DOT and file an official complaint.

The official DOT complaint process is pretty easy. It consists of filling out a simple form and returning it to the DOT. Alternatively, you can submit a letter outlining the details of the incident to the DOT at the address listed here. Personally, I recommend using the complaint form, as the specific questions are designed to gather pertinent information that is often overlooked or omitted. You can get a copy of the complaint form online in PDF format at airconsumer.ost.dot.gov/forms.htm or contact the DOT.

Department of Transportation
Aviation Consumer Protection Division
400 7th St., SW, Room C-75-D
Washington D.C. 20590
(202) 366-2220

Don't expect an answer or acknowledgment to your complaint. Because of the volume of complaints, the DOT tends to address trends rather than individual complaints. Still, don't let this discourage you from submitting a complaint, as it is the only way to effect change. In any case, if your complaint is addressed you will not receive any monetary compensation for your losses. DOT complaints usually result in an adjustment to airline policies and practices. They do not include monetary compensation for damages to the complainant. You must address this issue directly with the airline within the required time period.

And finally, when dealing with violations of the ACAA, you may have some slight redress for monetary damages through a civil lawsuit. In theory, you are always free to sue anybody you choose; however, you may have problems finding an attorney willing to take an ACAA case on a contingency basis because there are no real provisions in the ACAA for the recovery of legal fees.

Most likely, you will have to pay a retainer up front and then continue to pay hourly costs every month. This could become quite expensive, and technically it's not a recoverable cost. I say technically because the August 1999 amendment to the ACAA allows for consequential damages in cases of wheelchair damage. Could consequential damages be interpreted as legal costs? Time will tell, as this most likely will be decided by precedent. For now though, civil litigation is a costly and somewhat ineffective way to deal with ACAA violations.

Airports

IT WOULD BE nice if there was one federal agency or department set aside to deal with access in U.S. airports. This is not the case, however, because the presiding enforcement agency depends on many factors, including when the airport was built, where it is located, and what type of funds were used to construct the facility. It's also not uncommon to have different areas within the same facility fall under the jurisdiction of different enforcement agencies. It's confusing at best, but here's the basic rundown of how it all works.

Airports that receive federal funding are subject to Section 504 of the Rehabilitation Act of 1973 and the implementing regulations developed by the DOT. Airports that are owned or operated by state or local governments (considered public entities) are subject to Title II of the ADA. This regulation applies even if the airport in question also receives federal funding. Title II also covers any fixed route transportation system (such as airport parking shuttles) within a public entity airport. Complaints addressing violations to either of these regulations may be filed with the Federal Aviation Administration at this address:

> Federal Aviation Administration
> Office of Civil Rights (ACR-4)
> 800 Independence Avenue, SW
> Washington D.C. 20591
> (202) 267-3270

Privately owned public-use airports are subject to Title III of the ADA. Violations found in these facilities should be addressed to the Department of Justice (DOJ) at this address:

U.S. Department of Justice
Civil Rights Division
950 Pennsylvania Avenue, NW
Disability Rights Section - NYAV
Washington, D.C. 20530
(800) 514-0301

And finally, all terminal facilities owned, leased, or operated by an air carrier at a commercial airport are subject to provisions in the ACAA. See the Air Travel section in this chapter for details on how to address an ACAA complaint.

Ground Transportation

GROUND TRANSPORTATION ACCESSIBILITY is covered under the ADA. In regards to enforcement of the law, ground transportation is divided into two categories: publicly owned transportation and privately owned transportation.

Access standards for public transportation in the U.S. are mandated under Title II of the ADA. For the purpose of this discussion, public transportation includes city bus lines, paratransit services, commuter rail lines, subways, and Amtrak. The U.S. Access Board developed the access guidelines for public transportation mandated under Title II of the ADA, and public transportation authorities must follow these guidelines and adhere to the accessibility requirements for newly purchased vehicles.

The Federal Transit Administration (FTA), a division of the DOT, provides for enforcement of Title II of the ADA with respect to public transportation. Call the FTA ADA Assistance Line for more information or mail your inquiry to the FTA office at this address:

FTA Office of Civil Rights
400 7th Street, SW, Room 9100
Washington D.C. 20590
(888) 446-4511
ada.assistance@fta.dot.gov

Privately owned vehicles, such as those owned by hotels and private bus companies are covered under Title III of the ADA. Title III complaints should be directed to DOJ at this address:

U.S. Department of Justice
Civil Rights Division
950 Pennsylvania Avenue, NW
Disability Rights Section - NYAV
Washington, D.C. 20530
(800) 514-0301

You may also enforce your rights under Title II and Title III of the ADA through a private lawsuit. Provisions in the ADA allow for the payment of reasonable legal expenses on Title II and Title III cases. Because of these provisions, it's much easier to get an attorney or an advocacy organization to take a Title II or Title III case on a contingency basis. This makes private lawsuits a realistic solution for many people, but unfortunately it also opens up the door for legal malpractice. Always use great care when choosing a attorney.

Cruise Ships

TECHNICALLY, CRUISE SHIPS are covered under the ADA. Realistically, compliance is difficult to enforce in this area. The reason for this difficulty is that the U.S. Access Board has not yet established any accessibility standards for cruise ships. Look for that to change in the next few years though, as the U.S. Access Board is currently working to remedy this matter. The U.S. Access Board is responsible for developing accessibility guidelines under the ADA, and the Passenger Vessel Access Advisory Committee (PVAAC) was created to make recommendations for the final guidelines.

The PVAAC completed their work in December 2000, when they submitted their recommendations to the U.S. Access Board. These recommendations are currently under review by the U.S. Access Board. Once a proposed rule is developed by the U.S. Access Board, it will be submitted to the Office of Management and Budget (OMB) for review. This can take up to 90 days.

The proposed rule is then published in the *Federal Register*. At that time, the proposed rule is open for public comment, usually for a period of 60 days. After the public comment period ends, the U.S. Access Board takes another 4 to 6 months to review the comments and modify the rule. The final rule goes back to the OMB for review, which takes up to 90 days. The final rule is then published in the *Federal Register* and can either take effect immediately or at a specified time in the future (i.e., in 30 days or on a specific date).

As you can see, even though the rule-making process has begun, it may still be a while before official rules are on the books. Once the regulations are developed, passenger vessels operated by private entities (most cruise ships) will fall under Title III of the ADA, whereas passenger vessels operated by state and local governments (some ferries) will fall under Title II.

Even though most cruise ships are not U.S. registered, the final rule will most likely cover all ships that call on U.S. ports. For now, any access provided by non-U.S. registered cruise ships is somewhat voluntary on their part. For more information on U.S. Access Board activities, including updates of the PVAAC, visit the U.S. Access Board website at www.access-board.gov. The U.S. Access Board also publishes *Access Currents*, a free bimonthly newsletter.

Hotels, Restaurants, and Tourist Attractions

THE LION'S SHARE of tourist facilities are covered either under Title II or Title III of the ADA. Title III covers public accommodations: those facilities which are privately owned but open to the general public. This includes privately owned hotels, restaurants, bars, theaters, recreation areas, museums, and tourist attractions. Title III of the ADA is enforced by the DOJ, and complaints should be sent to this address:

U.S. Department of Justice
Civil Rights Division
950 Pennsylvania Avenue, NW
Disability Rights Section - NYAV
Washington, D.C. 20530
(800) 514-0301

No official Title III complaint form is available, so just submit a signed letter that details the alleged ADA violation. Remember to include all pertinent information such as dates, names, and addresses. You may also include other documentation, such as receipts and photos, with your letter. Never send original receipts or documentation, as they won't be returned to you and you may need them for future action.

Title II of the ADA covers access to services, programs, activities, facilities, and buildings owned or operated by state or local governments. This could include facilities such as state-owned museums, recreation areas, or tourist attractions. Additionally, if you are unlucky enough to end up in a local or county court (watch those speed traps!), those facilities are also covered under Title II. You can get a copy of the Title II complaint form on the DOJ website at www.usdoj.gov/crt/ada/publicat.htm. Return the completed form to the DOJ address given earlier.

You may also enforce your rights under Title II and Title III of the ADA through a private lawsuit. Provisions in the ADA allow for the payment of reasonable legal expenses on Title II and Title III cases. Many advocacy organizations that specialize in disability rights law will either help you put your case together, or represent you outright. Alternatively, you may hire a disability rights attorney of your choice to litigate this matter for you.

National Parks

A LOT OF confusion exists about access requirements for U.S. National Parks. You may have heard that the ADA does not cover access in U.S. National Parks. This is true; however, some people interpret this fact to mean that U.S. National Parks are not required to be accessible. This is not true. U.S. National Parks are required to be accessible.

Access in U.S. National Parks is covered under Section 504 of the Rehabilitation Act of 1973, legislation that actually predates the ADA. Additionally, concessionaires in U.S. National Parks are responsible for providing appropriate access to all programs, services, and facilities. This is important to remember because many U.S. National Parks have concessionaires who provide lodging, food, and tour services. The National Parks Service (NPS) is ultimately responsible if these concessionaires are in violation of any access laws.

Where do you go if you encounter an access problem in a U.S. National Park? Common sense would tell you to talk to the Access Coordinator for the park, and that's fine if you just want to talk about access. The Access Coordinator is actually a NPS employee, and although he may be interested in access solutions, he's not in any position to implement them.

Consider the Access Coordinator something akin to an access advisor; he merely makes recommendations. Many Access Coordinators have great ideas and are very helpful, but when it comes to action, most don't have enough influence to actually facilitate access improvements. Access mandates come from above, and they are usually the result of official complaints.

Official complaints should be directed to the Department of the Interior. Write a letter describing your access problem and state that you are making an official complaint under Section 504 of the Rehabilitation Act of 1973. Try to be as inclusive and detailed as possible when describing your access problem. Send your complaint to:

U.S. Department of the Interior
Office of Equal Opportunity
Director
1849 C St. NW, MS-5214
Washington D.C. 20240-0002

Technical assistance and general information about access in U.S. National Parks can also be obtained by calling the National Center on Accessibility's Technical Assistance Line at (812) 856-4422. The National Center on Accessibility has done a great deal of work in this area, and they are really the experts. They also have a very informative website at ncaonline.org.

Often Overlooked Laws

MANY PEOPLE THINK only of the ADA when addressing access violations in the United States, but the ADA is far from the only law mandating access. It's one of the newer access laws, and perhaps that's why it gets so much press. In truth, many laws actually predate the ADA, and sometimes these useful laws are overlooked when addressing access violations. It pays to be on the lookout for all access laws that may apply to your particular case. Remember, sometimes more than one law may apply. Here are a few often overlooked access laws you might want to consider.

The *Architectural Barriers Act of 1968* (ABA) mandates accessibility in certain buildings financed or leased by the federal government. Buildings that were constructed or altered with federal funds may be subject to this legislation. The key words here are *federal funds*, so follow the money trail to determine if a building falls under ABA jurisdiction.

The current access standards for the ABA are detailed in the Uniform Federal Accessibility Standards. The U.S. Access Board is responsible for enforcement of the ABA, and all complaints should be directed there. For technical assistance call (800) 872-2253.

U.S. Access Board
1331 F St., NW, Suite 1000
Washington D.C. 20004-1111

If the U.S. Access Board determines a violation of the ABA has occurred, they will notify the responsible agency and request removal of the access barriers. The U.S. Access Board monitors the progress of the removal and updates the complainant of the status. In rare cases, the U.S. Access Board has sought court action to enforce ABA violations; but that's usually not necessary because the U.S. Access Board has an excellent record of achieving voluntary compliance.

Another often overlooked access law is Section 504 of the *Rehabilitation Act of 1973*. Although I touched on this law briefly is some earlier sections in this chapter, be aware that many avenues exist to enforce Section 504. Section 504 states that no qualified person with a disability shall be denied access to programs or services that receive federal financial assistance. So once again, follow the money trail to determine if your access problem is covered under this law.

The confusing part about Section 504 is that each federal agency has its own set of 504 regulations that apply to their particular programs. Each department also has its own contact person, and Section 504 complaints must be filed with the appropriate federal agency. Section 504 complaints can also be pursued in civil court. For information on how to file a Section 504 complaint with the appropriate agency, contact the DOJ.

Finally, don't overlook any state or local civil rights laws that may pertain to your access complaint. For example, in California, the *Unruh Civil Rights Act* prohibits businesses from discriminating against certain individuals, including people with a disability. So a California tourist attraction would be in violation of the Unruh Civil Rights Act if it charged people with a disability a higher admission price, or refused them access or entrance to their establishment. Many states have some type of civil rights legislation that may pertain to discrimination against people with a disability. Check with your State Office of Civil Rights for more information.

Lawyers and Court

BECAUSE TITLE II and Title III cases provide for the payment of reasonable legal fees, more and more attorneys are willing to take these types of cases on a contingency basis. In fact, many law offices actively solicit these types of cases through fancy websites and slick disability rights pamphlets. Although I'm all in favor of the distribution of accurate disability rights information, be forewarned that you do need to exercise some caution when searching for an attorney to represent you.

First and foremost, always remember that you are the boss, even if you don't pay your lawyer any money up front. The attorney you hire is working for you even if you have a contingency arrangement. Some attorneys may imply that they are taking your case (at no cost to you) out of the kindness of their heart. Remember, they will recover their expenses and fees if they win the case. It's also not unusual for attorney fees to sometimes exceed the plaintiff's award. Just keep things in perspective and remain in control of your legal proceedings. Your lawyer works for you.

And now a few words about choosing an attorney: Be careful. Obviously, you shouldn't choose an attorney just because he will take your case on a contingency basis. Ask for references and ask what types of disability rights cases he has tried in the past. Try to find an attorney who has experience with cases that are similar to yours. Disability rights is a very broad category. And finally, don't be afraid to ask your attorney what percentage of disability rights cases he has won. If the cases are closed, the settlements should be a matter of public record, so also ask him for specific case names. Spend some time selecting your attorney and don't let anybody rush you into a decision.

Alternatively, you can represent yourself and file your own pro se ADA Complaint in Federal District Court. The Pennsylvania Coalition of Citizens with Disabilities has compiled some easy-to-understand instructions along with the forms required to file your own complaint. You can find these on the Internet at www.ragged-edge-mag.com/archive/pro-se.htm. If you need further assistance, or have any questions about the process, contact the Pennsylvania Coalition of Citizens with Disabilities at (717) 238-0172.

For More Information

A LOT OF good information is available about disability rights legislation. Here are a few of my favorite resources.

Air Carrier Access

This free guide is published by the United Spinal Association. It explains consumer rights and airline responsibilities under the ACAA in simple language. It also includes some good photographs of airline boarding procedures for nonambulatory passengers. A good primer on the ACAA. Call (800) 444-0120 for your copy.

The Americans with Disabilities Act
Your Personal Guide to the Law

Published by the Paralyzed Veterans of America, this 53-page booklet contains general information on the different titles of the Americans with Disabilities Act. Information about enforcement and tax incentives is also included. Call (888) 860-7244 for your free copy.

A Guide to Disability Rights Laws

This 17-page guide presents a good overview of eight federal access laws. Laws covered include the ADA, ABA, the Rehabilitation Act of 1973, and the ACAA. This free guide also contains a helpful list of disability rights resources. It's available from the Consumer Information Center at (888) 878-3256.

ADA Technical Assistance CD

This Technical Assistance CD contains a complete collection of the DOJ's ADA materials, including DOJ regulations, architectural design standards, and technical assistance publications pertaining to the ADA. Order your free copy at www.usdoj.gov/crt/ada/ or call (800) 514-0301.

DOT Consumer Hotline

The DOT operates an aviation consumer disability hotline at (866) 266-1368. Travelers are invited to call to obtain information and assistance if they experience disability-related air service problems.

Beyond the USA | 11

ACCESS DOESN'T MAGICALLY disappear once you venture beyond U.S. borders, but it does change. These changes can be good or bad, depending on your perspective. With that in mind, there are a number of things to consider if a foreign destination is on your travel calendar.

First, you should become familiar with the access laws of your destination country. The United States is not the only country that has rules and regulations that govern access; in fact, some countries have even stricter laws with higher access standards. It's true that the Americans with Disabilities Act (ADA) won't protect you on foreign soil; however, don't rule out the existence of local access laws.

Of course, some countries are at the other end of the access spectrum and have *no* human rights or access legislation. Whatever the case, it pays to find out about the laws (or lack thereof) before you hit the road. This not only helps you understand local customs, but more important, it also gives you a good idea of what to expect in the access department.

Canada

BECAUSE OF ITS proximity to the United States, Canada is a popular destination for many Americans. Canada presents a welcome air of familiarity, as English is widely spoken throughout the country. But there are many differences, too. As far as access laws go, it's a fifty-fifty split: Some are very familiar whereas some are drastically different. Here's a breakdown of what to expect.

On the strikingly familiar side is the Canadian Transportation Act of 1996 (CTA), which covers access on transportation throughout Canada. Among other things, the CTA mandates access at airports and on Canadian airlines (on aircraft with 30 or more seats). The air transportation regulations under the CTA are very much like our own Air Carrier Access Act (ACAA). Basically, the regulations mandate access and prohibit disability-based discrimination at Canadian airports or on Canadian airlines.

So, although Americans are not protected by the ACAA on Canadian airlines, most travelers feel comfortable with the protection afforded them under the CTA air transportation regulations. For more information on the CTA, or for a copy of the CTA air transportation regulations, contact the Accessible Transportation Directorate at the Canadian Transportation Agency in Ottawa. An electronic version of the CTA air transportation regulations is also available online at www.cta-otc.gc.ca/access/regs/air_e.html.

Another good transportation resource is the Access To Travel website at accesstotravel.gc.ca. Developed by the Canadian government, this resource was developed in partnership with provincial governments and nonprofit organizations to provide centralized information on accessible transportation throughout Canada. It includes detailed access information on bus, rail, air, and ferry transportation and gives visitors the heads-up on accessible public transportation, paratransit, and even accessible van rentals.

It should also be noted that some glaring differences exist between Canadian access laws and the ADA. For example, even though disability-based discrimination is prohibited under the Canadian Human Rights Act of 1976-77, no building codes address physical access. This results in much confusion for uninformed Americans who assume that Canadian access standards are identical to those mandated under the ADA. They are not. In fact, no disability legislation in Canada actually regulates physical access to buildings.

To address this problem, the Hotel Association of Alberta

founded Access Canada, a voluntary rating program for Canadian hotels and motels. The Access Canada rating system is divided into four levels, with level four having the highest level of access. Level one has basic pathway access, whereas level four requires properties to have a roll-in shower and a trapeze bar over the bed. In truth, very few level four properties exist.

Participating establishments are inspected by an Access Canada specialist to determine their access rating. After inspection, the property can then display the Access Canada logo along with their access rating. Although not widely used in Canada, Access Canada is the only official access rating system for Canadian hotels, so it's a good idea to become familiar with it. Most of the Access Canada properties are located in Alberta and Victoria. For more information about Access Canada, visit the Alberta Hotel Association website at albertahotels.ab.ca.

In the absence of official access regulations, sometimes it's best to take the cue from disability organizations within the country. What do they consider accessible when it comes to hotel rooms? Well, here's the access criteria that the Canadian disability organization Keroul uses to define an adapted room.

"Accessible entrance is ground level or gently sloped, the threshold is less than two cm. high and the door is wider than 76 cm. The bathroom has a door at least 76 cm. wide, enough space to circulate (1.5 m. by 1.5 m.), grab bars, and enough clearance under the wash basin (68.5 cm. or more). If there is one bedroom, it is large enough to move around in easily."

As you can see, it's not exactly an ADA definition of accessible, but it's pretty much what you can expect to find when you see that little blue wheelchair pictogram in Canada. One final note about access in Canada: roll-in showers are not as commonplace as they are in the United States. It's somewhat unusual to find a property that has a roll-in shower, so even if a property touts its accessible bathroom, be forewarned that a roll-in shower is probably not considered part of the access package. Remember to always ask specific questions about access. Never assume anything.

Europe

EUROPE IS ANOTHER popular vacation spot. The good news is that travelers can expect to find a high degree of access in most Western European countries. On the other hand, there are a few differences between access in Europe and access in the United States. It goes without saying that it pays to be aware of those differences. For purposes of clarity, when talking about access it's usually best to divide Europe into two parts: the United Kingdom and Continental Europe.

In 1995, Britain passed the Disability Discrimination Act (DDA), which made it illegal for most providers of goods, services, and facilities to discriminate against any person with a disability. The DDA applies to public accommodations such as hotels, airports, and

Figure 11.1.
Thanks to the strengthening of Britain's Disability Discrimination Act in October 2004, there are now many more accessible things to do in London.

entertainment venues as well as to most ground transportation providers. In October 2004, the DDA was further modified and strengthened to include even the smallest businesses.

It's important to note that the DDA excludes domestic air carriers in Britain. Domestic air carriers can voluntarily provide accessible services, but they are not required to do so. This point is well illustrated by the following tale of Disability Rights Commission Chief, Bert Massie.

Bert ran into some problems at London City airport, when he tried to board a Scot Airways flight to Edinburgh in late 2000. Massie, who uses a wheelchair, checked in for his flight, went through security, and proceeded to the gate. He was later told by the gate agent that he couldn't board the plane if he wasn't able to walk. Mr. Massie tried to make the best of the situation and offered to crawl up the three steps to the aircraft or to have a friend carry him on board. Scot Airways refused his requests.

Merlin Suckling, Scot Airways' director and owner claims that "It's a well-publicized policy that Scot Airways does not allow wheelchair-bound people to fly on its planes." Well-publicized or not, there's no mention of that policy anywhere on the Scot Airways website. The bottom line is (unfortunately) Scot Airways was operating within the law. Yes, it would have been nice for Scot Airways to notify Mr. Massie (before he bought his ticket) that they wouldn't be able to accommodate his needs, but I expect that's a customer service issue.

On the other hand, some European airlines have voluntarily agreed to abide by the provisions in the European Commission's Airline Passenger Service Commitment. This document suggests a number of non-legally binding provisions designed to deliver a defined standard of service to air travelers. Access provisions include requirements for airlines to publicize their accessible services and assist disabled passengers in an appropriate manner.

In any case, some British domestic carriers do accommodate people with disabilities, but it is a voluntary service. Remember to ask a lot of questions regarding access before booking any domestic flights within the United Kingdom. Make sure you will be able to get on and off the plane!

As far as accessible lodging goes, you may encounter two access rating systems in the United Kingdom. The three-tiered Tourism for All (TFA) scheme is being replaced by the four-tiered National Accessible Scheme (NAS). These programs work much like the Access Canada program. Properties are first inspected by a trained professional to determine their access rating. This rating is then noted in guide books, tourism department publications, lodging brochures, and travel websites.

Of the three categories in the TFA access rating system, category one has the highest level of access.

- **CATEGORY ONE:** Accessible to an independent wheelchair user.
- **CATEGORY TWO:** Accessible to a wheelchair user with assistance.
- **CATEGORY THREE:** Accessible to someone with mobility difficulties, but able to walk up a minimum of three steps.

Roll-in (no rim) showers are required in all Category One and Category Two properties, which have a "shower only" (rather than a tub or a tub and shower combination).

Of the four mobility categories in the newer NAS scheme, category M4 has the highest level of access.

- **M1:** Typically suitable for a person with sufficient mobility to climb a flight of steps but would benefit from points of fixtures and fittings to aid balance.
- **M2:** Typically suitable for a person with restricted walking ability and for those who may need to use a wheelchair some of the time.
- **M3:** Typically suitable for a person who depends on the use of a wheelchair and transfers unaided to and from the wheelchair in a seated position.
- **M4:** Typically suitable for a person who depends on the use

of a wheelchair and transfers to and from the wheelchair in a seated position. They also require personal/mechanical assistance to aide transfer (e.g., caregiver/hoist).

Sound confusing? Well it is. That's just how it goes when you introduce a new access scheme. Just be aware that you may encounter two drastically different access schemes in the United Kingdom. More important, make a mental note that the number one doesn't always indicate the highest level of access.

Another unique thing about access in the United Kingdom is the availability of accessible public toilets. The good news is that thousands of accessible public toilets are available throughout the United Kingdom. The bad news? They are locked and are only accessible with a National Key Scheme (NKS) key. NKS keys are available to the public but you do have to plan ahead. Make sure you get the appropriate NKS keys before you leave home.

Figure 11.2.
Rooms in the M4 category, such as this one at the Copthorne Tara, in London, offer the highest level of access.

Britain's NKS covers over 6,000 accessible public toilets throughout the United Kingdom, and the best place for visitors to get their NKS key is from The Royal Association for Disability and Rehabilitation (RADAR). The cost is $6.35. RADAR also has a NKS guide that lists the locations of the accessible public toilets. It's available for $8.16.

If your travels include the Republic of Ireland, a different key is available from the Access Department of the National Rehabilitation Board in Dublin. This key will open 99% of the locked accessible public toilets in the Republic.

A lot of Internet resources cover access in the United Kingdom, but one of my favorites is Ann Litt's Undiscovered Britain. This excellent website includes information about access to the theater, driving, the NKS toilets, and lodging in Britain. It also features lots of photos that illustrate access throughout the United Kingdom. Ann is a destination specialist for the United Kingdom, and she's an expert on all things British, including access. You can find her informative website at www.UndiscoveredBritain.com.

Two good books about access in the United Kingdom are *Access in London* and *The Level Guide to the South West*.

Access in London was researched by a London-based nonprofit organization and released in its fourth edition in 2004. This handy resource includes information on accessible tourist attractions, toilets, accommodations, recreation, and transportation in the London area. All information in this guide was compiled from site inspections conducted in 2002. This 438-page guide is advertised as free, however an $8.16 donation is requested for each guide, to help defray the cost of research, printing, and postage.

The Level Guide to the South West presents accurate access information on hotels, restaurants, and attractions throughout Southwest England. The access information is presented in a narrative format with detailed contact information included with each listing. Peter Watts, a wheelchair-user himself, personally visited all sites covered in the book. Peter hopes to publish more Level Guides, so keep a look-out for his new titles.

And finally, be sure to check out Holiday Care for a wide variety of access publications. They publish numerous fact sheets and information guides that include information about accessible accommodations, transportation, and tourist sites around the world. Since they are based in London, they have a large amount of information on the United Kingdom. Visit their website at www.holidaycare.org.uk for a list of their current publications.

On the Continent, access standards and laws vary from country to country, but some things apply across the board. Although different from the United States, access terminology is pretty standard throughout Western Europe, although the differentiation between an adapted room and an accessible room is a new concept for most Americans

An accessible room is defined as a room that presents no obstacles to entering and moving about in a wheelchair, but offers no other specific access amenities. An adapted room is a room in which the bathroom, shower, and toilets are adapted to comply with access standards. So, if you need a roll-in shower or a raised toilet, don't ask for an accessible room. Roll-in showers are quite common throughout Europe, but you need to specify your needs. They are sometimes called *level-entry* or *no-rim showers*. Also remember, in Europe the first floor is not at street level. If you want a room at street level, ask for a room on the ground floor.

There is also a different key scheme for accessible public toilets in Continental Europe. The Euro Key scheme is administered by CBF, a German disability organization. In 1986, CBF started the Euro Key scheme in Germany, and today it has expanded to include many other European countries. The Euro Key is available for 15 Euro from CBF.

Another good European resource is *Rick Steves' Easy Access Europe*. Penned by Ken Plattner and Rick Steves, this 2004 release contains general information about European travel and includes listings for accessible hotels, restaurants, and attractions in London, Paris, Bruges, Amsterdam, and Frankfurt. All listings are rated for access, but because of the off-the-beaten track focus of Steves' titles, the majority of the listings are only appropriate for slow walkers. Still, it's a useful resource for budget travelers and for people who can make do with less than perfect access.

Down Under

WITH THE PASSAGE of the Disability Discrimination Act (DDA) of 1992, access for people with disabilities in Australia has greatly improved in subsequent years. The DDA states that it is unlawful for providers of goods, services, and facilities to discriminate against a person with a disability. This includes public accommodations such as restaurants, lodgings, transportation, and entertainment venues. The Human Rights and Equal Opportunity Commission (HREOC) is the enforcement authority of the DDA.

In practice, Australia offers good access to lodging and most tourist facilities. The big exception is public transportation. In fact, this exception gained international attention in October 2000, during the run of the Sydney Paralympic Games. The Paralympic Games created the biggest demand for accessible transportation ever experienced in Australia, and the Olympic Roads and Transport Authority (ORTA) was responsible for coordinating that transportation. How'd they do? Well, according to many disability rights advocates, "not very well."

The situation came to a head in June 2000, when ORTA applied to the Australian HREOC for a temporary exemption from the DDA. The rationale behind the application was that since there were not enough accessible buses in New South Wales to serve the expected Olympic crowds, ORTA would have to procure them from public and private bus operators throughout the country. ORTA sought to protect these cooperating operators from any liability that might arise from the temporary transfer of their accessible buses to Olympic- and Paralympic-related services.

Disability advocates were outraged at ORTA's request, but in the end the exemption was approved by the HREOC. Buses were pulled from other areas and sent to Sydney for the Olympics and

Paralympics. Of course, many residents went without accessible transportation during that time. The reason? Accessible transportation was still in its infancy in Australia, and there just weren't enough buses to go around.

To be fair, access has improved since the 2000 Olympics, although accessible transportation can still be difficult to find in some parts of the country.

On the positive side, Australia does have some very unique access resources. At the top of the list is NICAN, a national database that contains access information on accommodations, tourist attractions, and recreational facilities throughout Australia. NICAN maintains over 4,500 disability-related resources in their database. Access information is available free from NICAN by phone, fax, e-mail, or in person. You can also search the NICAN database online at www.nican.com.au.

Another great Australian innovation is the mobility map. These city maps depict the access features of local business districts, and they are usually available through city tourism departments. The maps include information on accessible routes, telephones, toilets, and parking. They also include local landmarks, tourist attractions, and street gradients. The city of Melbourne publishes an excellent mobility map, which is also available online at www.access-melbourne.vic.gov.au. I'd love to see this concept catch on in other countries, but so far Australia is the only place that has really developed this access resource.

Australia also has an accessible public toilet key scheme called the Master Locksmith Access Key (MLAK) Scheme. Patterned after Britain's successful NKS, the MLAK scheme was first introduced in Australia in 1994. Today, over 170 public toilets have MLAK locks. Anybody with a disability can purchase a MLAK key from a locksmith who is a member of the Master Locksmiths Association of Australia (MLAA).

Two excellent books about accessible travel in Australia are *Easy Access Australia* and *The Wheelie's Handbook of Australia*.

Easy Access Australia is packed full of helpful access information about hotels and major tourist attractions throughout Australia. Author Bruce Cameron includes approximately 600 accommodations and 300 bathroom floorplans in this handy resource. Information on accessible transportation is also included, along with lots of contact information, phone numbers, and maps.

The Wheelie's Handbook of Australia, authored by Colin James, contains hard-to-find access details on over 500 accessible accommodations throughout Australia. Properties are listed by city and divided by geographic region. Each listing contains a detailed description of the property, plus access features, contact information, and (sometimes) unexpected extras.

Third-World Travel

WHAT ABOUT TRAVEL to third-world countries? Is this really a possibility for wheelchair-users and slow walkers? It depends. To be honest, there really isn't a pat answer to that question.

I know a number of wheelchair-users who love this kind of off-the-beaten-track travel, but they all admit it's not easy. It takes a lot of planning and in the end these adventuresome folks set out well prepared with very realistic expectations. On the other hand I also know people who have attempted this type of travel with grossly unrealistic expectations and even a certain degree of naiveté. These poor souls set out ill-prepared for what they will encounter along the way, and as expected they don't fare very well. Indeed, the key to any successful trip lies with proper preparation, and proper preparation in this case also means familiarization with the access realities of your destination.

What should you realistically expect as far as access goes in third-world countries? In many cases human rights and access laws are scant or nonexistent, so you have to be prepared for access obstacles. In most cases, you should be prepared to be carried up steps and through narrow doorways. Accessible toilets and bathrooms are few and far between, and accessible transportation is usually nonexistent.

That's the downside. The upside is that in many cases there are work-arounds. As far as physical access goes, travel with a light-weight manual wheelchair whenever possible. It's also a good idea to travel with a companion who is able to lift you, carry you, and bump you up stairs. Alternatively, you can hire a local (usually for a very low price) to assist you.

As far as transportation goes, you will have to transfer (with help or by yourself) to a standard vehicle, as accessible vehicles are few and far between in most third-world countries. Take a transfer board and whatever manpower (or womanpower) you need to accomplish this task. Many drivers and tour guides are also willing to help, but you should tip them for their assistance.

You might also consider taking along a portable suitcase ramp to help make some of those two or three step entrances more accessible. Handi-Ramp manufactures a wide variety of sizes and styles of portable ramps. They are great for travel and very durable. Visit their website at handi-ramp.com for more information.

The best all-around resource for third-world world travel is *The Practical Nomad: How to Travel around the World* by Edward Hasbrouck. Now in its third edition, this comprehensive volume includes authoritative information on everything from air and surface transportation to baggage, budgets, and health issues. Although the book contains a few paragraphs and some resources on accessible travel, it's not really an accessible travel title. Still it's a must-read for any off-the-beaten path traveler. Additionally, Mr. Hasbrouck has a very enlightened attitude about accessible travel in third-world countries, an attitude that serves to encourage rather than discourage people from giving it a try.

Electricity and Converters

ACCESS STANDARDS AREN'T the only differences you'll encounter when you travel outside of the United States. One difference of major importance to many wheelers is the electrical voltage outside of North America. In short, if you travel with a rechargeable battery, you need to learn how to safely recharge your battery while you're on foreign soil. It goes without saying that you also need to formulate a contingency plan, just in case something goes wrong.

The United States, Canada, and most countries in the Western hemisphere operate on 110-volt electricity. Most other countries operate on 220-volt electricity. Additionally, some countries also have plug configurations that are different from those in the United States. So, you need two things to safely charge your battery overseas. First, you need a converter or transformer to safely convert the foreign electricity. Additionally, you may also need an adapter so that your U.S.-style plug will fit in the foreign socket. What happens if you don't use a converter? Quite simply, you will fry your battery charger. Although it sounds pretty basic, many people get into trouble because they don't think before they plug in their equipment.

For example, some countries have that familiar two-prong outlet found across the United States; however, they also operate on 220-voltage. The plug fits in the socket nicely, but if you don't also use a converter you'll fry your charger. Remember, the only thing an adapter does is change the shape of the plug. It does nothing to convert the electricity.

Many people get into trouble when they only use an adapter. Just because the plug fits into the socket, doesn't mean that it's safe to plug in your equipment. Before you plug in your battery charger, always ask yourself, "Do I need a converter?" Don't plug in your equipment until you know the definitive answer. Nothing ruins a vacation faster than a fried battery charger.

What kind of a converter do you need? First, find out the voltage, amperage, and wattage of your battery charger. This information is usually written on your charger, but if you can't find it consult your owner's manual. If you still can't find this information, write down the make and model of your wheelchair, then call the manufacturer and ask for the technical support department.

Says scooter-user Carol Randall, "Of all the calls I've made, I have found these technical support people to be the most knowledgeable and helpful. They can usually tell you exactly what you will need, and where you can get it." It's a good idea to consult your wheelchair manufacturer in this situation, as they are the experts on your particular wheelchair, and they will recommend the most appropriate converter for your needs.

You'll probably also need some adapters to go along with your converter. Which adapters should you buy? Well, that depends on where you plan to travel. A good information resource for adapters is Magellan's, a mail-order catalog for travel supplies. They have a good table on adapters and lots of valuable information on their website and in their print catalog. Additionally, they will answer individual questions about specific needs. Of course, they also carry just about every adapter known to man.

If you travel a lot, or you just don't want to bother with thinking about converters and electricity, you might want to consider buying a universal battery charger. They are available through a variety of companies and can be installed on your wheelchair. Check with your wheelchair manufacturer to see what model will work best for you.

The advantage to a universal charger is that you don't have to carry a special converter to use electricity in a foreign country. It's the safest way to proceed, but most universal chargers run over $250. You may still need some adapters to use with your universal charger, depending on your destination. A universal charger is a good idea if you plan to travel overseas frequently.

What do you do if, in spite of all your efforts, you do fry your battery charger? It happens to the best of us, including experienced travelers like Carol Randall, so you should at least think about a contingency plan. Fortunately, Carol's quick thinking provided her a creative solution that saved her trip.

Says Carol of her experience, "After I fried my charger in London, I headed over to the local automotive supply store and bought an inexpensive 12-volt, low-output battery charger for $20. The drawback was that we had to disconnect the batteries, and it would only charge one battery at a time. This meant we had to get up once during the night to change the charger—but it did work, and it saved the trip."

Other helpful suggestions include carrying a photo of a battery charger and the words "battery charger" written in the local language. These items will help you if you need to go in search of a battery charger in a country where you don't speak the language.

Other Concerns

MEDICAL ISSUES ARE a concern no matter where you travel, but they take on an added importance when you travel outside the United States. While your medical insurance will most likely cover you throughout the United States, it may not cover you in a foreign country. Check with your insurance company before you depart. If your insurance does cover you outside of the United States, be sure to carry the appropriate medical cards and insurance forms. Find out how to file an overseas claim. Although nobody plans to seek medical care while on a vacation, accidents do happen. The best strategy is to be prepared.

You'll also want to find out if your destination country has some sort of national health care program that also covers travelers. Some countries do, and they provide free emergency medical care to anyone, even visitors. It pays to ask a few questions, as it may prevent you from buying unneeded medical insurance.

If you don't have any other coverage, you may want to buy some travel medical or health insurance that will cover you overseas. Some travel agents sell this, but it's really best to check with your insurance agent. After all, they are the experts about insurance issues. Make sure that any travel insurance you purchase doesn't exclude pre-existing conditions.

One of the biggest costs of a medical emergency overseas is the cost of medical evacuation. If you should have an accident and can't fly home on a regular airline, you'll need to hire an air ambulance. Some types of insurance already cover this. For example, my Travel Medical Protection Plan from American Express covers up to $100,000 for emergency medical evacuation. The premium is incredibly affordable, and it covers me for the entire year, no matter where I travel. Of course, I carefully inspected the policy before I made my purchase decision.

Check with your insurance company about travel insurance plans. They are affordable, and some even include trip cancellation and accidental death coverage. Again, it's very important to make sure that your policy does not exclude pre-existing medical conditions. Additionally, it's usually more economical to buy a policy that covers you year round, as opposed to a short-term policy that only covers you for one trip.

Many travel agents also sell all sorts of trip cancellation and travel insurance. Some travel agents even make you sign a form that states you declined to purchase coverage from them. They are not doing this to scare you, but rather to protect themselves from liability should something happen to you. They also like everybody to have travel insurance, because they don't want unhappy clients— and when clients have to cancel a trip and don't get their money back, they are unhappy. Although most travel agents are reputable, it's best to see your own insurance agent regarding any travel insurance issues. Again, they are the experts in all insurance matters.

Of course, always take a copy of all your prescriptions with you when you travel. Pack them in your carry-on baggage. Some people also take a brief medical history with them in case they have a medical emergency and are unable to communicate. You might also want to check into getting a Medic Alert bracelet if you have a special medical condition or unique medical needs. And finally, if you are going to a foreign country, learn a few words of the language. At the top of the list is "wheelchair." If you can't manage the pronunciation, then just write it down and carry with you. It may come in handy.

Where to Begin

WHERE DO YOU begin your research for your overseas trip? The first rule of thumb is to try to deal directly with organizations or people in your destination country. Although many people in the United States are experienced with overseas travel, the locals have the most updated and accurate information.

Wherever you travel, there will most likely be some set of rules governing access, and the best way to find out about these is through a national disability organization. Disabled Peoples' International, an international cross-disability network, has a good list of worldwide disability organizations on their website at www.dpi.org.

Another good resource are the foreign counterparts of U.S. disability organizations. For example, if your travels take you to the United Kingdom, you might want to check out the MS Society of the United Kingdom. The Internet is a great tool for this type of research. Post notices in travel forums and on disability-focused websites. The goal is to find a local contact. Generally speaking, if you ask enough people, sooner or later you will find a good contact.

And finally, don't forget about foreign tourist bureaus. Some offices now have access information and some even publish access guides. It never hurts to ask, as they may even be able to give you a local access contact.

The Travel Agent
Friend or Foe? | 12

YOU'VE FINALLY DECIDED that it's time for a vacation. So, what's the first thing you need to do? Well, according to most other books about accessible travel, you need to "Find a good travel agent." To be honest, that's pretty useless advice. After all, nobody wants to find a bad travel agent.

Sarcasm aside, you need to understand several things before you go in search of that perfect travel agent. First, you need to determine if you even need a travel agent. To do this, you need to understand how travel agents work and what they can and can't do for their clients. In the long run, this will also help you work more effectively with your agent.

You also need to know how to find a travel agent that best suits your needs. To do this, you need to learn a little bit about the industry, so that you will know how to recognize a good travel agent. Additionally, you need to be able to recognize a bad travel agent, along with some of the pitfalls and scams that seem to proliferate in this industry. As with everything else, it's definitely a case of buyer-beware.

Travel Agent 101

TRAVEL AGENTS WORK in a variety of ways, but in the simplest form they book travel for clients and receive commissions from suppliers (cruise lines, hotels, airlines, tour companies). The products they offer depend on their business relationships and commission arrangements with the suppliers. So in theory, two different travel agents could work with a number of different suppliers and, as a result, offer their clients different travel options. I say *in theory*, because it doesn't always work that way.

In practice, many mainstream travel agents only work with the suppliers that pay the highest commissions. Unfortunately, only a limited number of suppliers provide accessible services and, since most of them don't pay large commissions, they are somewhat unknown to mainstream agents. Those agents who specialize in accessible travel are ultimately those who are familiar with these specialty providers. The big problem is finding these specialist agents. More on that later.

The truth is that many small accessible tour operators would like to be able to pay commissions, but they just can't afford it. So, these small guys are effectively left out of the booking loop. Travel agents and tour operators both need to make money. Travel agents can't afford to work for free, so they have to work with suppliers that can pay commissions. Small tour operators need to make a living, so most can't afford to pay out commissions. Sometimes it's a vicious circle.

But it's not just the small tour operators that don't pay commissions to travel agents. Years ago, most airlines paid out hefty commissions, but over the years those commissions have also dwindled. Now, it's hard for many travel agents to even pay for their reservation software with the meager commissions offered by most airlines. The result is that some agents no longer work with air-only clients, while others now charge a minimal processing fee for domestic air tickets. Generally speaking, travel agents still receive a decent commission on international airline tickets, so most are still willing to offer this service.

As a result of dwindling commissions, many travel agents found different ways to address the travel market. The professional organizations encouraged travel agents to find profitable niche markets, such as accessible travel. Many travel agents became accessible travel specialists overnight. I say this sarcastically because, officially, there is no such thing as a certified accessible travel specialist. Of course, you can print whatever you want on your own business cards and in your own promotional literature, so I have seen this claim in a number of advertisements.

On the other hand, there are a number of genuine accessible travel specialists out there, and most of these experienced agents have served this niche market long before it was ever fashionable. But, with so many Johnny-come-latelys popping up, sometimes it is hard to find the real accessible travel experts.

Then there are the destination specialists and itinerary planners. These are highly trained experts, and I encourage you to actively seek them out. Destination specialists focus on a particular destination, and they are experts about everything related to that destination. Many of these destination specialists are also knowledgeable about access. Some destination specialists also do itinerary planning.

Itinerary planners charge their clients for their services. Sometimes they also get commissions from suppliers, but these travel agents don't exclusively work only with suppliers that pay out commissions. These travel professionals are worth their weight in gold, but be on the lookout for impostors. Nobody can be a destination specialist for all areas of the world, so be wary of any travel agent who makes that claim.

In truth, I know a lot of good travel agents; in fact some of my best friends are travel agents. Unfortunately I've also heard horror stories about the bad travel agents, so I know they are out there. Good travel agents work hard for their money and offer their clients valuable first-hand knowledge about products, services, and destinations. The bad ones? They can ruin your trip and make you swear off travel forever.

Do You Need One?

DO YOU NEED a travel agent? There's not really a blanket answer to that question. In truth, it depends on many factors, including your travel needs and your own personality type. This book gives you the tools to cut out the middleman and in a sense, be your own travel agent. But do you really want to do that? Some people do and some people don't.

Many people work with travel agents because they want somebody else to take care of all the details. If you don't want to deal with the hundreds of minor details that can pop up before, during, and after your trip, then by all means delegate the task to a competent travel agent. But planning and knowledge are two different things; so remember, just because you delegate trip planning to a travel agent, doesn't mean you shouldn't also educate yourself about the logistics of accessible travel and the accessibility of your destination.

Regardless of who makes your travel arrangements, you still need to know your rights and understand the process. Why? Because the real proof of a genuine accessible travel specialist lies with her knowledge about the rules, regulations, and realities of accessible travel; and the only way to judge her expertise is to become an expert yourself.

As I pointed out earlier, many travel agents don't want to bother with domestic air-only tickets because it's simply not profitable, so if you are just looking for the lowest fare to Cincinnati, then it's usually best to bypass the travel agent. Let's face it, sometimes the logistics of accessible travel are time intensive, and most agents can't afford to spend this time with clients pro bono. Like everybody else, they need to be paid for their time, and if the airlines won't pay them, they simply can't afford to work for free. Nobody can.

On the other hand, travel agents can be quite helpful with international travel, package tours, cruise travel, or group tours. These are pretty competitive markets, so make sure your agent is well versed in the finer aspects of accessible travel. For example, don't just use any cruise travel agent—use one that can tell you about the accessibility of the ports.

Additionally, don't feel you are married to one agent forever, because different agents have different specialties. One agent may be a great cruise agent, but know very little about land tours in the

United Kingdom. Again, nobody can be an expert at everything, so choose an expert who works best for your particular trip.

Giving equal time to travel agents, some travel agents do go above and beyond the call of duty for regular clients. As one travel agent confides, "I've done some ridiculously time-consuming things for long-term clients, just as favors because they've used me for years." Truthfully, the best reason to work with any travel agent is to take advantage of his destination and access knowledge. A good travel agent is a very valuable resource.

The Search

THE SEARCH FOR a travel agent begins much the same way as the search for any other professional. The best strategy is to gather a list of potential candidates and then interview them over the phone. Where do you find the candidates? Personal referrals are great, so ask your friends and family if they know of any good travel agents. Be sure to specify that your definition of a good travel agent is one who is well educated about accessible travel.

Scan through national disability magazines, search the Internet, ask people in your support group, and look for advertisements in the yellow pages. Learn to read between the lines of advertisements though. I recently spied an advertisement in a national disability magazine that didn't even list a phone number, company name, or address. The only contact information for this advertisement that touted accessible tours of Ireland was an e-mail address.

After a little investigation, I learned that this individual was ill-equipped to organize accessible tours, because he wasn't even aware of the accessible transportation situation in Ireland. The big tip-off should have been the lack of contact information. Skip over any advertisement that just doesn't have a professional look.

Soon your list of candidates will grow, and you'll be ready to begin the interview process. Before you pick up the phone, remember that it's important to ask all the candidates the same questions. Try to talk to at least five candidates. Even if you absolutely love the first candidate, continue to call everybody on your list. You never know, you may just find somebody you love even more.

Feel free to eliminate anybody you just don't like, even if they seem to have the appropriate professional qualifications. Go with your gut feeling. This is a personal service, and you need to feel comfortable with your travel agent. You don't have to become best friends, but you can't really work effectively with somebody if you have a personality conflict.

Be sure to inquire about what kind of training the agent has, as well as how long they have worked with accessible travel. Nobody is born with this knowledge, so remember we all have to learn it at some time in life. Don't rule out real life experience either, as some agents are very experienced in accessible travel because they have a disability and they love to travel. This type of experience is valuable, but by itself it is not enough. The agent also has be familiar with the travel industry. Ask about their professional qualifications. If they have a lot of initials after their name, ask what they mean, and how they got them.

It's also a good idea to throw in a test question, just to make sure they have the requisite knowledge about accessible travel. Now, I'm not saying you should cross-examine and badger each candidate, but ask at least one question that tests their accessible travel expertise.

If you have a specific destination in mind, ask about their expertise on that destination. Additionally, ask them how many clients they book to that destination annually and when they last visited that destination.

Most important, ask them if they have experience dealing with clients with your specific disability. Ask for references, and call up those references and inquire about their travel experiences. Now, to be honest you may run into some travel agents who won't give you references.

Some travel agents are gun-shy about giving out references. Says one long-time travel agent, "I used to give out references (with my clients' permission), until I had a bad experience. A few years ago a lady requested references and then she badgered the heck out my client. She kept calling her up and just wanted to chit-chat and be her best friend. My client didn't want anything to do with her, and she had a hard time getting rid of her. I don't give out references any more. I just can't risk another experience like that one."

So, don't automatically disqualify a potential candidate just because she won't provide you with references, because sometimes there is a very good reason behind this decision. And let's face it, no travel agent is going to use the client who had the disaster trip as a reference.

In the end, you'll just have to rely on your own judgment in this matter; however, if the travel agent doesn't have the time to answer your questions, then move on. Answering a few personal questions is easy, compared to the intricacies of researching and arranging accessible travel.

Some Red Flags

ONCE YOU'VE COMPLETED the interview process, how do you evaluate the answers and pick the best travel agent? The personality factor will serve to screen out some candidates. In fact, you will probably run across a few agents whom you just don't like. They are easy to scratch off the list. But what about the rest? Your final decision should be based on the candidates' destination and access knowledge, but a few responses should throw up a red flag.

Be wary when somebody tells you they are a "certified" accessible travel expert. There's nothing wrong with somebody saying they have experience in this specialty, but as I pointed out earlier, there is no official certification training program or credentialing process. Ask them how many hours of training they received, who gave it, and what it covered. Ask them how long they have been in the industry and how long they have been working with accessible travel. Some people call themselves experts after an afternoon training seminar.

Watch out for candidates who tout their membership in a professional organization as their primary qualification as an accessible travel specialist. Ask about the organization's membership requirements. A large number of professional organizations exist for travel agents and, while some have rigid membership criteria, others merely require members to write out an annual check.

A red flag should go up if a candidate guarantees you something that is simply not within his power. For example, if someone guarantees you bulkhead seats, "no matter what," this only serves to illustrate their own ignorance about the Air Carrier Access Act. Additionally, be wary of any agent who guarantees you a problem-free trip. Travel is unpredictable, and nobody knows when problems will arise.

Stay away from anybody who uses that dreaded h-word. It's all right to use this word to describe horses and golfers, but not to describe people with disabilities. It shows a general lack of knowledge and sensitivity about the market—and that lack of knowledge usually doesn't stop at terminology. Most likely this person is also lacking in essential knowledge about the logistics of accessible travel.

Some agencies advertise that they are "owned and operated by a person with a disability." Although there's nothing really wrong with stating that fact, be wary if that in itself is the agent's only qualification. Of course, you should also ask what their disability is, if they make it a point to include this fact in their advertisements. Look for somebody who is experienced and knowledgeable about your specific disability. For example, just because a person is blind, doesn't mean they have a good working knowledge about wheelchair travel.

Watch out for agents who use broad generalizations, such as "everything is accessible." This indicates a general lack of knowledge on the subject.

Finally, be wary of travel agents who don't travel. If they don't travel, ask them why (sometimes there is a good reason), and then ask them what they do to keep up with the industry. The ideal agent should have also traveled to your destination recently, although this isn't always possible.

Additionally, be wary of travel agents who always travel. Some people get into the travel business just so that they can write off their own travel expenses. Although there's nothing wrong with that per se, your travel agent should be available to answer your questions and deal with problems as they arise, and that's just not possible if they are always on the road.

Buyer Beware!

YOU NEED TO be extra cautious about a few things when searching for a travel agent. I hate to blatantly call them scams, however they deserve more attention than the red-flag items. By far the worst one is the "you too can be a travel agent" scam. And yes, I do classify this one as a scam.

Also known as a card mill, this scam is incredibly damaging to consumers and professionals alike. Many people unknowingly fall prey to it even if they aren't in the market for a job. In fact, the biggest market for card mill operators is people who like to travel, not just people who need a job. This scam works in a variety of ways, and indeed some are quite slick.

Typically, the con man tries to convince you that it's in your best interest to become a travel agent, because you can save money on your own travel. He'll also tell you about how you can book travel for your friends and family and make big bucks with little or no effort. And then he'll rave about the free and discounted travel you can receive as a official card-carrying travel agent. What's he selling? Not much, usually just a card saying you are a travel agent and maybe a manual of some sort. Both items are pretty worthless.

Card mills can present themselves in a variety of ways, including self-employment opportunities. This is perhaps the most straightforward approach, as at least you know what they are selling. Other approaches aren't so straightforward and can include advertisements that read "travel for free" or "save big money on travel."

Additionally, card mill operators take full advantage of the underemployment in the disabled community because they actively solicit people with disabilities. They entice their marks with promises of a turn-key home-based business that makes big bucks. Be careful when somebody offers you something that sounds too good to be true.

The truth is, real travel agents work very hard for their money and most have had some kind of hands-on training. It's not easy work, and many travel agents take years to turn a profit and establish their business. As for the travel agent discounts and fam trips—well, travel suppliers are familiar with card mills too, so card mill travel agents are routinely screened out of most offerings.

Be wary of anybody who tries to sell you a home-based travel business, because they could in fact be a card mill operator. Unfortunately, many people fall for this scam and, as a result, there are a number of card mill travel agents out there. Worse yet, some of these untrained travel agents specialize in accessible travel. All the more reason to carefully screen your travel agent candidates!

Another thing to be on the lookout for are travel agents or tour operators who operate as nonprofit agencies. This practice isn't something that I actually classify as a scam, but it can be pretty misleading. True, some legitimate nonprofit organizations do offer accessible trips and tours; however, some businesses operate as nonprofits in name only. It's merely an accounting method for some. They still make money and take a salary. There's really nothing wrong with that, unless they imply otherwise.

If your tour operator or travel agent claims nonprofit status, ask about the services they provide for the community. If the best they can come up with is, "We negotiate good deals on travel," then you may be dealing with a nonprofit in name only. Remember, operating a nonprofit organization doesn't necessarily guarantee altruistic motives. To some, it's just a marketing tool. Ask a lot of questions whenever a travel agency or tour operator touts their nonprofit status.

And finally, be wary if something just doesn't sound right. Recently, a travel agent told me this horrifying story. A man called her after he had booked a group tour to Europe with another travel agent. The man used a power wheelchair and required assistance to transfer. He was feeling a little anxious about his upcoming tour because no arrangements for accessible transportation or lodging had been mentioned. He confronted his travel agent with his fears and she told him, "Don't worry, all of Europe is completely accessible." This should have sent up a big red warning flag! Fortunately, the second travel agent told the man the truth.

So ask around, do your research and, if something just doesn't sound right, use your common sense and investigate further. And if somebody tells you, "All of Europe is completely accessible," run (or roll) as fast as you can in the opposite direction!

Travel Agent Etiquette

CHOOSING A TRAVEL agent is only half the battle. Now that you understand how the travel industry works, you can use this knowledge to work more effectively with your travel agent. Here are a few pointers to help you along the way.

First and foremost, don't waste a travel agent's time. For example, don't call up a travel agent and just ask for a list of accessible hotels. Remember what travel agents do. They are not a public information resource. They book trips and use their expertise for their clients. Says one travel agent, "Last week one caller took up about 3 hours of our time. She wanted detailed information on accessible ships, accessible ports, and ports where her service dog could come ashore. She asked for multiple rates on different ships and cabins. Then her traveling companion decided she felt more comfortable booking locally, so she took all the information she gleaned from us and booked with another travel agent. I now understand why so many specialists require nonrefundable goodwill deposits."

Of course, if your travel agent is making travel arrangements for you, then it's perfectly acceptable to ask for a choice of hotels in a particular city; but don't just call up any agent, ask for the information, and make the arrangements yourself. If you want to make your own travel arrangements, find another information source.

Be well prepared when you first contact your travel agent. Have some idea of where you want to go, when you want to go, and how long you want to stay. Have a general idea about your travel budget.

It's all right to go to your travel agent with a few choices and ask for an opinion, but don't just walk in and expect them to find the right trip for you. Do some advance research and make a list of destinations that interest you, and then inquire about their suitability when you talk with your travel agent.

Be honest with your travel agent (and yourself) about your disability. It won't benefit anybody if you hide important information; in fact, anything short of full disclosure can be disastrous. Consider the plight of Judy, who ended up stranded at Denver International Airport, because of a failure to disclose. Judy, a 52-year-old woman with multiple sclerosis (MS), was no longer able to travel independently due to progressive cognitive difficulties. Unfortunately, when Judy's daughter made the travel arrangements, she neglected to mention her mom's cognitive difficulties to the travel agent. She only said that her mom needed some wheelchair assistance.

After Judy landed in Denver, she got confused and didn't know where she was. She missed her connecting flight to Bismark. Of course, she assured everybody she was all right and that she was just waiting for her daughter. Finally, security stepped in and came to Judy's aid. Unfortunately, by this time, Judy's pants were soaked with urine, and her daughter was worried sick in Bismark. The whole situation could have been easily avoided with a little honesty.

Now, I'm not saying that you need to give out a complete medical history, but don't hide important facts. For example, if you can't transfer independently, then you need to be honest with your travel agent about this fact. It won't prevent you from going on a trip, but it will help your travel agent plan a trip that is appropriate for you. Most likely, your travel agent will have a questionnaire for you to complete. Try to answer all the questions as completely as possible; however, if a particular question makes you uncomfortable, talk it over with your travel agent and ask why they need to know that information.

Remember, "I don't know," is sometimes an acceptable answer; in fact it's better than a wrong answer or a guess. Nobody knows all the answers, but a good travel agent has the resources to find them. Allow your travel agent time to research your question, and be glad you have a travel agent who is willing to do the research. However, if your travel agent continually answers "I don't know" to your questions and is unwilling to do the research, then perhaps you need to look elsewhere.

Don't call your travel agent for daily updates about your travel arrangements. Remember, you are not their only client. Admittedly, you will have questions, so write them down and consolidate them into one phone call. I'm not saying you should never call your travel agent. For example, if your agent promised to call you back on a certain date, and that time has passed, then by all means pick up the phone.

On the other hand, calling for daily updates only tends to frustrate travel agents, because time is a very important commodity to them. Give them a fair chance to do their job. If you don't trust your travel agent to make the appropriate arrangements, then perhaps it's time to find somebody who you do trust.

Don't blame your travel agent because your dream destination is not accessible. Instead, work with your agent to find a suitable alternative. The truth is, some countries are just not very accessible, and it will take more than your travel agent to change that fact. You should expect an honest evaluation about access from your travel agent, but don't blame your agent if it's not exactly what you want to hear. In other words, don't shoot the messenger!

If your travel agent is working on a package tour or cruise for you, remember to inquire about the access of *all* facets of your trip. This includes transportation, transfers, accommodations, and day trips. For cruises, it's very important to ask about the accessibility of shore excursions. Outside the United States, few accessible shore excursions are available, so work with your travel agent to arrange your own accessible shore excursions.

Finally, remember it's standard practice for travel agents to ask for a deposit. If they are making independent travel arrangements for you, the deposit will be deducted from your final bill. If you cancel, they will most likely retain the deposit to cover fax and phone costs. If you're a booking a package tour or cruise, the deposit requirements are set by the supplier. Make sure you have a good understanding of the deposit agreement. Don't be afraid to ask your travel agent for clarification before you write out that check.

The Way It Should Be

IDEALLY, ALL TRAVEL agents should have a working knowledge of accessible travel. But, what if your long-time travel agent doesn't have this knowledge? This question comes up often from people who are recently injured or newly disabled and who want to work with the same travel agent they have been using for the past 20 years. What do you do in this case?

If your travel agent seems willing to learn, and you feel comfortable dealing with her, then I say give it a try. But, don't expect perfection overnight. Your agent will be learning something new, and it may take a while to learn all the ins and outs of accessible travel. It is, as you know, an extremely complex subject. The advantage to working with your present agent is that you have developed a relationship over the years. But remember, it will be incumbent upon you to update your agent about your new access needs.

In truth, everybody has their own definition of the perfect society. My Utopia comes equipped with all the standard features (universal health care, courteous cab drivers, and an unlimited supply of chocolate), but it also has an few added options. In my Utopia, all travel agents (not just the specialists) have a good working knowledge of accessible travel and disability issues. Furthermore, every travel agent is able to book accessible tours, rooms, and transportation for anybody who happens to walk or roll into their office. That's just the way it should be!

But, as you may well know, that's not exactly the way things work today. Perhaps someday soon, all travel agents will have a working knowledge of accessible travel. Until then, take care when selecting your travel agent—your research, time, and effort will pay off in the long run.

Shopping the Net

The Truth about Online Booking | 13

NOBODY IS AMBIVALENT about the Internet. Some folks claim it's the greatest thing since sliced bread, while others blame it for the downfall of modern society. Regardless of your feelings about the Internet, it's a great tool for travel junkies. But, is online booking a realistic option for wheelers? The answer is a conditional yes.

In reality, there isn't a one-click method, but you can use the Internet to save money and ensure appropriate access. What's the best way to do this? Well, there's not a blanket answer to that question. In truth, it depends on what type of travel arrangements you are booking, because the best method varies drastically from reserving a hotel room to making an airline reservation.

Reserving a Room

THEORETICALLY, BOOKING A hotel room online should be a fairly easy process. In practice, however, it doesn't quite work that way. This is especially true when you throw access issues into the equation. Unfortunately, a few problems inherent in the hotel industry make it difficult to book an accessible room online. Not impossible, just difficult.

Two basic roadblocks exist to booking an accessible room online. First, we go back to that age-old problem of defining access. Most hotel websites, travel portals, and consolidators don't list the specific access features of their accessible rooms. At best, they define their rooms as being accessible or ADA compliant. What access features do these rooms have? Sometimes it's hard to tell. Does the room you're booking have a roll-in shower? Is it on the ground floor? How wide is the bathroom door? How high is the toilet? Unfortunately, these important details are not listed on most websites.

It requires a bit of research (and sometimes a few phone calls) to find out what features are included in an accessible room at a particular property. And, of course, the criteria can change from property to property. The first rule of online booking is to always contact the property directly for the most accurate access information.

Second, it's hard to determine if a property will block their accessible rooms just by looking at their website. Is this important? You bet your bottom dollar. It's useless to reserve an accessible room, if it's not there for you when you arrive. Contact the hotel directly regarding their policy on this matter, and don't do business with hotels that won't block their accessible rooms.

Although these roadblocks make it harder to book an accessible room online, they don't make it impossible. Three main ways are possible to book a hotel room online: by using either a hotel consolidator, a professional interface, or the hotel's own website. Although these methods each have different advantages and disadvantages, it's a good idea to keep the basic roadblocks in mind while using any online booking system. That way, you'll be able to circumvent the inherent problems and book an accessible room that's right for you.

Hotel Consolidators

IF YOU'VE EVER searched for travel websites on the Internet, you've probably visited your fair share of hotel consolidator websites. Hotel consolidators buy blocks of hotel rooms and resell them to the public at substantial discounts. You've probably also seen advertisements for hotel consolidators in the Sunday travel section, under a headline such as "save up to 50% on hotels."

The good news is that you can indeed save anywhere from 20% to 50% off the rack rate by booking through a consolidator. The bad news is that it's virtually impossible to book an accessible room through a hotel consolidator. Worse yet, some consolidators are not very up front about their cancellation fees; so, besides being impossible, it can be downright costly. The best advice is to steer clear of hotel consolidator websites.

Sometimes it's hard to recognize hotel consolidators, because many travel portals use them as booking engines. This is commonly referred to as an *affiliate relationship*. Basically, the travel portal uses the hotel consolidator interface and receives a commission for rooms booked from the portal website. The hotel consolidator interface is incorporated into the travel portal website, and sometimes it appears that you are booking directly with the travel portal, when in fact you are using a hotel consolidator.

It's pretty easy to recognize consolidators and their affiliates once you understand why it's impossible to use them for booking accessible rooms. First, consolidators don't guarantee accessible rooms. You can state that you need an accessible room on the reservation form, but it's only treated as a request. In other words, you will get an accessible room if it's available when you arrive. To add insult to injury, this fact is usually only disclosed in the fine print.

Additionally, you must prepay your room charges when you book through a hotel consolidator, plus there's usually a substantial cancellation fee. So basically you pay in advance, but you aren't guaranteed anything. If you get to the hotel and they don't have an accessible room for you, you're still on the hook for the cancellation fee. In short, it makes no difference why you cancel, even if the room doesn't suit your access needs.

One of the worst things about dealing with a consolidator is that you don't deal directly with the hotel. If you call the hotel to confirm your reservation, they usually won't find a reservation under your name. The consolidators book big blocks of rooms, so your reservation is technically under the consolidator's name, until the last minute. So, it's impossible to communicate directly with the property about the specifics of your reservation, because as far as the property is concerned your reservation doesn't exist. Of course, this makes it impossible to confirm the amenities of your accessible room. Are you starting to understand the problems associated with using a consolidator?

Unfortunately, many people do fall prey to the evil hotel consolidator, including yours truly. Before I really learned about hotel consolidators, I used one to book a room online. It seemed like a good deal at the time, even better than I could get by booking directly with the hotel. So, I typed in my credit card number and clicked on the send button. I figured that if I found a better deal, I could just cancel the reservation. I didn't see anything on the website about a cancellation fee. Of course, the hotel consolidator claimed differently, but apparently the Javascript warning about the cancellation fee didn't work on my browser.

In any case, after I made my reservation, I called the property directly to confirm that I had booked a nonsmoking room. That's when I learned how consolidators work, because the hotel had no record of my reservation. I also found that they didn't have any nonsmoking rooms available on the days of my stay. So, I decided to cancel. Well, I couldn't cancel with the hotel because they didn't have a record of my reservation. I called the hotel consolidator to cancel. Of course, the reservation agent warned me about the $75 cancellation fee. I almost dropped the phone when I heard that—after all, I was canceling several months in advance.

The cancellation fee seemed rather excessive to me, so I explained the situation to the reservation agent. It didn't matter. In fact, she told me "Even if you died we wouldn't waive the cancellation fee." That seemed like a rather drastic solution to me. The story does, however, have a happy ending, because once the hotel consolidator found out that I was a travel writer, he mysteriously agreed to waive the cancellation fee. But the bottom line is that I was let off the hook because of privilege, and the solution to my predicament effectively does nothing to change the unreasonable cancellation policy.

Remember, never do business with hotel consolidators. In fact, never do business with any property or service that imposes an unreasonable cancellation fee. You really need the flexibility to cancel your reservation, especially when you're dealing with access issues.

The Professional Interface

THE SECOND WAY to book a hotel reservation online is through a professional interface, the same type of a reservation system that many travel agents use. Apollo and Sabre are two of the most popular interfaces, and they both have lite or consumer versions.

These scaled-down versions are pretty easy to use, because they don't require any great technical expertise. You just need to know when and where you want to stay. The major advantage of using a professional interface is that you deal directly with the hotel. You request a reservation, the request goes to the hotel, and you get a confirmation number back; all within a matter of seconds. It's a pretty efficient system.

The downside to all this is that sometimes it's hard to tell a professional interface from a hotel consolidator just by looking at the online booking form. Both forms ask you for the same information. There are, however, two big differences. One is that, aside from a no-show fee, you won't encounter a cancellation fee when using a professional interface. And two, when you use a professional interface, you don't have to pay the hotel charges in advance.

The professional interface can work well for booking an accessible room, however, the success rate is directly dependent upon each individual property. You can search the database for available rooms based on date, location, hotel chain, price range, and special preferences (including wheelchair access). Your search will return a list of available accessible rooms for that date and location. So far so good; however, your ability to actually book an accessible room depends on the amount of access information that each individual property enters into their own reservation system.

Some properties enter specific details about their accessible rooms, whereas others don't even separate the accessible rooms from the rest of their inventory. In some cases, you can book an accessible room with a roll-in shower using the professional interface, but that's a best-case scenario.

The positive side of this situation is that most of the properties that actually take the time to enter access details about their inventory are pretty access conscious. So, in a way, you're not only booking an accessible room, but you're also screening for the most proactive properties. The down side is that sometimes it is a very long search. Still, the professional interface can be a very useful tool in the search for an accessible room. Of course, you should always check with the hotel directly to confirm that they do in fact block their accessible rooms.

Hotel Websites

THE BEST WAY to book an accessible room online is to make a reservation directly from the hotel's website. Of course, it's not as simple as it sounds; in fact, you should follow a very specific procedure to make sure you get an accessible room.

The first step is to visit a number of hotel websites and check their rates for the dates of your visit. Pick the best rates and then call those properties directly to inquire about the specific features of their accessible rooms. Ask about each hotel's policy about blocking accessible rooms upon reservation. And, while you're on the phone, go ahead and inquire about their rates. If they offer you a better rate than on the Internet, and the room suits you needs, then by all means make a reservation. If not, then go back to the Internet.

By now, you've eliminated a number of properties: those that can't meet your access needs and those that won't block their rooms. Of the remaining properties, pick the one that has the best Internet rate. Go to that property's website and book your reservation online. Make sure to specify your access needs. It never hurts to mention your access needs twice, so go ahead and also mention them in the comments section. Get a confirmation number and call the hotel directly to confirm your booking. If the reservation is not to your satisfaction, or you find out that the property cannot block an accessible room for you, then cancel the reservation. Of course, you'll now have to start the whole process all over again.

In truth, this whole process takes an awful lot of legwork. As I said earlier, it's not exactly a simple procedure. Indeed, sometimes your long-distance phone charges will far exceed that 5% Internet discount. It helps to work with properties that have previously demonstrated a progressive attitude towards access issues. Unfortunately, it's takes time and experience to recognize these properties.

Still, some people find substantial savings online, and unfortunately many of these discounts are only available online. In the end, you'll have to determine if the savings is really worth your time and effort. But if you do decide to use the Internet to book your room, remember to use the hotel website. For now it's the safest way to book an accessible room online.

Finding A Flight

ADMITTEDLY, BOOKING AN accessible flight online is much easier than booking an accessible room online, quite simply because there are fewer choices. But it does require some advance planning. Before you even begin to shop for airfares, you need to learn your rights under the Air Carrier Access Act (ACAA). Among other things, the ACAA mandates that a passenger with a disability cannot be denied boarding solely because of their disability. In theory (and under AIR 21), the ACAA also covers foreign air carriers; however, in practice this legislation is difficult to enforce on foreign soil. Learn the law, and fly on U.S. air carriers for the best access.

Even among U.S. carriers, accessibility still depends on the aircraft, airline, and airport you choose. Size does matter, so learn a little bit about the different types of commercial aircraft. Many of the ACAA regulations regarding aircraft accessibility and boarding depend on aircraft size. The ACAA mandates level boarding whenever possible on all aircraft with 30 or more seats. On aircraft with fewer than 30 seats, level boarding is not required. Some airlines have aircraft diagrams available on their websites. You can also call the airlines directly to find out about the seating capacity and access features of specific aircraft types.

Seating is another important access issue. Wheelchair-users are not always guaranteed seating in bulkhead areas. Contact each airline directly to find out about their specific seating policies for wheelers. Some airlines will seat you in the bulkhead section, and some won't. Seating is addressed in the 1998 amendment to the ACAA, which was published in the March 4, 1998 issue of the *Federal Register*. Learn the rules, then contact airlines in advance to find out about their seating policies. Do business only with those airlines that can provide you with appropriate seating.

Finally, do some research on your departure and arrival airports, because boarding options can be dependent on airport size. Not all airports have jetways to enable level boarding. Some regional airports board directly from the tarmac. Many airports have print access guides, and some even have access information posted online. Some airports have neither, so you'll just have to pick up the phone and call to find out about their accessibility.

Basically, there are three major places to book flights online: on travel portals, auction websites, or airline websites. It's only possible to make accessible flight arrangements in two of these places, however.

Travel Portals

HERE'S WHERE THINGS get confusing. Although it's usually a bad idea to book an accessible room through a travel portal, it's a great idea to use a travel portal to book an accessible flight. The reason is simple. Most travel portals use hotel consolidators for hotel reservations, but they use a professional interface for airline reservations. When you book a flight on a travel portal, you are most likely dealing directly with the airline.

After you've completed your initial research, search the travel portals for flights on U.S.-based airlines. Prices may vary from portal to portal, because each portal has strategic partnerships with different airlines. Some portals may only display prices from select airlines; while others may feature all airlines but only have competitive prices on a select few. Shop around for the best price, but keep your access needs in mind. You'll want to avoid small airplanes, regional airports, and multilegged flights. It's important to note that the best price for your access needs may not necessarily be the cheapest price.

Book your flight when you find the best price. Airfares are somewhat volatile, so there's no guarantee that the same fare will be available next week. Most fares are based on load factors, and when fewer seats are available, prices usually rise. Make note of your access requirements when you book your flight online. It's also a good idea to make note of any cancellation penalties.

After you book your flight, call the airline and speak with the special services department to confirm your access requests. This is also a good time to request any special seating (if you qualify for it), or to request an onboard wheelchair. Additionally, remember to reconfirm all access arrangements 24 hours in advance.

Pig-in-a-Poke.Coms

ALTHOUGH THE INTERNET is a great tool for booking travel, people with disabilities should steer clear of one type of travel website: the auction website or the name-your-price website. These websites go by many different names and are promoted by scads of celebrities, but collectively I call them pig-in-a-poke.coms. Why? Well, because you buy merchandise (in this case airfares) sight unseen, without the benefit of important information that determines flight accessibility. It may seem like a good idea at the time; however, reality will quickly set in when you arrive at the airport and find out you're booked on a turbo-prop that makes seven stops between Boise and Atlanta.

Pig-in-a-poke.coms all operate in much the same way. Basically, you log on and either name your price or bid against other users for airline tickets and hotel rooms. Sounds pretty good, right? I mean, who wouldn't like to name their own price for an airline ticket? Well, the catch is that you can't choose your carrier, routing, aircraft, or even the time of day you travel. In fact, you don't find out these details until after your bid is accepted and you pay for the ticket.

Although this may be acceptable for travelers who don't have access needs, it's a big gamble for anybody who does. Unfortunately, these websites are hyped heavily across cyberspace as being the best places to find cheap airfares. Indeed, they may be cheap, but many times the tickets are not useable by people with disabilities. The sad part is that most people don't find this out until it's too late.

A hybrid type of a website includes both an auction interface and a traditional booking engine. While the booking engine may be OK to use (although I wouldn't pay a fee or commission to use it), steer clear of the auction or name-your-price options.

The bottom line is, stay away from pig-in-a-poke.coms, as they don't offer choices of airlines, aircraft, or routes, all of which are important factors in airline accessibility. Remember, a cheap airfare is no longer a bargain when you can't get on the airplane. And of course the tickets are nonrefundable.

Airline Websites

THE AIRLINE WEBSITES are good places to book air tickets online. In fact, it's a good idea to develop a relationship with one specific airline. It doesn't really matter which airline, and indeed the choice will be different for everybody. The advantages to working exclusively with one particular carrier are manyfold.

First, you can collect frequent flyer miles and cash them in for free flights. Second, if you live near an airline's hub city, you'll be able to get more nonstop flights on that airline out of the hub city. This means fewer connections and fewer plane changes, which is a great plus for wheelchair-users.

And finally, if you travel on one particular airline, you'll be more familiar with their policies regarding people with disabilities. This includes everything from pre-boarding to seating. In short, you'll know what to expect. You'll know immediately when something is wrong, and you'll be able to voice your complaint before it's too late.

There are many benefits of one-carrier loyalty; however, you may need to shop around until you find the airline that best suits your needs. Once you find that carrier, it pays to book online at the airline's website.

Most airline websites also offer special online deals or special promotions. If you book consistently with one airline, you can theoretically shop the sales. Of course, this requires some advance planning and familiarization with the airfares. After all, how do you know when you're getting a good deal on something unless you know the regular price? Plan your route, check the fares, and book online when the fares fall. Again, bear in mind that the best deal is not always the cheapest fare; the best deal should also include appropriate access for you.

Using an airline website to buy your ticket online just makes good sense, and (relatively speaking) it's a pretty simple procedure. Once you've found the right flight for you, purchase your ticket on the airline website. A drop-down menu is usually provided to indicate if wheelchair assistance is needed. Additionally, it doesn't hurt to make note of any special access requirements in the comments area.

One word of caution: Before you hit that send button, make sure you are familiar with the aircraft type used for the flight. Additionally, it doesn't hurt to have a look at the seating diagrams and even the cargo door dimensions. Many airlines have this information available online. SeatGuru.com also features seating diagrams for many airlines, and although accessible seats are not noted, you can still get a good idea about aircraft size and configuration.

After you get a confirmation number, call the airline directly to make sure your access needs are properly noted and to request special seating (if eligible) or an onboard wheelchair. Finally, make sure to call the airline to reconfirm all access arrangements, 24 hours prior to your flight.

Cruises

CAN YOU ALSO save money by booking a cruise online? More and more cruise websites offer some type of discount booking option, but what about access? Can you really book an accessible cabin online at those discount cruise websites?

According to accessible cruise expert and travel agency owner Connie George, none of the major cruise lines release their accessible cabins to the discount cruise websites. This is done to ensure that the accessible cabins go to people who need them. Says George, "If you want to book online, you have to book a nonaccessible cabin and then call the cruise line or dot com agency to see if an accessible cabin is available in that category. Then you have to change your reservation."

Is the savings worth the hassle? That depends on how you define savings. Yes, you may pay a lower cruise fare if you book with a discount cruise website, but that's only part of the total cruise price. Most dot com agencies operate on volume and their agents (who aren't usually trained in disability travel) can't afford to spend time on the telephone fielding questions. In short, customer service is slim to nonexistent.

If you book through a discount cruise website, you'll have to follow through with the cruise line regarding any special needs, such as medical equipment allowed on board, rental equipment delivered to the ship, specific access features of your cabin, and accessible transportation to and from the port. You'll also have to research each port, determine its accessibility and, in most cases, plan your own accessible shore excursions. The cost of these calls alone (many of which are international) can far outweigh any money saved by booking online.

When comparing savings, it's important to compare the bottom line costs of both options. This includes the extra time and money it takes to make the accessible arrangements after you book your cruise. The cruise fare is just part of the total cruise cost. In most cases, discount websites don't really offer any substantial savings on accessible cabins. Your best bet is to book directly through the cruise line or deal with a travel agent who specializes (really specializes) in accessible cruises.

The Solution

IN TRUTH, THERE is no one perfect solution for booking accessible travel arrangements online. Different people have different preferences and different needs. The best solution for many people may be a combination of the methods outlined in this chapter. It pays to be creative, so don't be afraid to customize a method that works best for you.

Learn your rights, plan your route, watch for special deals, and then book your best price online, or shop around for a travel agent to do it for you. After all, the Internet isn't for everybody. The choice is yours. And as I said earlier, there isn't a one-click solution to online booking. Be wary of any website that claims otherwise. In reality, the Internet is great tool for travelers, but it's not the only tool.

Accessible Recreation
A World of Choices | 14

OR MANY PEOPLE, recreation is an integral part of travel. In fact, for some people it's the main reason for travel. People go to great lengths to enjoy their favorite recreational activities at home and while on holiday. In the past, most recreational facilities only focused on able-bodied travelers, but today many facilities are accessible to people with disabilities.

Additionally, many companies, facilities, and services now use universal design to achieve barrier-free access. These welcome changes allow travelers with disabilities many new options for vacation-time recreational fun. Although there's literally a world of choices, here's a sampling of some accessible recreation possibilities.

Trails and Boardwalks

LET'S START WITH the basics: accessible nature trails. They come in all shapes and sizes. It's great to be able to roll along a trail and get an up-close-and-personal look at nature. Unfortunately, accessible trails are not the norm today, and you do have to search them out.

Additionally, finding an accessible trail that meets your specific access needs can be difficult. Although there are legal definitions for access, there are also personal definitions of what access means. What may work for one person, might be inaccessible to the next. For this reason, the best strategy is to ask specific questions relating to your particular access needs. This applies to the outdoor environment as well as to any unfamiliar place you are traveling.

On the positive side, more developers are now incorporating the principles of universal design into trail construction whenever possible. Of course, some folks have been doing this for years. Take the National Sports Center for the Disabled (NSCD) for example.

Founded in 1970, the NSCD is a nonprofit organization based in Winter Park, Colorado. They provide a wide range of recreational opportunities for children and adults with disabilities—everything from skiing to sailing. They are truly the leaders in adaptive recreation in the United States. Among other things, they constructed the Bonfils Stanton Outdoor Center at their Winter Park location. This unique outdoor center includes a variety of accessible trails. It's the perfect venue for a bevy of accessible activities including camping, fishing, hiking, and picnicking.

Variety is the keyword at Bonfils Stanton, especially when talking about accessible trails. Besides a 1.2-mile boardwalk, they also

Figure 14.1.
Accessible boardwalk at NSCD's Bonfils Stanton Outdoor Center in Winter Park, Colorado.

have the Challenger Trail. This undulating dirt trail has grades from 2% to 6% and was designed for those people who want to work up a sweat. There is no charge for admission or camping at Bonfils Stanton, but advance reservations are required for camping. The campground features raised tent platforms, accessible restrooms, and is open from May 29 to September 30.

A little further south in Kenosha Pass Colorado, Wilderness on Wheels (WOW) operates what they call a "Model Wilderness Access Facility." The WOW facility has an accessible boardwalk and cabins, plus camping and fishing facilities. All facilities were constructed by volunteers, and most of the materials were donated.

The WOW boardwalk is 8 feet wide and winds around a well-stocked trout pond. This fishing pond is reserved for people with disabilities. A nearby stream is for able-bodied fishermen. The boardwalk follows the contour of the land, and it's lined with willow trees and natural vegetation. Pack a picnic lunch and spend the day with nature at the WOW boardwalk or plan to camp overnight.

Figure 14.2.
Accessible campsite at WOW in Kenosha Pass, Colorado.

The WOW facility offers accessible campsites for overnight guests. All campsites have raised tent platforms and one even has a covered dining area. There is no charge for admission or camping at the WOW boardwalk, but advance reservations are required. The WOW facility is open from April to October.

Another accessible trail option are Rail Trails; trails that are built on abandoned rail corridors. More than 700 Rail Trails exist across the United States, and many are accessible. Most Rail Trails are flat or have a minimal grade, so they are excellent for wheelchair-users and handcyclists. The Rails to Trails Conservancy in Washington D.C. has several guide books, plus online information about Rail Trail accessibility.

Additionally, you can search for accessible Rail Trails on the Trail Link Database at traillink.com. This searchable database contains information on Rail Trails throughout the United States. You can search the database by state or by activity ("wheelchair access" is included as an activity). Each entry includes a description of the trail, including the length and surface composition, along with parking and trailhead information.

Many state, regional, and local parks also have access information available. Of course, this comes in a variety of forms. Some parks have access information on their websites and some even have access guides.

And when all else fails, pick up the phone and ask to talk to the accessibility director or somebody who is familiar with the access features of the park or facility. Remember, just because access information isn't prominently displayed doesn't mean that it doesn't exist; in fact, sometimes it's hidden behind the counter, or in a forgotten corner of the office. Always remember to ask for access information!

National Parks

NATIONAL PARKS CAN also be good places for accessible recreation, although some parks are better than others. In truth, most parks have at least some facilities or services that are accessible, even if it's just a visitors center. Indeed, a very wide variety of accessible trails and facilities is available in our national parks. Here's a sampling of what you will find.

Rocky Mountain National Park has some nicely done accessible trails and accessible campsites. The nicest accessible trail is the Coyote Valley Trail, located 5.4 miles from the west entrance to the park. It's made of hard-packed dirt and winds along the river and through a meadow. This interpretive trail is very accessible, and it's an excellent place to view wildlife. Other accessible trails are located at Bear Lake, Sprague Lake, and Lily Lake.

Trails are made accessible for different reasons. Over in Florida, the Everglades has a number of accessible boardwalks and a new accessible visitors center. These facilities were rebuilt to be accessible after they were destroyed by Hurricane Andrew.

The boardwalk Anhinga Trail is one of the most accessible trails in the park. This half-mile boardwalk winds through sawgrass pines and Taylor Slough and is the home to a wealth of bird life. You'll see blue herons, white ibis, and snowy egrets along with the namesake anhingas. The anhingas (also called water turkeys) can be seen in abundance drying their colorful wings in the sun, or perched peacefully in trees along the trail. The Anhinga Trail is also an excellent place to get a close look at alligators.

Other accessible trails in the Everglades are the Pahayokee Trail, the Mahogany Hammock Trail, and West Lake Trail. These boardwalk trails are all less than 3/4- mile long, and each offers a slightly different view of the Everglades. The Pahayokee Trail, located 12.5 miles from the southern park entrance, is a good place to see alligators hidden among the sawgrass and cypress vegetation. A short boardwalk leads to an elevated observation tower, which has an accessible ramp.

Seven miles down the road, the Mahogany Hammock Trail winds through a magnificent tropical mahogany jungle. There are a few slight inclines on this trail, and it's a much easier roll if you follow the trail in a counterclockwise direction. West Lake Trail, located 30.5

miles from the south park entrance, offers a nice stroll through the mangrove forest that surrounds the shallow West Lake. Raccoons, lizards, and snakes are the prevalent wildlife along this trail.

Out west, Yosemite National Park also offers a variety of accessible trails. Happy Isles trail is a prime example of how an accessible trail can be integrated into the existing landscape without impacting the environment. This gently sloping trail crosses the Merced River in two spots and is made of decomposed granite.

Another nice trail is the trail to Mirror Lake. Although this trail gets a bit steep at the top, visitors with a disabled placard are allowed to drive on the trail. The trails around the lake vary in accessibility, but most wheelers can access some of them. It's a very peaceful place, with beautiful views.

Speaking of great views, one of Yosemite's newest access upgrades is located at Glacier Point, about 45 minutes from the valley floor. Glacier Point is the place to get a spectacular view of the entire park, and many recent improvements, including new ramps and trails,

Figure 14.3.
Glacier Point in Yosemite National Park offers good access and a spectacular view.

have (finally) made this Yosemite landmark nicely accessible.

Although the natural entrance to Carlsbad Caverns is not accessible, visitors can reach the Big Room by elevator. A large section of the Big Room (where you'll find some spectacular rock formations) is accessible. A few areas are roped off to wheelchair-users (for safety reasons), but it's still possible to see most areas of the Big Room. Additionally, accessible nature trails and picnic sites are located near the visitor center and at nearby Rattlesnake Springs.

No matter which national park you choose to visit, advance research is a must. The best place to start is the national parks website at nps.gov. Some parks have access information listed, while others only have contact phone numbers. Sometimes you have to pick up the phone and talk directly to a park employee to find out about access.

Park rangers can be a good source of access information. For example, I've been going to Yosemite for over 40 years, but just last year I found out about Washburn Point from a ranger. Located about a half-mile below Glacier Point, it's nicely accessible, has a spectacular view, and is less crowded that nearby Glacier Point. The ranger knew about access because his sister is a wheelchair-user. It never hurts to ask.

Finally, if a visit to a National Park is in your future, be sure to get your free Golden Access Passport. This lifetime pass is good for free admission to all national parks, monuments, historic sites, recreation areas, and wildlife refuges. Pass holders also receive a 50% discount on campsites. The Golden Access Passport can be obtained at any national park entrance or Bureau of Land Management (BLM) office. There is no charge for the Golden Access Passport, but proof of disability (such as a doctor's letter or SSDI check stub) is required. For more information about the Golden Access Passport, visit nps.gov or call your local BLM office.

Campsites and Cabins

MANY PEOPLE LIKE to stay in or near recreation areas. Accessible lodging choices range from camping and rustic cabins, to luxury lodges and resorts.

Although camping is the traditional way to enjoy the great outdoors, campgrounds are not always accessible. Additionally, if a campground is listed as accessible, it's a good idea to inquire about the specific access features. Most often accessible means that the campground has a level campsite, accessible parking, and an accessible bathroom. Raised camping platforms are not the standard, so be prepared to sleep on the ground.

Some campgrounds will reserve accessible campsites in advance and some won't; it pays to check in advance. A number of accessible facilities like Bonfils Stanton and WOW have gone the full nine yards to make their campsites fully accessible.

If pitching a tent isn't exactly your style, then consider a USDA Forest Service Cabin. They're a bit rustic, and indeed some are very basic, but they're a great choice if you love the outdoors. They are located across the United States, and some are accessible, depending on when they were built or remodeled.

For example, in Alaska barrier-free Forest Service cabins are located at West Point, Kah Sheets Lake, Heckman Lake, Green Island, and Virginia Lake. Each cabin includes a table and benches, plywood bunks, a wood or oil heating stove, a broom, and an outhouse. The cabins don't have electricity, bedding, or cooking utensils. Reservations for Forest Service cabins can be made up to 180 days in advance through the National Recreation Reservation Service.

State parks are also good resources for accessible cabins. For example, Smallwood State Park is doing a great job of providing accessible lodgings. This Maryland state park has four accessible cabins; two cabins are located in the woods and two cabins overlook the Potomac River. The cabins all have electricity and air conditioning. Visitors can also enjoy the accessible facilities of the park, including the floating marina, fixed docks, boat launch, fish cleaning stations, and the pedestrian walkway along the shore.

The Wisconsin Department of Natural Resources (DNR) has accessible cabins available at Kettle Moraine State Forest, Buckhorn

State Park, Mirror Lake State Park, and Potawatomi State Park. Each cabin has one bedroom equipped with two hospital beds and a Hoyer lift, a living room with a full-size sleeper sofa and two cots, and a bathroom with a roll-in shower, a fold-down shower bench, and a shower-commode chair. All cabins have heating and air conditioning, lowered kitchen counters, an attached screened porch, and an outdoor fire ring. The cabins rent for a very affordable $30 per night.

And then there are yurts; Oregon's version of luxury camping. Yurts are permanent domed structures with plywood floors, framed doors, electricity, and skylights. They are furnished (you supply the bedding) and can sleep up to five people. They are located in many of Oregon's state campgrounds and are a bargain at just $27 per night.

Cooking is not allowed inside the yurts, but there are picnic and barbecue areas outside. Bathroom facilities are available in accessible community bathrooms. Some yurts are accessible, but you

Figure 14.4.
Accessible yurts are available at many state campgrounds in Oregon.

need to specify that you need an accessible yurt when you make your reservation. Reservations are a must, as yurts are popular and sell out quickly.

And if you really want to get up-close-and-personal with nature, consider Mala Mala safari camp in South Africa. The Mala Mala main camp is set in beautiful surroundings on the banks of the Sand River. The thatched roof buildings are located on manicured lawns and surrounded by mature shade trees.

Mala Mala main camp has an accessible suite complete with ramps, wide doorways, wheelchair-height furniture, and a bathroom with a roll-in shower and shower seat. The facilities were designed with the assistance of the Quadriplegic Association of South Africa to meet international standards for accessibility.

And for a safari experience a little closer to home, check out Safari West in Santa Rosa, California. This 400-acre game preserve is home to a bevy of exotic animals and birds, most of which roam free inside the gated compound. Safari West has two accessible lux-

Figure 14.5.
Accessible tent cabin at Safari West game preserve in Santa Rosa, California.

ury tent cabins with hardwood floors, canvas sides and tops, indoor plumbing, and electricity. Just like the upscale safari camps in Africa.

Access features in each accessible tent cabin include a ramped entry, wide doorways, ample room to maneuver a wheelchair, a roll-in shower with a fold-down shower seat, a hand-held shower head, and grab bars in the shower and around the toilet. Both tent cabins have a roomy porch with great views of the giraffe enclosure. It's the ideal place to watch the sunset and enjoy a glass of wine.

Hit the Beach

A LOT OF recreational activities revolve around the water. Indeed, the beach is a popular recreational venue. You can choose to simply sit and enjoy the sand and surf or opt for a refreshing dip in the ocean. Beach access varies and includes everything from beach chairs and hard-packed sand to barrier-free access by ramps. But many beaches are not accessible at all.

One way to access the beach is in a beach wheelchair. These specially made wheelchairs have wide plastic tires that are designed to navigate sandy beaches. The major drawback is that most beach wheelchairs are not self-propelling, so you need somebody to push you.

The exception to this rule can be found at San Diego's Mission Beach, home of the world's first motorized beach wheelchair, the Beach Cruzr. Although the Beach Cruzr looks like a standard beach wheelchair, it's powered by two 24-volt motors. This allows wheelchair-users independent access to the beach. Two Beach Cruzrs are available for free loan on a first-come basis at the Mission Beach lifeguard station.

Alternatively, a variety of companies manufacture standard beach wheelchairs, and you can buy your own and take it with you to the beach. They are made to disassemble easily, so they fit nicely into a car trunk or in the cargo bin of an airplane. Remember though, you will need somebody to push you.

Many state parks, beaches, and resorts also provide beach wheelchairs for loan. Although there isn't a master list of venues that provide them, some beach wheelchair dealers have this information, so ask if they have a list of recreation areas that use their equipment. Some dealers also provide this information online. Do an Internet search under "beach wheelchairs" and see what you find. Additionally, many state beaches and national recreation areas have beach wheelchairs for loan. When in doubt, always ask.

Beach wheelchairs are OK, but direct access to the beach is even better. Unfortunately, not many beaches have ramp access, but those that do are very well done. Take Luquillo Beach in Puerto Rico, for example. The sand is hard-packed and negotiable in a scooter and there is also a ramp to the water. An accessible walkway runs along the shore, with access to outside showers, picnic areas, and a playground. Accessible parking places, changing rooms, showers, and restrooms are located at the far end of the parking lot. Luquillo Beach is one the most beautiful beaches in the Caribbean. It's also the most accessible.

Another way to access the water is via beach mats. Although this concept hasn't exactly taken off full throttle yet, some cities are installing beach mats at their public beaches. These portable rubberized pathways provide a firm and flat trail over the sand. Currently, beach mats are available at Ala Moana Regional Park in Honolulu, several of Chicago's Lake Michigan beaches, and Hilton Head Island's Coligny Beach Park. Hopefully, this concept will catch on at other public beaches.

A very unique approach to beach access is found at the Yaquina Head Tidepools on the central Oregon coast. This coastal headland area was established by Congress in 1980; in 1992-1994, the Bureau of Land Management (BLM) reclaimed the Yaquina Head rock quarry and converted it to a rocky intertidal area.

The BLM also made the intertidal area wheelchair accessible—a first for the Oregon coast. Accessible pathways allow wheelchair-users to roll along and explore the tidepools. Wheelchair-users can park in the lower parking lot and just roll on down to the tidepools. The paved paths go right into the intertidal area. There are also a few raised tidepools that are just the right viewing height for wheelers. Yaquina Head gets high marks for barrier-free design.

Water Sports

FROM FISHING TO sailing, the water attracts professional athletes and weekend amateurs alike. Fishing continues to be a popular recreational activity. For those who prefer to fish from shore, many choices are available. In fact, access doesn't have to be elaborate. Over in Frasier, Colorado, the local Lions Club constructed a very simple accessible fishing area around their local fishing hole. They did two things; first they built an accessible dock so that wheelchair-users can just roll on and fish.

Second, they constructed some safety barriers that allow wheelchair-users to fish safely from shore. The wheelchair-height barriers have one rail across the top and, although they prevent wheelers from rolling into the water, they don't obstruct the view. Of course, they are made of natural material, so they blend in with the environment.

Sailing is another fun way to enjoy the water. Passengers can sit back and enjoy a leisurely sail or they can actively participate in the navigation of the vessel. NSCD is a leader in adaptive sailing and, in 1999, they added yet another dimension to their already popular sailing program, with the addition of *Sea Legs* to their fleet.

Sea Legs is a customized sailboat, specially constructed so that it can be fully operated from a seated position. Fitted with an accessible fiberglass mold, all sailing operations can be completed from two swivel seats that allow access to the entire boat. You don't have to be able to walk to learn to sail; sailing lessons are available at the NSCD, and no previous sailing experience is required. Graduates of the course (or any sailing course) are also eligible to rent *Sea Legs* for their own sailing experience on Lake Granby.

And if you've ever dreamed of sailing a tall ship, then check out the Jubilee Sailing Trust (JST), a British nonprofit organization.

The JST operates two accessible tall ships, the *Lord Nelson* and the *Tenacious*; and JST participants are not just passengers, they are members of the crew. Wheelers and able-bodied crew members work side by side.

Accessible features on board JST ships include flat wide decks suitable for wheelchair-users, lifts between the decks, wheelchair tie downs, and accessible living quarters. JST stresses integration and inclusion in all of their programs.

Another British organization, the Disabled Sailors Associations (DSA), is working hard to provide accessible sailing opportunities to more people. Their goal is to make sailing accessible for everyone. DSA designed and built the *Verity K*, the world's first wheelchair accessible 35-foot cruising yacht. The *Verity K* is available for hire by any disabled sailor, at very reasonable rates. A skipper can also be provided by the DSA for those who lack the proper sailing experience.

A good one-stop resource for sailors is The Sailing Web (www.footeprint.com/sailingweb). This comprehensive website includes loads of information about adaptive sailing, from sailing clubs and accessible sailboats, to competitions and ports of call.

For those who want to explore the undersea world, scuba diving is a great choice. The Handicapped Scuba Association (HSA) sets standards and trains instructors in adaptive techniques. They also arrange dive trips for members, and they are very knowledgeable about accessible dive resorts around the world.

Although many divers choose land-based vacations, another option is to live on a dive boat. Live Dive Pacific operates two accessible live-aboard diving boats, the *Fiji Aggressor* and the *Kona II*. The *Fiji Aggressor* is the most accessible boat. It has a specially designed hydraulic skiff lift, a wheelchair elevator, and shower stalls with seats. Both boats were evaluated by members of the HSA.

And although it's not exactly a sport, if you want to get up-close-and-personal with a dolphin (or two), then check out the Dolphin Research Center (DRC) in Grassy Keys, Florida. This marine research center offers an excellent half-day dolphin interaction program. This popular program begins with a dolphin education workshop and culminates with a structured dolphin-swim.

Access at DRC is excellent, with an emphasis on integration and the removal of physical barriers. Says Marry Stella of DRC, "We don't have only one program that is accessible. Instead, if a person wants to participate in any of our programs, we do our best to make it possible."

Fun in the Snow

SKIING IS A POPULAR winter activity, and a ski vacation makes a great winter getaway. The good news is that a wide variety of adaptive equipment helps people with all types of disabilities enjoy the excitement of downhill skiing and Nordic sports. Truly, there is something for just about everybody.

Downhill skiers can either stand up or sit down to ski, depending on their ability. Stand-up skiers use outriggers for balance. Outriggers are modified ski poles with mini-skis attached to the ends. Three-track skiers use one ski and two outriggers, while four-track skiers use two skis and two outriggers. Sometimes a ski bra is also used in conjunction with this technique, to help skiers control the position of their ski tips.

Sit-down skiers can use either a mono-ski, a bi-ski, or a sit-ski. A mono-ski is a fiberglass shell and a monoshock, mounted on top of a single ski. Mono skiers use two shortened outriggers to steer and turn the mono-ski. Mono-skis are a good choice for people who have disabilities affecting their legs, but still have some upper body strength.

A bi-ski is constructed much like a mono-ski, except the bi-ski is mounted on two skis. This extra ski offers added stability and balance. Bi-skis are used by people who have limited upper body strength, along with limited or no lower body strength. A bi-skier may ski independently or may be tethered (pulled) by an instructor.

A sit-ski is a sled-like piece of adaptive equipment, which is used by people who have very limited or no mobility. The sit-ski is tethered at all times, but sometimes skiers are able to assist in steering the sit-ski by using a ski pole.

Cross-country skiing is great exercise for both stand-up and sit-down skiers, and it can be adapted for a wide range of disabilities. It gets you away-from-the-madding-crowds and, depending on your luck and location, it can allow you an up-close-and-personal glimpse of the local wildlife. Remember to pack your binoculars, as you never know what you will see. Many handcyclists and wheelchair racers take up cross-country skiing to stay in shape during the winter, but you don't have to be a super athlete to enjoy this sport.

Participants who can stand up use traditional cross country skiing equipment: long narrow skis with bindings that attach to the toe of the boot. Skiers who can't stand up, walk, or have problems maintaining their balance use a sit-ski. Sit-skiers propel themselves with shortened ski poles in this adapted sled-like device.

Equipment makers are developing new sit-skis that add kick to each push, resulting in more slide for each arm movement. Of course, most adaptive ski schools are pros at altering and tweaking existing equipment to meet individual needs, so don't be afraid to call them up and ask what they can do for you.

Adaptive snow sports are available in the United States, Canada, Europe, New Zealand, and Australia. Two good adaptive skiing resources are Disabled Sports USA (DSUSA) and the NSCD. Additionally, the Emerging Horizons website (EmergingHorizons.com) has an updated list of adaptive ski schools around the world. Most adaptive ski schools will custom tailor equipment to meet individual needs. For best results, check with the facility in advance, explain your disability in detail, and find out what equipment is available.

Before You Go

IT GOES WITHOUT saying that advance research is necessary before you hit the road, however there's another important aspect to consider whenever recreation is a major part of your holiday. Always remember to take any recreational equipment or adaptive devices with you.

Says wheelchair-athlete Sharon Myers, "Athletes who use wheelchairs need to be aware that some airlines may charge them a fee for bringing along their extra sports wheelchair. These chairs would be in the same category as a surf board, skis, or other device used for sports by the able-bodied."

Indeed, sometimes figuring out how to take all your equipment with you can take just as much planning as your travel arrangements. But it's well worth the added effort. This point is aptly illustrated by the following story from Patty, an above-the-knee amputee who wanted to enjoy the water on her family vacation.

"We planned to spend a week at a lakefront resort in upstate New York. My son's baseball team was playing a tournament in Cooperstown, so this wasn't only a family vacation, but also a vacation for the families of all my son's teammates. As we made our plans, I realized that most of our non-baseball time would revolve around fun in the pool and lake. We have two young boys, and I didn't want to be a spectator to their activities; but as a bilateral above the knee amputee, I wasn't sure how much I could participate.

"Sure I swim at home. In fact, I have a set of water legs that are specifically designed for water activities. My water legs allow me to swim, water ski, jet ski, sail, and generally enjoy the water. I used my water legs at home, but I had never traveled with them before. My problem was pretty simple; I just couldn't figure out how to transport my water legs from California to New York.

"I couldn't imagine my husband carrying them down the aisle of the airplane. I wasn't even sure if they'd fit in the overhead bin. If not, I wondered if they would survive the trip in the cargo bin. I've had nightmare airline experiences with my wheelchair, and I didn't want to repeat those with my water legs. Would insurance cover damage to my water legs? Who would take responsibility if they were damaged? I had a lot of questions, and very few answers. So, I called my prosthetist.

"'How do I get my water legs to New York?' I asked. 'Simple,' he responded, 'we'll ship them.' As instructed, I delivered my water legs to my prosthetist, 1 week before we left. Upon arrival, they were waiting for me when I checked into the hotel. There was also a return-shipping label, a roll of packing tape, and even a pair of scissors inside the box. It was obvious they had done this before! I enjoyed my water legs during my vacation. I spent a considerable amount of time in the pool, and I was glad I brought them."

So, even if it takes a little extra work before and after your trip, make sure you take along everything you need to make your vacation enjoyable. You'll be glad you did. And, don't be afraid to ask others for advice. They may have just the solution you need!

Budget Travel | 15
Is It Really Possible?

IS IT REALLY possible to travel on a budget? That depends on your budget. Seriously though, it never hurts to stretch your travel dollar, and to some people, budget travel simply means getting the best deal possible. To others, budget travel has a more concrete definition, usually a dollar amount per day or per trip. Is it really possible to travel on a limited budget without sacrificing access? The answer is a qualified yes. It is possible to put a cap on travel expenses and still get the accessible services you need; however, don't expect to get five-star service for a two-star price. Like everything else, budget travel requires planning and research, and sometimes a little compromise. But the good news is, it is possible. Access and affordability don't have to be mutually exclusive.

What Is Budget Travel?

TO BETTER UNDERSTAND travel costs, let's take a look at two different trips to the same destination. The first trip is a hotel and air package deal, and the second trip is an all-inclusive guided tour. Both tours are accessible, and they use the same hotel. The guided tour includes private tours each day in an accessible minivan, and the hotel package includes a half-day sightseeing tour on an accessible bus. The hotel package costs $800 per person, and the guided tour costs $1,500 per person. Why?

Well, in this case you are paying for service; more specifically, the service of your own personal tour guide in a private vehicle. Is it worth the extra cost? It depends on what you want. If you truly want an all-inclusive escorted tour, then it's usually easier to join a guided tour than to arrange things on your own. On the other hand, if you just want to explore the city yourself, you're probably paying for unneeded services if you join a guided tour. At first glance, the hotel package seems like a deal, but if you plan to tour the city extensively, the hotel package becomes less of a bargain. The first rule of budget travel is to pay only for the services you need, but don't forget to figure in all the associated costs before you pick the best deal.

Choosing Your Destination

PEOPLE CHOOSE VACATION destinations for a variety of reasons, including wheelchair-access. Although it pays to choose an accessible destination, sometimes that just isn't possible. Not every country is as accessible as the United States, and even within U.S. borders some cities are just more accessible than others. On the other hand, you should be aware that the level of access at your destination can raise or lower your vacation expenses.

For example, let's say you choose to go to a relatively inaccessible third-world country. Let's also assume no accessible public transportation is available in this country, but one tour company has an adapted van. In short, that's the only way you will be able to tour that country—in the adapted van. You will also need the services of a tour escort because many of the attractions and hotels have steps, and you'll need to be lifted up and down them in your wheelchair. Is this a budget trip? No, and quite frankly the only thing you can do to change that is to find a more accessible destination.

Remember this rule: The relative accessibility of any destination, along with the availability of local accessible transportation and tour services, is a major factor in determining the cost of any trip. In the above case, the cost will be higher because of the high level of personal assistance required and because of the lack of competition among accessible tour operators. This is usually true in any country that does not have a high level of accessible facilities and services.

If, however, you can make do without accessible transportation and a minimum of personal assistance, you may be able to do it on a budget. Generally speaking, labor is very cheap in third-world countries. In other words, it might not cost very much to hire an attendant to help carry you up the stairs and get you in and out of taxis. The key here is to deal locally and not through a U.S. tour operator. This option is not for everyone, but I do know people who have gone this route.

Choosing a more accessible destination usually helps to lower your travel costs. This doesn't mean that you have to stick with U.S. destinations, but you may have to compromise to find something that fits your budget. Truly, if your dream vacation is to go to the furthest reaches of Nepal, then go for it; however, realize that this is not the budget option.

The more flexibility you have destination wise, the more money you'll save. It's often a good idea to pick several destinations and then go with the one that offers the best travel deal.

Timing Is Everything

IT GOES WITHOUT saying that travel costs rise during peak travel times, so for the best deals it pays to travel in the off season. So when is the off season? That depends on a number of things, including your destination.

Travel prices rise drastically during the holidays, in fact it's the most expensive time to travel, even if you stay with family. It's hard to postpone the holidays, however, so sometimes travel during this time is essential. What do you do then? If you must travel around the holidays, then start shopping early for your air ticket. Watch the airfare sales and snap up your ticket early in the year. Don't wait until the month before Thanksgiving to buy your air ticket.

If you don't have to travel during Christmas and Thanksgiving, and your schedule is flexible, then a little research can help lower your travel costs. The first step is to determine the peak travel season for your destination. This varies from destination to destination. A good way to determine the peak season is to look at lodging and resort rates for your destination. Most have high, low, and shoulder season rates listed, along with a definition of each season. Check several resorts in the same area to get a good idea of when the peak and low seasons occur.

Generally speaking, the best time to travel is in the shoulder season. Remember, the low season is usually the low season for a very good reason. Many times, it's weather related. Additionally, in some resort areas, many of the attractions are closed during the low season.

Then there's what MSNBC's Peter Greenberg calls the dead week, the 10 days following New Years Day. During this time virtually every segment of the travel industry offers substantial discounts. It's a great time to take a vacation. You'll find good deals on hotel rooms, air fares, and cruise packages. It's also a nice time to travel because not many people travel during this time. In fact, that's why there are so many deep discounts.

It's a simple case of supply and demand. During this time, people are just returning to work from their holiday excursions. The Christmas bills are coming in and most people just don't think about travel at this time. So, if you want to grab a really good deal, plan ahead, be flexible, and travel during the dead week.

Airfares

THERE IS NO magic formula for finding the lowest airfare. Of course, that statement is nothing short of blasphemy to many people. Everybody has their own tried and true method. I have friends who subscribe to virtually every airline e-mail list, and those who use complicated software programs. I even know people who call up 12 different travel agents every week until they find a bargain. And they all have their own rules, like, "Never book a ticket on the third Monday of any month that begins with the letter 'J'."

Of course, they all swear that their own method is the only real way to good deal. I don't buy it. I mean, why don't I just swing a garlic necklace over my head three times, face north, and hit the "book your fare now" button. To me, it all seems like a lot of trouble. Life is just too short.

I use the common sense approach. In my book, there are two simple rules for finding the lowest airfare. First, you have to know the regular price of the airfare to your destination. Second, you have to accept the fact that somebody on the airplane probably got a better deal than you did. Otherwise, shopping for a bargain airfare becomes an obsession.

My method is pretty simple. After you decide when and where you want to travel, find out the regular price of the airfare to your destination. Why? So you will be able to recognize a good deal when you see it. After all, how can you tell if something is a bargain if you don't even know the regular price? Check the prices on the Internet weekly until you find your best fare. Then buy the ticket, and don't look back.

Where is the best place to check airfares online? I prefer the airline websites because I know what I'm getting. I know I'm not comparing apples to oranges when I'm looking at two different airfares. I'm able to see the aircraft type, routings, and seating diagrams on the airline websites, and these are all critical factors when I choose a flight. In most cases, you do get what you pay for, in regards to airfares.

In my opinion, an airfare is no longer a bargain if I have to fly in a turbo prop and change planes three times. You'll also find sales and special deals on airline websites, deals that you won't find in other places. It really doesn't matter which airline website you use. Choose your favorite airline or check several competitors, but, remember to use a U.S. flag air carrier to ensure access mandated under the Air Carrier Access Act (ACAA).

Of course, it pays to fly in the shoulder or low seasons. Additionally, try to fly midweek. Tuesdays and Wednesdays are usually the best days for the lowest airfares. Business travelers pay the highest airfares, so flights on Monday and Friday are usually the most expensive. Finally, shop around for airfare and hotel packages, as sometimes these deals offer hefty discounts on both the airfare and the hotel rates. If you choose this option, you'll need to find out what hotels are used by the airline and then investigate their access on your own. A word of warning here: Never rely on the airlines for hotel access information!

Attendant Airfare Discounts

WOULDN'T IT BE great to get free airfare for your attendant? Now, that would really reduce your travel costs, wouldn't it? Well, it's a nice dream, but in reality that's all it is, a dream. The cold hard truth is that no airlines offer this perk.

Although there's no such thing as free air travel for attendants, a few airlines do offer discounted travel. As with everything airline-related, some restrictions apply, so contact the air carriers directly for more information. Currently no U.S. airlines offer discounted attendant travel, but here's the latest rundown of non-U.S. air carriers that do offer some sort of attendant fares.

Air Canada offers some reduced fares for attendant travel. The attendant must be able to care for the passenger during the flight, and the reduced fare is limited in availability. Additionally, this special fare is only offered on flights within North America. Contact Air Canada for details and restrictions.

Quantas Airlines offers the Qantas Carer Concession Card scheme, which enables people with high support needs and their attendants to travel at reduced rates. Through this scheme, both the person with high support needs and their attendant are able to travel at 50% off any full-priced domestic Qantas flight.

To be eligible for this fare, you must require one-on-one support with meals, drinks, transferring to the bathroom, and communicating with the crew. People who only need assistance boarding and deplaning or wheelchair assistance at the airport are not eligible for this fare. The Qantas Carer Concession Card scheme is administered by NICAN. The fee for the card is $27.50 (Australian) and the card is valid for 3 years.

Lodging

ANOTHER WAY TO stretch your travel dollar is to rein in those ever-escalating lodging costs. According to PKF consulting, a San Francisco-based travel research firm, hotel rates have increased 37% since 1995. The good news is, it's still possible to find lodging that's both affordable and accessible. I've already covered some budget lodging options such as hostels and home exchanges in the "Finding the Right Room" chapter, however there are few other ways to lower your lodging costs.

First, consider the location of your hotel. Generally speaking, you will pay more for downtown hotels rather than those out in the suburbs. However, make sure it won't cost you more in transportation costs to get downtown if you choose a suburban hotel. Sometimes it's just more economical to pay the higher downtown hotel rates if there are no accessible public transportation options nearby. Additionally, don't forget to ask about senior discounts, auto club rates, or other special deals when booking a room. Some special discounts aren't widely advertised, and it never hurts to ask.

Many hotel chains, such as Microtel and Motel 6, offer accessible rooms at reasonable rates. Microtel gets the highest marks for consistent access, as all Microtel properties are constructed from the ground up with access in mind. Their goal is to be the preferred motel chain for travelers with disabilities. So far, they've done a great job, and their rates start at a very affordable $39.95.

Motel 6 can also offer good access, but unfortunately they're not very consistent. When they're good, they're very good; however, when they're bad, you have to almost be a contortionist to use the toilet. Most of their newly constructed (post ADA) properties are nicely accessible, so look for properties constructed after 1992. Their remodeled properties are access nightmares, so make sure to ask a lot of questions before you book a room.

And if your travels take you across the Big Pond, you can't beat Travel Inns for access and value in the United Kingdom. Says Ann Litt of Undiscovered Britain, "All Travel Inns have at least a couple of adapted rooms which have wide doorways, grab bars, adapted bathrooms and low rise tubs. They're not luxury properties, but they are clean, affordable, and accessible." Rates start at $85 per night.

Of course, you can always look to the great outdoors for some budget lodging options. If that's your choice, don't leave home without your Golden Access Passport, a free lifetime pass available to any U.S. resident with a permanent disability. Pass holders get free admission to all national parks, and a 50% discount on campsites. For more information about the Golden Access Passport, contact your local Bureau of Land Management office or visit the National Parks Service website. Golden Access Passports are available at all national park entrances.

Transportation

ONE OF THE most expensive components of any trip is accessible ground transportation. Many people don't even consider this as a cost of travel because sometimes it's added into the cost of a group tour. But even if you don't see it as an itemized cost, the high cost of accessible ground transportation helps push up the price of many tours.

Why is accessible transportation so expensive? According to one veteran accessible tour operator, skyrocketing insurance costs are to blame for the high cost of accessible transportation. This tour operator bought a bus, converted it, and made it accessible. She then had to let it sit because the insurance was so expensive. She eventually sold her bus to a bus company that gutted it and converted it back to its original nonaccessible incarnation.

One option for many accessible small tour operators is to lease an accessible bus. The down side is that accessible buses are in short supply, and the leasing companies also have to pay high insurance costs. The result? These high costs are passed on to the tour operator and ultimately to their customers.

Although U.S. tour operators are not allowed to charge a person with a disability more than an able-bodied person for the same tour, sometimes accessible specialty tours are more expensive to all customers. The reason is that once you make a tour vehicle accessible, you lose a number of seats, and for tour operators to make a profit, sometimes they have to raise the price per seat.

It's hard to fault the tour operators for this, as they are really caught in the middle. Additionally, some accessible tour operators provide an excellent service and, in the end, that's really what you are paying for, the service. So shop around for accessible tours, but realize that if the tour involves transportation in an accessible bus, it will most likely raise the price. In truth, tour operators are caught between a rock and a hard spot here. Ultimately, it's the insurance companies that are raking in the dough!

So what's a traveler to do? If you're on a budget, consider booking a few day tours in an accessible vehicle instead of opting for a fully escorted tour. Check around for accessible public transportation options in your destination city.

Taxis can sometimes be hired for half-day sightseeing tours, and many taxis are accessible. Additionally, you might want to rent your own self-drive accessible van for a few days. This is not a cheap option as most accessible vans run $100 (or more) per day; however, you may only need to rent one for a few days if you organize your activities appropriately. Research makes the difference, so investigate your accessible transportation options long before you depart for the airport. Your pre-trip research could translate into valuable savings.

Cruises

CRUISES ARE A popular travel option and, like everything else, it pays to be flexible with your travel dates and destinations for the best cruise deals. Additionally, you should understand a few things about cruise pricing to maximize your savings.

First, the brochure price of a cruise is comparable to the sticker price of a car. In short, it's like the suggested retail price, and most cruise passengers pay less than the brochure price. In fact, some passengers pay substantially less than the brochure price. How do they do that? The best way to get a good price on your dream cruise is to work with a travel agent who monitors cruise prices (at least) weekly.

It's also important to remember to compare like products when shopping for a cruise. Although many discount cruise websites offer bargain-basement cruise fares, it's important to note that these Internet companies do not offer any level of service beyond booking the cruise. To get information on accessible cabins, airport transfers, and shore excursions you need to work with a travel agent who specializes in accessible cruises. Truly, a knowledgeable travel agent can be your ticket to the best overall cruise deal.

Cruise prices rise and fall like the stock market, even though the general public isn't always aware of these fluctuations. It's a simple case of supply and demand, and most price fluctuations are based on cabin availability. Once you book a cruise, you're locked into that price; however, if your travel agent finds a lower rate before you sail, she can re-book you, lock you into the lower price, and save you big bucks.

This plan of action only works if your travel agent monitors cruise prices frequently. Additionally, it works best when you book your cruise at least 6 months to a year in advance. It's also important to note that even though your cruise price can't increase once you're locked into a specific rate, other fees such as government taxes, port charges, and airline fuel surcharges can still increase.

Another way to save some bucks on a cruise is to look for repositioning cruises. These are fairly well publicized by the cruise lines, and they usually occur at the end of the season when the cruise lines move (reposition) their ships to different routes. The cruise lines have to get their ships from port A to port B to start their new cruise schedule, and it's a great marketing move to also sell the cabins at bargain prices. The downside of a repositioning cruise is that open-jaw airfares (when you fly into one city and out of another one) are sometimes rather expensive. In fact these higher airfares can sometimes offset any cruise savings.

It also pays to let your travel agent know as much about you as possible. Let her know where you live, how old you are, and if you have ever cruised before. These seemingly mundane details can actually be the ticket to big savings in the form of special regional fares, senior specials, or alumni fares. And finally, don't forget to tell your travel agent if you plan to travel with some friends, as sometimes you can earn a free cabin just by putting together a group cruise.

Be Your Own Tour Guide

ANOTHER WAY TO save a few bucks on your travel costs is to be your own tour guide, although this is only a realistic option for those people who have the time and inclination to thoroughly research their destinations. To some people, it's just more trouble than it's worth and, quite frankly, some people would rather pay for the services of a tour guide than spend their valuable time researching access. To others, it's the ticket to savings.

The first step to being your own tour guide starts well before you ever leave home. In fact, valuable time can be lost just getting your bearings in a strange city. To that end, pre-trip research is essential.

I'm constantly reminded of the saga of my friend John, who spent five days in Paris last spring. Indeed, many tour companies told him that this would be an adequate amount of time for him to see his favorite attractions. Unfortunately, John wasted his first two days in Paris just looking for a good city map. He did not do any pre-trip research. The result? He spent most of his time getting his bearings, trying to figure out if the metro was accessible (it's not), and showing up at attractions that were closed. It was a very disappointing trip for John.

The moral of the story is to have your itinerary pretty well mapped out before you hit the road. Study a city map in advance and have a good idea about public transportation options and the operating hours of the major attractions. And don't forget to pack the map!

So, where do you start with your pre-trip research? A good first stop is the local convention and visitors bureau. In addition to

---

detailed city maps and information on local attractions, some convention and visitors bureaus also publish access guides, so don't forget to ask about access information. You might also want to check with the local chamber of commerce.

Contact these resources well in advance and have them mail the tourist information to you. Additionally, you also may want to stop in at the visitors center once you arrive, just to make sure there's nothing you missed. How do you find a local convention and visitors bureau? One good resource is the online directory at ChamberofCommerce.com.

Of course, it also pays to surf the Internet and ask friends and family for resources too. Don't forget to look for free factory tours. A wide variety of businesses offer these free tours, from jelly bean factories to breweries, and many are accessible.

A good resource for searching out accessible factory tours is *Watch It Made in the USA*, by Karen Axelrod and Bruce Brumberg. This handy guide contains detailed information on over 300 factory tours across the United States. Every listing includes general information about the tour, plus details on everything from free samples to wheelchair access.

Many major museums also have free days every week or month. Find out when these are in order to cut down on sightseeing costs. And remember, the free Golden Access Passport is good for free admittance to national monuments, too.

It never hurts to ask about unpublished specials or discounts. Some special rates only apply to certain days or hours—this is where that pre-trip research adds up to some big savings.

Deal Direct and Save

NO MATTER WHAT the product is, the best way to get the lowest price is to deal direct and save. As far as travel is concerned, sometimes that's easier said than done. To maximize your savings, the best plan of action is to hire your own local tour operator. Tour operators usually pay a commission to travel agents, and many times if a commission is involved, it's just cheaper to deal direct.

The first step is to hunt down the local tour operators. One way to do this is to browse through U.S. tour company brochures. Sometimes they mention the name of the local tour operator or sometimes there is a photograph of a tour vehicle with the local company logo. It doesn't hurt to ask the U.S. agent who the local tour operator is, but don't expect any type of useful reply. In fact, you may meet with some resistance from the U.S. agent, but it never hurts to ask. Sometimes agents are willing to give out this information, even if it's only to get you off the phone.

And finally, ask friends, family, and business contacts if they have any resources. Don't forget to investigate every possibility, as you never know when something will pan out. I've made many good contacts from questionable referrals. The goal is to find somebody at your destination who has access to information on local tour operators. Sometimes this involves quite a number of contacts, but don't give up, as the Internet has truly opened up the world. The best advice is to be persistent and remember to be methodical in your quest.

Appendix | A
Resources

YEARS AGO, TRAVEL opportunities for people with disabilities were pretty limited. Today, things have changed, and more and more wheelers are hitting the road. Due to this change, the demand for accurate access information has reached an all time high, and (fortunately) new access resources are popping up every day. So where do you begin your search for these resources?

My favorite resource is *Emerging Horizons*. In fact, that's why I founded the magazine, to provide updated information on barrier-free travel. Along with legal updates and access news, I give *Emerging Horizons* readers travel tips, new resources, and specific access information about destinations.

And believe me, we do go out and research all of our destination pieces. Rest assured that we don't rely on second-hand access information or press releases. We actually investigate the access first-hand. If there's one thing I've learned about access information over the years, it's that you can't rely on third- or fourth-hand information. Something always gets lost in the translation.

So, the next time you read an article about access, find out if the writer actually visited the destination before you accept the information as fact. It will save you a lot of grief. All right, that's the end of my *Emerging Horizons* commercial!

Through the course of my research for *Emerging Horizons*, I've also stumbled across a number of other potential sources of access information. Take note that I said potential sources. In fact, sometimes you'll completely strike out with these sources, but it never hurts to ask.

One of my favorite sources for updated access information is the local Center for Independent Living (CIL). Check with the CIL in your destination city to see if they have any access information on local transportation, attractions, and lodging. You might also want to contact some national disability organizations to see if they have any access information.

Be sure to hit up any disability-related organizations that recently held a conference (or are planning to hold a conference) in your destination city. Many such organizations collect local access information for their conference attendees.

Don't forget about airports and public transportation providers, as sometimes they also provide print access guides. And finally, don't rule out the local Convention and Visitors Bureaus (CVB). Some CVBs incorporate access information in their own tourism publications, while other CVBs work with local organizations to provide this information in separate access guides.

Print Access Guides and Resources

ACCESS GUIDES COME in a variety of forms. For example, in 2000, Access Northern California published San Francisco's first access guide. Today, the San Francisco CVB continues to make this valuable resource available to all visitors. The newest guide contains detailed access information on hotels, restaurants, museums, public transportation, theaters, tourist attractions, and shopping centers. It's available free from the San Francisco Convention and Visitors Bureau at (415) 391-2000. You can also order a copy online at AccessNCA.com. Access Northern California continues to publish updated editions of the guide.

And down in Palm Springs, Palm Springs Tourism worked with the Palm Springs ADA Coordinator to produce *A Mobility Impaired Traveler's Guide to Palm Springs*. This guide features detailed access information on selected lodgings in Palm Springs, along with general access information on the major tourist attractions. It's available free from the Palm Springs Visitor Information center at (800) 347-7746.

The Virginia Tourism Corporation continues to publish yearly updates of *The Virginia Travel Guide* for Persons with Disabilities. This access guide contains travel resources such as dialysis centers, oxygen sources, and equipment-repair facilities, along with information on accessible transportation, attractions, lodgings, and restaurants. It covers the entire state of Virginia. *The Virginia Travel Guide for Persons with Disabilities* is available free from the Virginia Tourism Corporation at (800) 742-3935.

Accessible San Diego (ASD) also produces annual updates of *Access in San Diego*. This guide contains access information on selected hotels, restaurants, public transportation, and tourist attractions. There is a charge for the guide, and it's only available through ASD. For more information call ASD at (858) 279-0704.

Figure 16.1.
Many CVBs publish local access guides. Get your copy of *Access San Francisco* to find out about access to Alcatraz Island (pictured here), as well as other local attractions.

Internet Resources

EVEN THOUGH I think print guides are great, the best place to look for the most updated information is on the Internet. Because of the nature of the medium, the Internet is more conducive to frequent updates. I didn't make up the rules, I just report them. I fully realize that some people out there want nothing to do with the Internet; however, if you totally exclude this medium, you'll miss out on some great access resources.

That doesn't necessarily mean you have to run out and buy a computer. You can easily log on at your local library, or use a friend's computer. If you've never surfed the Internet before, it's best to give it a trial run before you decide to invest in your own equipment. And by all means, remember the Internet is just one source of information, and it's best used in conjunction with information from other media.

So where do you look on the Internet? Although an Internet search under "accessible travel" will return a bevy of selections, sometimes it's best to start out in a more directed way. How do you tell a good website from a bad website? Look for unbiased first-person information. Many websites just post press releases or offers from their advertisers. Just because a website comes up at the top of a search engine doesn't mean it contains the most accurate information.

Scrutinize the content carefully and make sure the person reporting the information actually visited the destination. First-person reporting is essential in barrier-free travel. Bigger is not necessarily better, either. In fact, it's better to have 200 good resources than 10,000 outdated ones. Three of my favorite websites are listed below.

* Wunago - wunago.com
* World On Wheelz - worldonwheelz.com
* Global Access - geocities.com/Paris/1502

And then there is *Emerging Horizons*. Of course, we have a website! In fact, we have a searchable database of accessible travel resources on our website at EmergingHorizons.com. I check the resources every month and delete outdated entries and add new ones. Feel free to drop by and browse our travel resources, and drop me an e-mail if you have a resource to suggest. Bear in mind that we don't accept any advertising on our website, and all *Emerging Horizons'* resources must contain specific information on accessible travel.

Chapter-by-Chapter Resources

HERE'S A CHAPTER-by-chapter rundown of the resources (along with complete contact information) that are mentioned throughout the book.

Up, Up, and Away
Air Travel

New Horizons: Information for the Air Traveler with a Disability
(888) 860-7244

DOT Aviation Consumer Disability Hotline
(866) 266-1368

On a Wing and a Prayer
Protecting Your Equipment

TravelMate Scooter
Amigo Mobility, Inc.
(800) 334-7274
amigoscooters.com

Care Vacations (Cruise Ship Assist)
(877) 478-7827
cruiseshipassist.com

Scoot Around North America
(888) 441-7575
scootaround.com

Haseltine Flyer
Haseltine Corporation
(888) 445-8751
haseltine.com

Other Air Travel Issues
Beyond Wheelchairs

Breathin' Easy
(707) 252-9333
breathineasy.com

Better Breathers Traveler
American Lung Association of San Diego
and Imperial Counties
(619) 297-3901
lungsandiego.org

All Go Here Airline Directory
everybody.co.uk/airindex.htm

International Ventilator Users Network (IVUN)
Post-Polio Health International
(314) 534-0475
www.post-polio.org

Air Travel for People with Disabilities
Free brochure from Northwest Airlines.
(800) 358-3100

PETS Travel Scheme Helpline
+44 870 241 1710
www.defra.gov.uk/animalh/quarantine/index.htm

Guide Dog Users Inc.
(888) 858-1008
gdui.org

Pets Welcome Database
petswelcome.com/milkbone/quarmap.html

Getting Around on the Ground

Super Shuttle
(800) 258-3826
supershuttle.com

Project Action
(202) 347-3066
projectaction.org

ECMT Transportation Resources
www1.oecd.org/cem/topics/handicaps/travel.htm

ILRU at TIRR
(713) 520-0232
www.bcm.tmc.edu/ilru/ilru-directory.html

Renting Cars with Hand Controls
users.actcom.co.il/~swfm

Enabled RVer
maxpages.com/enabledrver

Handicapped Travel Club
handicappedtravelclub.com

We Will Ride
Bus Travel

Greyhound Bus
ADA Assistance Line
(800) 752-4841

All Aboard
Train Travel

Amtrak
Office of Access
(877) 268-7252
amtrak.com

USA by Rail
John Pitt
usa-by-rail.com

VIA Rail
(888) 842-7245
viarail.ca

BritRail
britrail.net

National Rail Enquiries
+44 8457 48 49 50
www.nationalrail.co.uk

Eurostar
+44 1233 617 575
www.eurostar.co.uk

Smooth Ride Guide to the U.K.
+44 1279 777 966
freespace.virgin.net/july.ramsey/home.htm

SNCF
Freephone for Access Information
0800 154 753 (France Only)
voyages-sncf.com

Rail Australia
+61 8 217 4321
www.railaustralia.com.au

Rocky Mountaineer Railtours
(800) 665-7245
rockymountaineer.com

Finding the Right Room

Innseekers
innseekers.com

Take-Along Lift
(877) 667-6515
takealonglifts.com

Nuprodx
(888) 288-5653
nuprodx.com

Great Grips
greatgrips.com

Port-A-Bars
(651) 439-8028
grabitonline.com

Hostelling International
(202) 783-6161
hiayh.org

Stockholm CIL Vacation Home Swap Bulletin Board
www.independentliving.org/vacex/index.html

Taking the Kids

Accessible Rest Stops In Oregon
tripcheck.com/General/restareas.htm#hc

Baby B'Air
(800) 417-5228
babybair.com

National Parks Service
nps.gov

Watch It Made in the USA
Karen Axelrod and Bruce Brumberg
(617) 734.6184
factorytour.com

So You Want To Get Off the Ship?
Cruise Travel

U.S. Access Board
www.access-board.gov

Dialysis Finder
dialysisfinder.com

Global Dialysis
globaldialysis.com

The Cruise Ship Center
cruise2.com

Cruise Critic
cruisecritic.com

Cruise Mates
cruisemates.com

ERA Helicopters
(800) 843-1947
eraaviation.com

Wheelchair Taxi Service
Bermuda
(441) 236-1456

Anticipation Tours
Puerto Rico
(787) 630-3030
anticipationtours.com/taxi.htm

Wheelchair Getaways
Puerto Rico
(787) 883-0131

Dial-A-Ride
St. Thomas
(340) 776-1277

Dial-A-Ride
St. John
(340) 693-7600

Accessible Adventures
St. Thomas
(340) 776-4410
accessvi.com

Wheelcoach Services
St. Croix
(340) 719-9335
wheelcoach.com

Sam's Taxi Tours
St. Vincent
(784) 458-3686

Elite Limousine Services
George Town, Cayman Islands
(345) 949-5963

Lincoln Campbell
Ocho Rios, Jamaica
(876) 779-9211

American West Steamboat Company
(800) 434-1232
AmericanWestSteamboat.com

Delta Queen Steamboat Company
(800) 543-1949
deltaqueen.com

River Barge Excursions
(888) 462-2743
riverbarge.com

Stockport Canal Boat Trust (U.K.)
+44 161 430 8082
newhorizons.org.uk

Lyneal Trust (U.K.)
+44 1743 252 728
www.lyneal-trust.org.uk

Saoirse ar an Uisce (Ireland)
+353 45 529410

MV Dresden
Peter Deilmann EuropAmerica Cruises
(800) 348-8287
deilmann-cruises.com

Croisieres Canal Boats
+33 4 68 91 33 00
croisieres-handy.com

Le Boat
(800) 992-0291 (U.S. & Canada)
leboat.com

When Things Go Wrong

Department of Transportation
Aviation Consumer Protection Division
400 7th St., SW, Room C-75-D
Washington D.C. 20590
(202) 366-2220

Federal Aviation Administration
Office of Civil Rights (ACR-4)
800 Independence Avenue, SW
Washington D.C. 20591

U.S. Department of Justice
Civil Rights Division
950 Pennsylvania Avenue, NW
Disability Rights Section - NYAV
Washington, D.C. 20530
(800) 514-0301

FTA Office of Civil Rights
400 7th Street, SW, Room 9100
Washington D.C. 20590
(888) 446-4511

U.S. Department of the Interior
Office of Equal Opportunity
Director
1849 C St. NW, MS-5214
Washington D.C. 20240-0002

National Center on Accessibility
(812) 856-4422
ncaonline.org

U.S. Access Board
1331 F St., NW, Suite 1000
Washington D.C. 20004-1111
(800) 872-2253
www.access-board.gov

Air Carrier Access
(800) 444-0120

The Americans with Disabilities Act
Your Personal Guide to the Law
(888) 860-7244

A Guide to Disability Rights Laws
(888) 878-3256

ADA Technical Assistance CD
www.usdoj.gov/crt/ada

DOT Aviation Consumer Disability Hotline
(866) 266-1368

Beyond the USA

Accessible Transportation Directorate
Canadian Transportation Agency
(819) 997-6828
www.cta-otc.gc.ca

Access To Travel
www.accesstotravel.gc.ca

Access Canada
Alberta Hotel Association
www.albertahotels.ab.ca

RADAR
+44 207 2503222
www.radar.org.uk

National Rehabilitation Board
+353 1 668 4181

Undiscovered Britain
(215) 969-0542
UndiscoveredBritain.com

Access in London
Gordon Couch
accessproject-phsp.org

The Level Guide to the South West
Peter Watts
www.howtobooks.co.uk

Holiday Care
+44 208 760 0072
www.holidaycare.org.uk

CBF
+49 61 51 81 22 0
cbf-da.de

Rick Steves' Easy Access Europe
travelmatters.com

NICAN
+61 2 6285 3713
nican.com.au

Melbourne Mobility Map
www.accessmelbourne.vic.gov.au

Master Locksmiths Association of Australia
+61 3 9428 5222

Easy Access Australia
Bruce Cameron
avoca.vicnet.net.au/~bruceeaa

The Wheelie's Handbook of Australia
Colin James
home.vicnet.net.au/~wheelies

Handi-Ramp
(847) 680-7700
handi-ramp.com

The Practical Nomad: How to Travel around the World
Edward Hasbrouck
practicalnomad.com

Magellans
(800) 962-4943
www.magellans.com

Medic Alert
(888) 633-4298
www.medicalert.org

Disabled Peoples' International
www.dpi.org

Shopping the Net

Seat Guru
seatguru.com

Accessible Recreation
A World of Choices

National Sports Center for the Disabled
(970) 726-1540
nscd.org

Wilderness on Wheels
(303) 751-3959
wildernessonwheels.org

Rails to Trails Conservancy
railtrails.org

Trail Link Database
traillink.com

National Parks Service
nps.gov

National Recreation Reservation Service
(877) 444-6777
reserveusa.com

Smallwood State Park Cabin Reservations
(888) 432-2267

Wisconsin DNR
(608) 266-2621
www.dnr.state.wi.us

Oregon Yurts
(800) 452-5687

Mala Mala Game Reserve
+27 11 268 2388
malamala.com

Safari West
(707) 579-2551
safariwest.com

Yaquina Head Outstanding Natural Area
(541) 574-3100

Jubilee Sailing Trust
+44 870 4435781
jst.org.uk

Disabled Sailors Association
+44 7734 246 385
www.dsahq.org.uk

Sailing Web
footeprint.com/sailingweb

HSA International
(949) 498-4540
hsascuba.com

Live Dive Pacific, Inc.
(800) 344-5662
livedivepacific.com

Dolphin Research Center
(305) 289-0002
dolphins.org

Disabled Sports USA
(301) 217-0960
dsusa.org

Budget Travel
Is It Really Possible?

NICAN
+61 2 6285 3713
nican.com.au

Microtel
(888) 771-7171
microtelinn.com

Motel 6
(800) 466-8356
motel6.com

Travel Inn
+44 870 242 8000
www.travelinn.co.uk

Golden Access Passport
nps.gov

Chamber of Commerce.com
chamberofcommerce.com

Watch It Made in the USA
Karen Axelrod and Bruce Brumberg
(617) 734.6184
factorytour.com

Figure 9.1.
Emerging Horizons is the only magazine which focuses on accessible travel. It contains no advertising—just lots of information and resources. Subscribe today! Visit EmergingHorizons.com for more information.

Index

A

*NOTE: Boldface numbers indicate illustrations

BARRIER-FREE TRAVEL

personal care assistants (PCAs) and, 75-77

rules and regulations concerning accessibility in, 75-77

D

E

F

G

I

J

K

Q

R

Rail Trails, 220

railroad. *See* train travel

Randall, Carol, 184-186, 184

recreation, 217-234

    beaches, 227-229

    campsites and cabins, 223-227

    planning for your vacation and, 232-234

    safaris, 226

    snow sports, skiing, 231-232

    trails and boardwalks as, 217-220

    water sports, 229-231

recreational vehicles (RVs), 72

references from travel agents, 194-195

Rehabilitation Act of 1973, 167

rental vehicles, 65-70

    accessible adaptations to, 66-70

    Europe, 69

    insurance policies and, 68-69

    parking placards and, 65-66, 69

    van rentals, 69-70

researching overseas travel, 187-188

reservations, blocking (reserving) an accessible room, 107-109

resources, 249-269

rest stops and accessibility, 118-119

restaurants, accessibility complaints and, 163-164

Rick Steves' Easy Access Europe, 179-180

river and canal cruises, 151-154

River Barge Excursion Lines, 153

River Explorer, **152**, 153

Rocky Mountain National Park, 221

Rocky Mountain Railtours (RMR), 94-95, **94**

Ronald Reagan Airport, 61

Royal Association for Disability and Rehabilitation (RADAR), 178

Royal Caribbean International (RCI), 131-133

    children and , 121-122

Ryan International Airline, 12
Ryanair, 4

S

Safari West, California, 226-227, **226**
safaris, 226
Sailing Web, The, 230
sailing, 229-231
Salton Inc., 106
San Francisco Municipal Railway (Muni), 63-64, **64**
Saxman Totem Park, 148
scams concerning travel agents, 197-199
Scoot Around North America, 30
Scot Airways, 175
scuba diving, 230
Sea Legs, 229
seamless travel concept, 57
SeatGuru.com, 213
security issues
    air travel and, 23-24
    service animals and, 54-55
service animals, 52-56
    air travel and, 52-56
    cruising and, 128-129
    quarantine restrictions and, 55-56
    security issues and, 54-55
ship selection for cruising, 133-140. *See also* cruises
shore excursions, cruising and, 144-148
Shore Tender Accessibility Project, 143-144
shower chairs, 104-105
Skagway, Alaska, 149, **149**
skiing, 231-232
Smallwood State Park, Maryland, 224
Smithsonian National Air and Space Museum, 123